Velázquez

AND
THE SURRENDER OF BREDA

Velázquez

AND

THE SURRENDER OF BREDA:

THE MAKING OF A MASTERPIECE

ANTHONY BAILEY

A JOHN MACRAE BOOK

HENRY HOLT AND COMPANY

NEW YORK

Henry Holt and Company, LLC
Publishers since 1866
175 Fifth Avenue
New York, New York 10010
www.henryholt.com

Henry Holt® and ® are registered trademarks of Henry Holt and Company, LLC.

Library of Congress Cataloging-in-Publication Data

Bailey, Anthony, 1933–
   Velázquez and the surrender of Breda / Anthony Bailey.—1st ed.
       p. cm.
   "A John Macrae book."
   Includes bibliographical references and index.
   ISBN 978-0-8050-8835-9
   1. Velázquez, Diego, 1599–1660.   2. Painters—Spain—Biography.   I. Velázquez,
Diego, 1599–1660.   II. Title.
   ND813.V4B26 2011
   759.6—dc22
   [B]

Henry Holt books are available for special promotions and premiums.
For details contact: Director, Special Markets.

First Edition 2011

Designed by Meryl Sussman Levavi

Printed in the United States of America

10   9   8   7   6   5   4   3   2   1

Again for Margot, and for our daughters,
Liz, Annie, Katie, and Rachel

Stein says to Marlow:

"A man that is born falls into a dream like a man who falls into the sea. If he tries to climb out into the air as inexperienced people endeavour to do, he drowns—*nicht war?* . . . No! I tell you! The way is to the destructive element submit yourself, and with the exertions of your hands and feet in the water make the deep, deep sea keep you up. So if you ask me, how to be? . . ."

JOSEPH CONRAD, Lord Jim

Contents

ILLUSTRATIONS

COLOR ILLUSTRATIONS

All by Velázquez

The Fable of Arachne (The Spinners), c. 1656, oil on canvas, Museo del Prado, Madrid. Giraudon, The Bridgeman Art Library.

Mercury and Argus, c. 1659, Museo del Prado, Madrid. Giraudon, The Bridgeman Art Library.

Las Meninas (The Family of Philip IV), 1656, oil on canvas, Museo del Prado, Madrid. Giraudon, The Bridgeman Art Library.

V ELÁZQUEZ IS ONE OF THOSE GREAT ARTISTS WHOSE PERSONAL
life has to be sniffed out: Suggestion and association and guesswork are all needed. His professional career as courtier and painter is
fairly well documented but letters to do with how he felt and thought
and lived are in very short supply. Yet he is one of the top half-dozen
painters, and his paintings tell stories that allow a biographer to flesh
out a portrait; the paintings—we need to remember—also sprang from
his life. A good deal of information about their creator can be coaxed
from them. I have written about several artists whose lives are brief in
terms of surviving documentary material, and about several who come
with masses of intimate correspondence in train. It isn't easy to decide
which category contains the most difficult subjects. I have always preferred to treat the biographer's task as not only archival but reportorial,
the result of experience (through feet on the ground) as well as from
research (sitting in a library chair); the four senses as much as the intel-
lect are vital tools of the trade. So, too, of course is the ability or good
fortune to get at the right books and documents, and at the right people
who generously allow their brains to be picked.

Among the vital documents for Velázquez are the biographical
accounts left by his father-in-law Francisco Pacheco and the court
painter and scholar Antonio Palomino. Pacheco's treatise *Arte de la Pintura* was published in Seville in 1649 and Palomino's *Parnaso Español*

in Madrid in 1724; translated into English, both are printed in Enriqueta Harris's invaluable monograph, *Velázquez*, of 1982. Some crucial new facts about his life have been revealed in the years since by Jennifer Montagu of the Warburg Institute, London, by Peter Cherry of Trinity College, Dublin, and by Kevin Ingram of St. Louis University, Madrid. The complicated financial underpinning of his career, which may have been kept deliberately obscured, has been recently summarized by J. M. Cruz Valdovinos. My bibliography gives details of these sources and serves I hope as an acknowledgment to the many other authors who have provided grist for my Velázquez mill. Distinctions are invidious, but let me say here that the works of Julian Gallego, Jonathan Brown, John H. Elliott, and Geoffrey Parker were indispensable. For Spanish background, Cervantes's *Don Quixote* remains the essential guidebook—English-speaking people who don't get its humor and find it prolix and obscure should try the marvelous Everyman edition, which uses the 1706 English translation of P. A. Motteux, a French Huguenot who came to live in England. The traveler Richard Ford, in the first half of the nineteenth century, brought out handbooks and gazetteers that still convey the gritty essence of Spain. I have used one particular painting, one of Velázquez's greater pictures if not his greatest, as a touchstone and frequent means of entry into his work and his world. This could threaten now and then to overbalance my effort, but I plead the example of the master, several of whose paintings have a similar dual focus, like plays within a play, with a picture of one event visible inside the scenery of another. Both artistically and politically what was happening on the smaller stage of the Low Countries had a profound impact in the larger arena of imperial Spain. Two countries geographically distant from each other were intricately involved in each other's fortunes by way of the lifeblood of their soldiery, the cost in cash of their conflict, and—in relation to Diego Velázquez—by a work of art I am especially concerned with. I have perforce shifted the scene back and forth between them. Finally, I should make it clear that I have used a small amount of novelist's license in the first chapter, setting the ball rolling (or the butterfly's wing beating). But the facts on which I base my account of the turfship venture in the Netherlands are to be found in books and documents in the Breda archives.

My researches and reconnaissances were interrupted by the World Cup—the football/soccer championships—held in South Africa in 2010. In these, Spain and the Netherlands fought their way past the other countries' teams to the finals. They had never played against each other before in such a tournament and deep memories of their often hostile sixteenth- and seventeenth-century political and military entanglements suddenly surfaced, together with occasional appreciation of their mutual debts. War with Spain assisted in the formation of the young Dutch nation. War between the United Provinces and Spain helped complete the achievements of the Dutch golden age and, depleting Spain's fortunes, write *finis* to the Hispanic empire as a great power. Both countries have had long overseas histories, and both were by no means considerate colonizers, intolerance and even savagery abroad balancing their reputations for creativity and easygoing behavior at home. However, when the two national teams squared off against each other in the World Cup final, the stadium audience and television viewers worldwide were taken aback to find the allegedly now pacific and democratic Dutch playing with ruthless, unsporting aggression, while the more lately dictator-bossed Spaniards, playing stylishly if a bit quixotically, seemed unable to deliver a knockout blow. However, in overtime there came a long-deserved red card for the Dutch and an exquisite goal from the Barcelona midfielder Andres Iniesta: It was one-nil for chivalrous Spain.

My particular thanks to:

Katie Bailey for her help with reading and translating Spanish texts, Margot Bailey, Sergio Buenaventura, C. J. Fox, Dr. J. R. L. Highfield, Kevin Ingram, Martha Logan, Jack Macrae, the late Adrian Mitchell, Neil Olson, Kirsten Reach, Jon and Marianne Swan, and Lies Meijer Vonkeman.

Velázquez

AND
THE SURRENDER OF BREDA

I. THE TURFSHIP. BREDA. 1590

THE WING OF A BUTTERFLY BEATS, WE ARE TOLD, AND A MIL-
lion aftereffects later, far away, a tidal wave happens. In the chain
of causation that matters here, what could be taken for a starting point
was not an insect wing-beat but a spade cut, as a rectangular piece of
peat was sliced from soggy ground and placed onto a barrow from which
it was then loaded onto a high-sided barge, heaped up, turf upon turf,
in a pile that resembled an earthen shed, hollow inside, though only a
few were aware of this fact. From the riverbank, where the loading was
taking place, the ship's cargo looked like a solid stack. The river was the
Mark; it flowed northward through Brabant, a province in the Netherlands, to join the much larger river Waal, and thence out to the North
Sea. The time was the beginning of March, 1590, a gray morning, and
a war was going on. Despite this the scene near Zevenbergen seemed
utterly peaceful as, the next day, the barge's sails were hoisted and—
think of a painting by the Dutch artist Jan van Goyen—the turfship
set off up the Mark toward the town of Breda, past the diked green
meadows in which cattle grazed.

One man, one of the only two visible crew members, stood in the
bow while the skipper sat on a bench at the stern, holding the oak tiller
against his hip, and listening to the rustle of water as it curved around
the plump sides and the barn-door rudder and fell away astern without
disturbance. There had been a heavy frost the night before and the air

was damp. But during the next few hours the breeze freshened, the wet-
ness dissipated, and the mainsail was reduced in area by being brailed
up at the front bottom corner between mast and boom. Nevertheless
Adriaan van Bergen, the skipper, thought it better to keep going with
the flood tide under them. Every now and then a figure could be seen
on the riverbanks, probably a cowherd or farmer, so far at least no soldiers from the outposts of the Spanish Army of Flanders. Before the
ship came abreast of these strangers the man on the foredeck leaned
down and loudly whispered, seemingly at the peat, the word *"Silence!"*

Not that you could hear much up on deck. The seventy or so men
crouched below were indeed silent, pent up with their thoughts. They
huddled together in almost total blackness, communicating by nudges
and gestures, hands touching shoulders, occasionally reaching out to
make sure their weapons were still there, within reach, on the barge's
hefty ribs and the bottom boards that lined the hold. The few cracks in
the stacked-up peat gave just enough light and air. It was the lack of air
rather than of light that most affected the party; the strong thick smell
of the peat made it feel like being buried in a compost heap, and the
need to swallow or—worse—sneeze and cough occasionally overcame
them.

It was Adriaan van Bergen's turfship. But its mission had been an
idea floated before, by the late William of Orange, the revered if somewhat reluctant leader of the revolt against the Spanish overlords of the
Netherlands. William had taken note of the fact that turf skippers
could enter the walls of the occupied town of Breda most easily. Breda
had been the home territory of the Orange-Nassau family. William,
nicknamed the Silent because of his cautious habit of thinking a long
time before acting, lips sealed, had fallen to an assassin's gun in Delft
six years before, but his son and heir, prince Maurice, had taken up the
turfship idea. He had made inquiries about an experienced skipper
and van Bergen, one of a family of turf handlers from Leur, was recommended. Van Bergen also had a big enough ship. The Spanish had
captured Breda in 1581, killing six hundred of its citizens and plundering
the place; they had occupied it ever since, and Maurice was impatient
to regain it. It was not only his family seat but a key link in the ring of
walled towns and forts with which Spain encircled the northern rebel-

lious provinces. The winter still not quite over had been a tough one; it was a matter of waiting for the castle garrison or town council to order a new load of fuel, which they must do soon. Meanwhile an assault force was put together. An experienced officer from Cambrai in the southern Netherlands, the mostly Spanish Netherlands, thirty-four-year-old Charles de Héraugiere, who wanted to prove his loyalty to the Orange-Nassau family, was given the command. Several meetings took place at secret locations to work out how and when the men would be embarked on the turfship. The unit was recruited by Count Philip van Hohen-lohe, a relative of Maurice's by marriage, and Maurice from his palace at The Hague organized a force of about 4,600 men of the States army to be ready to take over the city if the surprise initial attack led by de Héraugiere was successful.

At the end of February 1590 it became known that a new shipment of peat had been ordered by Breda. Maurice—who was twenty-three—set off with his small army toward Dordrecht, although, because of spies everywhere, he attempted to get it known that he was going some-where else. Gorinchem was mentioned. The governor of Breda, an Ital-ian named Lanciavecchia, led an opposing force of the king of Spain's Army of Flanders toward Geertruidenberg, northeast of Breda, on the edge of the large area of river and swamp known as the Biesbos, think-ing Maurice was heading there. In this time of haste and flurries of misinformation, the first attempt to embark the assault force went wrong; the blame fell on the skipper for "oversleeping" though over-drinking was more likely. The river Mark was tidal up to Breda and very low water then kept the turfship immobile for several days. But on the afternoon of Friday, March 2, the decision was made to go for it. On the following day van Bergen's heavily laden ship sailed up the channel to the north of a small island named Reygersbosch. Here a moveable barrier or boom controlled passage to the canal surrounding Breda's castle. Here guards waited in an outpost, and a brief inspection took place led by an Italian corporal, the guards seeing that the ship obviously carried the expected peat shipment. Then there was an uneasy period of waiting for the tide to rise high enough so that the ship could be moved in through the water gate. This was the worst time, the Dutch soldiers uneasy under their stack of peat, the leaky ship's bilges slowly filling with water that would soon need pumping out, de Héraugiere murmuring encouraging words to keep spirits up. But just after three p.m. the tide served. The ship's mast was lowered and the vessel was poled toward the quayside. Van Bergen now pumped away, the noise disguising some coughs coming from within the peat. At the quay a squad of Italian soldiers hauled on warps to bring the turfship in through a sort of tunnel under the walls to a sluis or lock that controlled the water level and thence into the little harbor within the castle. There the ship was moored alongside the arsenal. An impatient squad from the garrison climbed aboard to start unloading the peat.

"What's the hurry?" Adriaan van Bergen wanted to know. The beginning of Lent was approaching and a drink or two surely wouldn't come amiss. There was all day tomorrow to unload the cargo. To reinforce this idea he doled out some coins to the soldiers and the suggestion worked. Most of the garrison men went off to a hostelry in the town or to their barracks. Only one Italian was left on guard but he too was plied with beer and by midnight he was asleep. It was a quiet night. When van Bergen gave the word that the time was right, de Héraugiere's band silently climbed out from their peat stack one by one, adjusting their helmets and cuirasses, unsheathing their swords and axes, priming their guns, and formed up in two groups. The sleeping guard was knocked on the head and rendered truly unconscious. One party went toward the bastion by the harbor and the northwest gate. The other, led by de Héraugiere, headed for the gate that gave entry into the town. On the way they encountered a guard, who, surprised, at least remembered to ask *"Qui va là?"* The Dutchmen seized him and questioned him about the garrison, its size and its whereabouts. The facts were that the town was guarded by six companies formed by citizens and five *vendels*, which were mostly Italian. The castle itself was garrisoned only by a unit of some fifty men, led by the son of the governor, Paolo Antonio Lancia-vecchia.

The Italian who was being questioned gave erratic answers: any number or location that came into his terrified head. He was killed. But the lethargic watch had now woken up. The alarm was sounded. Short battles took place at the guard houses by the outer gates. Those inside were shot through the windows. Young Lanciavecchia's men made a counterattack, but this was repelled. Their colleagues who had been partying in town tried to burn the outer gate but were forcibly prevented. Mopping up went on for some time, but by dawn the victory was evident. Thirty-seven Italians lost their lives and among the insurgents only one Dutchman, Hans van den Bosch, who fell into a canal and drowned. A number on both sides were badly injured. Paolo Lanciavecchia managed to negotiate the surrender of himself and some of his men, paying a hefty ransom. On the north side of the castle, the field gate was found to be frozen shut—warming it up by fire might have helped—but it was finally prized open and van Hohenlohe's vanguard let in, the first contingent of Maurice's small army. Trumpets sounded the Dutch anthem, the "Wilhelmus." Breda had been taken. The flags of Spain were hauled down and burned.

The burghers and magistrates of Breda thought it advisable to show how pleased they were. Bells were rung and thanksgiving services held in the Groot Kerk near the market square and in the many other churches in town. As the news spread, bonfires were lit in celebration all over the northern Netherlands. A feast was held in one of the town's best inns for the van Bergens, owners of the turfship, and its skipper, Adriaan van Bergen, who was given an annual pension and made a lockkeeper in Breda. De Héraugiere was given a set of pewterware, a gold-plated model of the turfship, and an even bigger pension. Many of the citizenry of the town who had enjoyed the royal, Catholic status quo tried to hide their chagrin at the turn of events, their fury at the failure of the king of Spain's army to defend Breda against the States rebels. Any remaining Italian or Spanish civilians fled town. The town had to cope with the sudden inrush of Maurice's 4,600 men, who included an English contingent under Sir Francis Vere, and a new governor (de Héraugiere for a period and then Maurice's half brother, Justin). The citizens of Breda were scared of looting and the imposition of fierce financial exactions. To alleviate their concern the town council negotiated a cash payment to take the place of the plundering generally permitted a victorious occupying force. Sixteen thousand guilders was the amount first agreed upon, but this was soon raised to 87,000 guilders. Breda couldn't afford this demand and the States General in The Hague had to make good the bill. The town moreover had to pay for the billeting, board, and lodging of the prince's troops. The citizenry also suffered the fate of collaborators everywhere; there was a decided loss of face; the feeling was common in the northern Low Countries that the Baronie, the name for the whole district of Breda, wasn't participating staunchly enough in the *opstand*, the revolt against Spain. As for the so-called defenders of Breda for the king of Spain, it was trouble. The royal governor of the Low Countries, the Duke of Parma, court-martialled those responsible. The Italian corporal accused of letting in the turfship and two of his superior officers were beheaded in Brussels. Young Lanciavecchia was dismissed from his command. Bolting the stable door after the surprise break-in, Count Karel van Mansfelt, the commander of the Army of Flanders, was ordered to ensure that Breda was properly locked up. One effect of this was that Adriaan van Bergen's turfship was stuck inside the city walls. Unattended, without constant pumping, it would have sunk and blocked the canal; it was therefore hauled out onto the quay by the castle, a roof built over it, and on every fourth of March for the next thirty-five years featured in civic celebrations.

IN 1590 THE conflict was already mature and getting older. What would become known as the Eighty Years War between the Dutch United Provinces and the Spanish empire had begun in 1568. Like many historic European wars, it would beggar understanding, causing as it did an immense loss of men's labor, the capital of nations, and human life; like many other such conflicts, it was sparked by rivalry over trade, control of overseas possessions, by religious dissent and dynastic dissatisfactions. The way royal families extended their power by inheritance was much to blame. A simplified family tree has Hapsburg possessions being first brought together in 1477 when Maximilian, son of the emperor of Germany, married Mary of Burgundy, and in time became regent of the Netherlands. Their son Philip married Juana, daughter of King Ferdinand (of Aragón) and Queen Isabella (of Castile). The elder son of Philip and Juana was Charles, born in the Netherlands and boasting the protruding Hapsburg lower lip, who married Isabella of Portugal and inherited an empire that, despite its pan-European and indeed eventually worldwide extent, had many fault

lines. Charles V ruled a diverse conglomeration of countries in which
what the historian H. A. L. Fisher called the "old medieval unity of
faith" was being tugged apart by vehement forces, sometimes under
monarchical leadership, sometimes in the guise of religion, sometimes
fired by early nationalistic fervor. Charles—who started out knowing
no Spanish—slowly became a Spaniard; keeping an empire together
and without heresy was a full-time job from which he finally abdicated
in 1555, worn out, immobilized by gout, and for the occasion leaning on
the shoulder of one of his Low Countries noblemen, the young Prince
of Orange.

Charles retired to a remote Spanish monastery, his cell decorated
with a Titian *Gloria*. His son Philip II was Spanish to the core, a devout
Catholic, keen on destroying heretics with the help of the Inquisition.
He insisted on only the plainest music. The times were hard on dissent:
The works of Erasmus were banned; the Utrecht painter Antonis Mor,
who had been working at the Hapsburg court, fled from Spain back to
Antwerp in the Netherlands. Philip II also had a formidable army, the
Spanish *tércios* providing him with the best infantry battalions in Europe,
and he possessed a massive navy. However, despite its success with
almost obsolete Mediterranean galleys at Lepanto in 1571, his armada
against England came up against skilled sailors in oceangoing ships in
the Channel and North Sea seventeen years later—resulting in an English
victory over Spain that had the effect of leaving the Dutch rebels in
command of the coasts of the Low Countries.

The Dutch had grasped the idea that free trade was the fount of
prosperity. Banking came as naturally to Amsterdam as it had to Antwerp. Spain was hopeless at finance, inept with taxation, both the
Spanish church and the nobility accustomed to exemptions, the country
expecting its trade to benefit from protection when what would have
most helped was freedom to ship anything anywhere. An increasingly
uncertain prop for Spanish power was furnished by the mineral wealth
of Mexico and Peru. These riches were diminished on their way to the
royal treasury by enemy fleets, shipwreck, peculation, inflation, and
sales taxes like the *alcabala*, which struck at the commercial energies of
the very people who most needed to be given heart.

In the Netherlands, the tax that did immediate harm was the tenth penny—the Spanish commander the Duke of Alba's local version of the *alcabala*. It was in Breda castle in 1566 that what was called a compromise but was in fact a statement of intent was signed by many of the Netherlands nobility, demanding the abolition of the Inquisition in the Low Countries. From there a delegation went to Brussels to ask the governor, Margaret of Parma, to convoke the States General assembly and moderate the injunctions against Protestants. It was there that Margaret's counsellor, Berlaymont, famously exclaimed to his distressed leader, "What, Madam, afraid of these beggars!"—an abusive term triumphantly taken on as a compliment by those who had signed the Breda Compromise. While opposition to Spanish financial exactions and religious persecution mounted, and as the counts Egmont and Hoorn, two noble dissidents, were tried in Alba's "Courts of Blood" and executed in Brussels in 1568, William of Orange tried to maintain that he was a rebel against misgovernment, not against his monarch, Charles V's son Philip II. The writer of the "Wilhelmus," the anthem written about this time that became the Dutch national hymn, declared for all to sing, as though making a distinction between disloyalty and necessary dissent:

> *Unto the Lord His power*
> *I do confession make*
> *That ne'er at any hour*
> *Ill of the King I spake.*
> *But unto God, the greatest*
> *Of Majesties, I owe*
> *Obedience first and latest,*
> *For justice wills it so.*

One further thing in common: The kings of Spain claimed to be ruling in direct succession to the kings of Israel, and the princes of Orange adopted a similar biblical camouflage, declaring their descent from the House of Judah. Both nations were therefore chosen people.

THE FACT THAT the Dutch revolt against Spain was a conservative revolt, against Spanish authority though not against the king of Spain, didn't prevent the Spanish crackdown from being terrifying. Fernando

Álvarez de Toledo, the Duke of Alva, was a believer in shock and awe. The duke thought Holland was "as near to hell as possible" and took it out on the inhabitants of the Low Countries. Property was seized, rebels and heretics arrested and executed, and entire cities such as Antwerp sacked. For many years after that in Spain itself any sort of inhuman behavior could provoke the question: *"¿Estamos aquí o en Flandes?"* Are we here or in Flanders? The troops of Alva and his son Don Fadrique raped, murdered, looted, and burned their way through Malines, Zutphen, and Naarden, though Haarlem took seven months to fall in 1573, and Alkmaar actually repulsed the Spaniards that same year: It could be done. Leiden also held out against a long Spanish siege. At Breda, the surprise Dutch turfship counterattack worked. By then the Netherlands were effectively sundered. In 1579 the Union of Utrecht brought together the northern provinces and three years later their representatives formally renounced their allegiance to the king of Spain. The southern provinces, united by treaty at Arras, developed a sort of autonomy under their new governors, Isabella, Philip II's daughter, and her husband, Archduke Albert of Austria. By 1590 indeed the era of Spanish beastliness was mostly past. The war seesawed on for another fourteen years. The Duke of Parma, an able and less savage general than Alva, was held up by the equally smart tactics of Maurice of Nassau, William of Orange's oldest son, by the fact that Philip of Spain made the great mistake of taking on at once the English and French (both of whose nations were involved in civil war), and by diverting Spain's strained resources into the armada. Parma was also impeded by the clever use the Dutch made of water, which seemed to be their natural element: whether the sea or the great rivers that penetrated deeply into the lowlands. Fresh or salt, water held up and diverted—even if it didn't stop—the armies of Spain. The States of Holland declared in 1596: "In the command of the sea and in the conduct of the war on the water resides the entire prosperity of the country." So much so that the Hollanders continued sending their ships to trade with the Spanish while the war went on.

Probably the biggest factor, at the turn of the century, that tilted the balance slightly in favor of the United Provinces was money, or in Madrid the lack of it. The Dutch flourished abroad, in the northern oceans and the Spice Islands, overseas trade creating great wealth at home. The Sea Beggars of Zeeland throttled the Scheldt, the approaches to Antwerp, and thousands of Antwerp's citizens (including Frans Hals's parents) left that city for the north, some for religious reasons, many because they had no longer any way of making a living there. (The Halses went to Haarlem.) Off Gibraltar in 1607 at the southwest tip of Spain a Dutch fleet convincingly defeated the Spanish. The northern united provinces consolidated as a federal entity, the Dutch Republic, governed from The Hague, with the province of Holland and the leaders of its oligarchy in prime control. Yet the Spanish weren't completely out of it. A three-year siege by their Army of Flanders succeeded in reducing Ostend, and the name of their Genoese general, Ambrogio Spinola, began to be much heard. (Genoa was in Spanish Hapsburg territory.) Spinola came from a great banking family, and often had to provide his own backing to finance Spain's armies, but he had a Renaissance condottiere's broad understanding of military endeavor, encompassing engineering, diplomacy, and hands-on skill in the field; this helped Spain stem the Dutch drive under Maurice to create a modern, efficient army, second largest in Europe and in receipt of helpful subsidies from France. By 1609 a balance of power was reached; successes and failures had canceled each other out; a new king in Spain, Philip III, had taken the place of his austere and autocratic father; in the Low Countries Philip's sister Isabella and her husband, Albert, ruled jointly in Brussels and introduced a new sense of moderation. The stalemate led to rumors of peace and then a truce. This lasted twelve years.

IN BREDA THE Dutch garrison of three thousand men sat tight. Many of the troops were in fact German, French, English, or Scots, and the "Spanish" Army of Flanders as noted was also cosmopolitan, containing many Italians and men from German principalities along the so-called Spanish Road that provided the Hapsburg line of supply from Lombardy to the Low Countries: in 1586 an army of Spanish recruits being sent to invade England with the armada's help was shipped by galley to Genoa and then trudged over the Alps on the long march to Luxembourg. Some of these untrained soldiers arrived barefoot but carrying their guitars. The hope of plunder kept many going, particularly as pay was fitful. The historian Geoffrey Parker tells us that in the period since 1567 the Spanish garrison at Breda "received goods and services worth over 40,000 florins from the shopkeepers and householders of the town" and left in 1590 after the turfship surprise without paying back a penny. Money was recognized by most authorities as the key to winning the war.

Restored to the Dutch, Breda's garrison was the largest in the almost uninterrupted ring of towns that formed a defensive horseshoe around the heartland of the Republic—a ring very similar to the *Randstad* of urban development that even now dominates Holland. To the south, the cavalry of the Army of Flanders conducted patrols but engaged in little fighting, levying contributions from villages in return for not pillaging them. In Breda the defensive life under the truce had its advantages. The Dutch troops received their pay fairly regularly from the province of Holland. The presence of a body of energetic men stationed in the town stepped up the sales of food and drink, especially of Breda's excellent beer. We can picture some aspects of those days with the help of two Dutch painters: Pieter de Hooch, with his early paintings of barracks and tavern scenes; and Johannes Vermeer, whose officers in broad-brimmed black hats were to be seen sitting at ease with goblets of wine as young women sat talking or playing musical instruments to them. After de Héraugiere, the long-serving governor of Breda through most of this period was Justin of Nassau, the illegitimate son of William of Orange and a Breda woman. Justin lived in the town with his wife, who was also from Breda.

Yet not all was harmony in the young Republic. The old religion went on being practiced by many citizens in Breda; after Vermeer's death, his wife, Catharina Bolnes, moved from Delft to Breda, it seems partly because she felt more at home there as a practicing Catholic. Throughout the United Provinces there was infighting not just between Catholics and Protestants but between the various Protestant sects, Arminians versus Gomarists, Remonstrants versus anti-Remonstrants; indeed, in Breda the theological feuding was so intense that the magistracy forbade church ministers from preaching on disputed subjects. Prince Maurice himself admitted that he didn't understand many of these quarrels. Moreover, not all Protestants were anti-Hapsburg. Count Enno III of

Friesland was a militant Lutheran and for the king of Spain. Amsterdam stayed loyal to Spain after much of the rest of the north of the country had gone Orange. And despite catchy slogans—"All this for freedom's sake" was a notable one—the Dutch proved just as able to use an ax on their own leaders, when those were regarded as too radical or too obstinate, as the Spanish "tyrants" had done in Brussels. Two generations or so after Egmont and Hoorn were beheaded by the Duke of Alba's regime, the Dutch decapitated their own seventy-year-old grand pensionary Johan van Oldenbarnevelt, a statesman accused of treason who had attempted to preserve the truce with Spain and thereby antagonized many Orangists and particularly Prince Maurice, who went on looking for paths to military glory. Maurice—who was regarded as both cryptic and devious—cited "Reasons of State" for Oldenbarnevelt's execution. By then the United Provinces was a state to be reckoned with, not just a land of beggars and freebooters.

In 1604 the Spanish poet and satirist Francisco de Quevedo wrote to a correspondent in the Netherlands: "In your country we consume our soldiers and our gold; here we consume ourselves." Four hundred years later it seems curious that two such seemingly dissimilar countries, linked largely by dynastic inheritance and war, should have had artistic golden ages at the same time. Both countries experienced a like flowering in adventurous expansion, an outgoing impulse that saw both exploring in Brazil and the Spice Islands. Both countries had great highs and lows, though it was the Spanish not the Dutch *siglo de oro* that Cervantes (who lived through it) could refer to as "these deprav'd Times." The Dutch golden age possibly lasted a little longer but both ages burned out before the seventeenth century was over, and the flame that also burned vividly within their greatest artists exhausted its fuel in both nations. Perhaps the most notable paradox where Breda was concerned—a city in which both countries had their interest—was that it was a Spanish not a Dutch painter who created a masterpiece out of a military campaign focused on it.

II. A Boy from Seville. 1599–1621

NINE YEARS AFTER THE TURFSHIP EPISODE, A THOUSAND KILO-meters away from Breda, a child was born in southern Spain. This arrival occurred in Seville, capital of Andalusia, through which the Guadalquivir, a much greater river than the Mark, bends its long course toward the sea. Above the quaysides the masts and rigging of oceangoing ships festooned the Seville skyline. A number of church bell towers climbed out of the packed shoulder-to-shoulder white houses with orange-red roofs between which one could just make out streets and alleyways. Among the highest buildings were the thirteenth-century Torre del Oro, from which a chain could be stretched across the river to keep out marauding vessels; the Giralda, the twelfth-century minaret of what had been one of the largest mosques in Islam; and the more conventional late-medieval pointed yet low-pitched roof of the tower of San Pedro church. The Muslim tide that had flooded Spain for seven centuries had now been at full ebb for 350 years, leaving a visible legacy of intricate architecture, fluent design, and a partly Moorish populace. It also left a Spanish language in which some 300,000 words came from Islamic terms, including "flamenco" and "*Olé*!" Proximity to Africa was evident in the hot, dry climate as well as in the number of dark-skinned workers. Seville at this point was the largest city in Spain. It held 150,000 people in 1598. It also had much of the lucrative trade with America. From Seville (fifty miles from the open sea) and Cádiz fleets of galleons sailed in convoy twice a year, escorted by half-a-dozen armed ships, taking out essential supplies of cereals, oil, and wine, and bringing back bullion. In Seville the silver fleet landed most of its rich cargoes from Mexico and Peru, booty that would in great part clunk into the coffers of the Spanish crown, providing about a fifth of its yearly revenues. As the sixteenth century ended, this easy source of income was starting to contribute toward inflation; prices were rising, the coinage was losing value. And when for one reason or other the silver fleet didn't make it home, the crown had less to pay its teeming court and all of Castile squealed. So did the soldiers in Flanders.

Nevertheless it was for some a *siglo de oro*, a golden age, if you ignored diseases and the black shadow cast by the Inquisition, the agency of clerical orthodoxy that was mostly bureaucratic but now and then malevolent and lethal. Seville was prosperous: For a century it had had the wealth of the Americas passing through it. It was either the new Rome or the new Babylon. It was a city where art followed trade, and high aspirations came in the wake of serious endeavor. And despite the onset of plague in 1599, Seville was a fortunate place to be born if you were Diego Velázquez, baptized on June 6 that year in San Pedro parish church—a church that showed *Mudéjar* influence, which is to say the effect of Muslim style after the Christian reconquest. It was the church where Diego's parents had been married at the end of December 1597.

The child survived infancy. He was given his mother's surname though he would later sometimes fit his father's name de Silva in front of it. His first name Diego honored the apostle James, Jesus's brother, who—legend had it—came to Spain to preach and left his body to be found by a miracle in Galicia in 813, making him an appropriate patron saint. For Velázquez's father, Juan Rodríguez de Silva, and his mother, Jerónima Velázquez, Diego was the first of seven children. Juan Rodríguez was a church scribe and notary, his mother the daughter of a garment worker who made trousers and stockings and did well enough to buy a few properties, which he rented out, and the family house in which Diego was born in the Calle Gorgoja, just off the Plaza Buen Suceso. It was a small two-story house in a maze of little streets, with an interior courtyard and small iron-barred and thick-shuttered windows that

balanced coolness against light; the house had something of the character of a cave, with dim recesses.

The child survived the plague of 1599, which apparently killed his
maternal grandparents. At what point his mother and father realized
they had a prodigy on their hands we don't know. Seville believed in its
classical connections: The city's legendary founder was the god Hercules;
the emperor Trajan had been born in Triana, the city district across the
Guadalquivir River. The city had been a western focus for the Roman
empire. The Velázquez boy had a proper grounding in the classics. He
grew up knowing that Seville's Giralda was the tallest tower in the
world at 322 feet and that the adjacent huge castlelike cathedral, built
using some of the material from the knocked down mosque, contained
the supposedly uncorrupted body of Ferdinand III, the king-made-saint
who liberated the city from the Moors and died from fasting. But Diego
would have been more aware of all the local convents and churches,
San Pedro his place of baptism, and San Vicente in the neighborhood
closer to the river his family next moved to. Seville took religious obser-
vance with fervent seriousness, with daily demonstrations of faith and
occasional spectacular processions devoted to the Virgin Mary. Possibly, although we have no way of saying precisely how they were made
evident, there may have been special reasons for Diego's family to pay
careful attention to showing they were good Catholics. Childhood meant
catechism, sacraments, communion, confession; many dark spaces, much
fear, and much beauty.

Their circumstances were modest but his parents also made a point
of letting it be known that they had, somewhere, an old Christian past.
The family decision to stress his mother's Velázquez name suggested
an attempt to follow Andalusian and Portuguese tradition, although
Diego's father and grandfather also had the name of Rodríguez, and
his paternal grandmother's de Silva provided a superior note. (Using
this name also followed Portuguese and Andalusian custom.) Diego's
father's work as a church scribe meant he was a skilled penman. His
mother was almost certainly illiterate. One suspects that the young
Diego heard a great deal about his distinguished ancestors and his roots
in "Portugal." The crowns of Castile and Portugal had been joined
in 1580, which had made for simpler emigration to Seville and the

prosperity it held out. At that time childhood was short. At the age of six, at the most seven, real life began. The Velázquez de Silvas' first child was evidently an apt pupil and there must have been early signs of a special bent for painting. Palomino, a court painter in Madrid who became in 1724 one of Velázquez's first biographers, tells us that "his school notebooks served him as sketchbooks for his ideas." His parents don't seem to have been bothered by any conflict between what Palomino later suggested was the boy's purported noble background and the artisan or craftsman aspects of his proposed occupation, that is, in a trade. Indeed, one has to credit them with perception, in seeing that their son had a special talent for drawing that could be nurtured. They were probably impelled not just by destiny but by the press of his younger siblings coming along into soon finding gainful employment for Diego. (Two of his younger brothers also trained as artists.) As a family, they had industrious habits—the habits, one might hazard, almost of the Jews and Moriscos rather than of the proud if impoverished and often indolent hidalgos who strutted their stuff throughout Spain. Many of them, as Gerald Brenan observed, preferred starvation "to the ignominy of working."

The young Velázquez may later have wondered if he really saw what he did in Seville in 1610, which was similar to what was happening then through much of southern Spain—or did he only think he had seen it? Was it simply a hot-weather mirage? But as a boy of ten, going on eleven, he would have been aware of the sadness and the horror of people from the streets around him as they were rounded up and forced to pack and go. Certainly afterward he was able to imagine, to *visualize*, on this and other occasions what it was like to be somewhere without being on the spot. He could identify with people and represent their feelings. In 1610 word spread fast, winged by fear if not terror. In his family's kitchen, he may have been aware of the panic showing in the countenances of one or other of the dark-skinned servant girls. But he may also have walked in person from his family's house in the parish of San Vicente to the close-at-hand riverfront and seen the waiting vessels, mostly oared galleys and lateen-sailed feluccas, tethered to the banks of the Guadalquivir, while on the floodplain outside the city walls, in view of Seville's resplendent spires and towers, some belonging to former mosques, the groups of tearful about-to-be emigrants were camped.

It had taken time to get the Moriscos' expulsion organized. It had been proclaimed in 1609 by the king, Philip III, seemingly brainwashed by his confessors, but such calls for the "Little Moors" to be thrown out of Spain had been heard for more than a century. After reconquering most of the peninsula from the North African Muslims, the Christian monarchs of the country had wavered between century-long periods of toleration and persecution of both Jews and Moors. Church leaders could be saintly like Archbishop Talavera of Granada, or hard-line fanatics, like Archbishop Jiménez of Toledo. Some Moriscos were in fact descended from Iberian stock, from people who had converted to Mohammedism on the arrival of the Moors in Spain. Many looked, dressed, or talked like Christians. Many spoke only Spanish. Both Jews and Moors, from notionally Eastern races, were visibly more industrious and productive than the Christian majority. As menial farmworkers or as literate and numerate lawyers and accountants, they pitched in, unashamed to work. Their energy made them invaluable, you would have thought, but also rendered them suspect for their Catholic employers. Suspicious, too, was their habit of washing themselves a lot. They were skilled producers; the Christians idle consumers. This also made for jealousy. Moreover, many in the Church wanted to keep the races apart—any friendship with infidels was a denial of Christ. So there were demands from time to time to get rid of them or mark them with badges or gather them in ghettoes, in specific areas of the city called *juderías* and *morerías*. (A *morería* was generally surrounded by a wall with only one door.) But even as *conversos* who had been baptized as Christians, could they really be trusted? Wouldn't they go on refusing to eat pork or drink wine, and practicing their horrid rites in secret?

The Spanish Inquisition, set up at episcopal behest in Castile by Queen Isabella in 1478, was fierce in its repressive measures, taken mostly against *conversos* who were thought to be backsliding into Judaic practices. In Seville alone, the Inquisition's tribunals ordered the burning of some seven hundred people from 1480 to 1488; thousands more were severely punished. Moorish religious books were burned. There was useful cash to be collected from fines, from confiscated property, and from denouncing neighbors. Mere arrest by the Holy Office was a savage punishment because its processes were secret and prisoners were held incommunicado. The tribunal's objective was clearly to rid the Church of all taint of Jewish and Moorish blood, "New Christians" included. Study abroad was prohibited for any who weren't of pure blood. Despite this, some Spanish scholars and artists fled to France and Italy. Under Philip II the Moriscos continued to be coerced into conversion, ordered to renounce their Moorish ways and give up their children to be educated by Christian priests. There was rebellion in Granada and many fled to North Africa, often taking a longer and supposedly lawful route through France to Tunisia.

What to do with the Moriscos became a serious issue after Philip III's expulsion order. Plans to put them in ships and scuttle the vessels at sea, and mass castrations of all males, were considered. Straightforward massacre was recommended by many clerics. Eventually nearly three hundred thousand Moriscos from Castille and Aragón were expelled, though many others—as the Jews had done in similar circumstances in 1492—chose to stay behind, to accept conversion and slavery, or, after converting, finding themselves expelled anyway. Some, getting no safe refuge in North Africa, decided to return to slavery and enforced conversion. In Algiers, a number of Christianized Moriscos were stoned to death on arrival. Many also died in Spain on the roads to the coasts, or were killed by locals who looted their possessions. (The population of Spain at this time was probably a bit more than eight million.) Many of the Andalusian Moriscos were sent from the Granada coast across the Mediterranean to Morocco. Those in and around Seville are thought to have been among the best integrated and were treated more charitably than, for example, the less assimilated Moriscos of Valencia. Many seem to have managed to duck back under the workaday surface of things, possibly by becoming slaves rather than employees of their long-term masters. As it was, after the expulsions the omens weren't particularly propitious: In Zaragoza, a vase full of fluid—miraculously retrieved from sweat exuded by religious images and faithfully kept since the forcible conversion of the Aragonese Moors in 1520—suddenly evaporated. Indeed it was soon evident that by the expulsion Spain had cut off its nose to spite its face. Few ambitious Spaniards claiming pure blood brought up their children to honest industry. Landlords now lost essential workers and tenants; many houses were left empty; some almost wholly Morisco villages were destroyed by their aggrieved inhabitants as they were forced to leave; fields were left unsown and cattle unfed. Meat became scarce in the cities; the roads between them were infested with vagabonds and thieves. In Toledo, whole districts were desolate and grass grew in the streets. Among Spain's occupied classes, the clergy alone had more rather than fewer people in its midst (Seville is said to have had some fifteen thousand priests in 1585, making up about a tenth of its population); church lands weren't subject to taxation; a petitioner to King Philip IV complained in 1621 that "It is only in the convents that people are not dying of hunger." Seville's population included at this date 7,503 Moriscos, but more were sent there to be loaded on the ships for a fee of ten reales a head—in all, 18,471 were shipped out from the Andalusian city where Velázquez had been born. His biographer Palomino later opined that the expulsion was "a well-deserved punishment for such infamous and seditious people." The Moriscos had often been coerced into conversion; they had been unfairly taxed; they were treated like spies in the house; and now they were to be compelled to leave. And many did so, though some stayed as slaves or after paying bribes.

AT AGE ELEVEN, the Velázquez boy was apprenticed to a master painter. Diego's father had performed legal services for the Herrera family, and Diego apparently went to work for the artist Francisco Herrera—the records aren't precise because Herrera wasn't yet a member of the Saint Luke's Guild and legally wasn't permitted to have apprentices. In any event, the arrangement didn't last. Herrera was said to have been so bad-tempered that his wife and children walked out on him: They claimed that life with him was hell on Earth. His daughter took shelter in a convent and his son fled to Italy. Herrera alledgedly counterfeited coins, just as Vermeer's grandfather did; artistic talent in deceiving the eye came forth in many forms. (Velázquez's maternal grandfather was also in jail for debt at one point.) For his crime, Herrera had to shelter in a monastery until the king pardoned him in 1624, after admiring an altarpiece Herrera had done of Saint Hermenegild, the sixth-century Visigoth king's son who converted from Arianism to Catholicism in Seville and was later beheaded. Diego was moved to another local painter, forty-seven-year-old Francisco Pacheco. The contract was definitely aboveboard this time, signed on September 17, 1611, for a five-year apprenticeship; since apprenticeships were generally for six years, the year with Herrera seems to have been taken into account. The customary terms were board and clothing—including two shirts, a hat, and a cape—and artistic instruction in return for the apprentice's labor: grinding pigments, preparing canvases and panels, and putting up with various indignities. Do this! Don't do that! Why on earth are you doing such-and-such? If you really want to become a painter, you're going to have to pull yourself together. . . . Between childhood and adolescence lay many humiliations. But he stuck it out and more than that, he won Pacheco's respect. He became a member of the master's family. His own parents, the Velázquez de Silvas, busy with further offspring, moved backstage, though there are occasional reminders of them. Diego's father later served as executor of Pacheco's estate.

Religious art was meat and drink for artists in Seville, as it was for painters and sculptors through most of Spain at this time. Spaniards took their religion seriously and its sacraments and saints, ceremonies and imagery, were central to human life. Velázquez was born into a world where for several centuries art had been inspired by the dogmatic and often doom-laden teachings of the Catholic Church. The art that was spawned by this fierce above-all-remember-heaven-and-hell devotion was to a large degree dourly or sentimentally conventional, although some of the practitioners were dutiful, and a few, like Velázquez's contemporary Zurbarán, were in their chosen tasks brilliant. Now and again there were lightning-lit pockets of perverse genius, such as that of El Greco, Cretan-born and Venice-taught, who was taken up by Philip II, lived for many years in Toledo, but was soon discarded by the court. (He died in 1614.) El Greco thought Michelangelo's works were indecent; the Greek's ecstatic and exaggerated mannerism was too disturbing and violent for the king. His pictures often seemed *carved* rather than painted. In that respect, Seville had its own unsettling close-at-hand talent in Juan Martínez Montañés, whose wooden statu-

ary provided the most exceptional examples of art that was at once religious, passionate, and necrophiliac—its liveliness seemed focused on
death; every work in its own way a crucifixion.

Pacheco wasn't a fire-eater like Herrera. He was a thoroughly com-
petent artist. He was evidently an excellent teacher and at the center of
an inspiring and influential group of men in Seville. His paintings
showed an earnest old-fashioned dedication, his portraits almost Dutch
or German in their dutiful realism, his religious paintings often more
religiose than spiritual, though there was substantial bread-and-butter
work for him in painting the statuary of Montañés in polychrome.
Pacheco was the immediate choice of local religious orders for portraits
of saints. He was appointed an official censor of religious art by the
Inquisition in Seville. It was a time in which many doctrines were being
vehemently disputed. Religious orders went to court on such matters as
how many nails were used to pin Christ to the cross, what age the Virgin Mary should be in depictions of her, and which friars had the right
to give or collect alms and were or were not allowed to preach. Theological nit-picking and hairsplitting were common. Pacheco was also
an inspector for the Seville branch of the Guild of Saint Luke, the union
for artists of sundry types, so when the time came he had the right to
attest to the qualifications of his apprentices. He was twice the elected
president of the guild. Meanwhile he and Diego Velázquez were in
daily contact in Pacheco's studio in what was then called the Calle de
Puerco, running southward from the Alameda de Hércules toward the
cathedral. In the last twenty years or so the area of formerly swampy
ground devoted to the Alameda had been turned into a rectangular
promenade, with two columns at one end, one topped by a statue of
Julius Caesar, one by a statue of the city's hypothetical founder—heroes
from times past, and they stuck in one's mind. The Alameda was long
and straight, something unusual in Seville, a city in which most of the
streets twisted and turned and allowed no view of the far end.

At Pacheco's young Velázquez had a traditional training: apart
from the menial practical jobs, there was much drawing and copying.
Drawing from life, drawing from nature. Pacheco recommended apply-
ing a priming layer of the local Seville clay on the canvas, "ground to a
powder and tempered on the stone slab with linseed oil." This the master

thought to be the best priming, making a base layer that did not crack, and giving Velázquez's early paintings the same dark reddish brown ground that most paintings from Seville had at that time. The hard-working boy also had to make chalk studies of casts and models and sketches of household objects. He had to copy *accurately* drawings Pacheco put in front of him, drawings done by Pacheco and prints Pacheco owned by the artists he most admired—Dürer, Lucas van Leyden, and of course the Italians. Drawing, according to Pacheco, was a fundamental element in what gave painters the right to claim a higher status than ordinary craftsmen, men who carried on a common trade. Painting indeed was a noble activity, as it was coming to be seen in Italy, and in his *Arte de la Pintura* years later Pacheco listed the painters who had been given royal recognition, from Apelles to Titian.

Although Pacheco in 1611 had just come back from a lengthy tour of Spain, looking at Spanish artworks, the Italian manner—*La buena manera*—was highest of all on his approval list, and so prints of the works of Michelangelo and Raphael were put before Diego; he didn't need to be told to draw, draw, draw—he drew insatiably. Despite the master's art duties for the Inquisition, Pacheco particularly admired Pietro Torrigiano's *Penitent St. Jerome*, a terracotta sculpture which was anatomically superaccurate. A Florentine contemporary of Michelangelo, whose nose he had broken during a student argument, Torrigiano had worked in England on the tomb of Henry VII and then in Seville, where, according to Giorgio Vasari, his choleric temperament got him into trouble again; insufficiently paid for a Madonna and Child commission by the Duke of Arcos, he furiously destroyed the sculpture. The insulted duke then accused Torrigiano of heresy. Torrigiano was taken to prison, writes Vasari, and "brought up [before the Inquisition] day after day, being sent from one inquisitor to another, and finally adjudged worthy of the gravest punishment. But meanwhile Torrigiano had fallen into a state of melancholy, and passed several days without eating, by which he brought himself to such weakness that he died, saving himself thus from shame, for it is said he had been condemned to death." Under Pacheco's mastership drawing the female nude wasn't encouraged. Lust was a danger, for the Church a mortal sin! If you needed to paint a woman's figure, Pacheco later wrote in his *Art of*

Painting, you should "take the faces and hands of virtuous women from life. And, for the remaining parts [whatever they might be] make use of good paintings, prints and drawings, and ancient or modern statues."

Diego came from an ordinary house, from a district where many of the activities were artisan. In his earliest neighborhood in San Pedro the workers in one nearby workshop shaped, cast, forged, and hammered metal with accompanying noise, heat, and flames, all memorable. Whatever the talk about his family's distant nobility, he was being trained in a craft for whose work he would be paid. He was at home with domestic things, and it was with such everyday objects and the work associated with them that most of his earliest surviving paintings were concerned. His early canvases were often stretched over thick wooden panels, on which he laid with a palette knife the local clay-based sizing followed by finely ground earth pigments tempered with linseed oil, as Pacheco recommended. This made a dull but durable brown foundation layer. (In time, Velázquez went for lighter grounds and developed a less constrained, more transparent technique.) Pacheco later described a peasant youth whom Velázquez occasionally drew who was good at adopting attitudes and expressions, "sometimes weeping, sometimes laughing." Pacheco went on: "He made many drawings of the boy's head and of many other local people in charcoal heightened with white on blue paper, and thereby he gained assurance in portraiture." With experience he appeared to need fewer preparatory drawings; fewer precise contour lines were to be found; and as his brushwork became freer and broader, his compositions grew more inventive, and more *pentimenti* were inherent in his works. The first paintings to be ascribed to him are of kitchen or tavern scenes, what were called *bodegones* from the word for the wine cellars in which taverns were often situated. In these pictures one or two figures generally appeared, but the artist seemed rather to dwell in an almost covetous way on the everyday objects at hand: mortars, pestles, water jugs, plates and bowls, particularly the brown earthenware pots known as *cazuelas* that were used for making *pisto*. Once again there was a Dutch flavor to all this concern with crockery. And it makes one wonder whether Velázquez was missing his own home.

Diego was one of several apprentices—another was Francisco

López Caro, a year older, who many years later claimed he had known Velázquez since he was nine years old; but Pacheco seems to have singled out Diego. He impressed Pacheco with what the older artist called "his virtues, integrity and excellent qualities, and also by the hopes which his happy nature and his great natural talents raised in me." The boy appeared tireless. The "happy nature" seemed to be demonstrated in the way he painted. He was the apple of his master's eye. He was allowed to browse through Pacheco's scholarly library and eventually permitted to choose books to add to it. (In the library that he himself later put together there were in time many scientific texts and works on perspective, artistic theory, optics, and geometry.) At Pacheco's, the young Velázquez was introduced to visitors: poets, men of letters, lawyers, canons of the cathedral, and Sevillian scholars such as Rodrigo Caro (1573–1647), writer, antiquarian, connoisseur. Pacheco had a sort of salon or informal academy, what Palomino was to call "a gilded prison of Art." The artist gathered together people who were devoted to the classical world and its works, and who came to one another's houses to talk poetry, philosophy, theology, and science. Optics were a fashionable interest; telescopes, cameras obscura, spyglasses, and viewfinders were all made in Seville, just as they were in a number of towns in the United Provinces.

Yet Seville was not all sophisticated thought and social refinement. The grittier side of life wasn't hard to discover, in markets, common taverns, brothels, and along the Guadalquivir riverfront where malefactors were led in chains to the rowing benches of the cargo galleys. The main prison near the Plaza San Francisco housed ruffians and ne'er-do-wells and also those sentenced for what are now called economic crimes. Miguel de Cervantes, a former soldier and writer of many unproducible plays, lived in Seville in the last part of the sixteenth century and was a prisoner here on several occasions. He had also worked as a civil servant and as a purveyor to the naval task force known as "the invincible Armada," helping prepare it for the attack on England in 1588. It was in the course of this service that Cervantes had allegedly seized supplies that belonged to the dean of the cathedral chapter in Seville and was excommunicated. Thereafter, working as a tax collector, he was thrown into prison when his accounts failed to pass audit.

In his cell he had leisure enough to start thinking about *Don Quixote*, which came out in Madrid in 1605, an original, laugh-out-loud combination of realism and surrealism. More Sevillian, perhaps, was his short picaresque tale *Rinconete and Cortadillo*, an "exemplary novel" about two young cardsharps and the thieves' den they worked out of.

Going through the narrow streets of Seville you were well advised to hang on tightly to your bag and keep it firmly fastened. Pickpockets abounded. Small boys went armed. The local argot, known as *germania*, contained a full vocabulary of thievery. Many people had their hands outstretched, beggars and alms collectors, peddlers and prostitutes, and the smallest change was welcomed by fruit sellers and water sellers. The streets of Seville were also the home of much theater, of religious processions and outdoor performances. However, along the waterfront, floods caused great damage in December 1603; serious epidemics occasionally wreaked havoc. And with the new century came hints of economic trouble. Things weren't helped when in 1609, on the very day that the government sensibly agreed to a truce with the Dutch rebels, it petulantly expelled the Moriscos—the three hundred thousand or so supposedly Christianized people of Moorish origin in Spain. In Seville's case, they amounted to seven thousand people who—as we've seen—did vital jobs, keeping shops, carrying goods, growing food. The city's prosperity was already being chipped away. The Guadalquivir was silting up and making passage difficult for ships from the Indies. San Lúcar at the river mouth and Cadíz a bit farther off waited to inherit the wealth-creating cargoes. It might have been taken as a sign of the times (though not many noticed it) when Miguel de Cervantes died on April 23, 1616, in Madrid, in the Calle de León, "old, a soldier, a gentleman and poor," according to staff of the French embassy who were surprised at how such a celebrated writer could live so unrecognized in the Spanish capital.

For Diego Velázquez the times continued prosperous. At age seventeen, he reached the end of his apprenticeship. He applied for membership of the Saint Luke's Guild and declared that he had been learning the art of painting with qualified masters. The plural "masters" presumably included Herrera, though on his own Pacheco would surely have sufficed, especially since he was one of his apprentice's examiners.

On March 14, 1617, young Velázquez was accepted as "a master painter of religious images, in oils and in everything related." He signed this as "Diego Velázquez de Silva." It was a good time for church painters, with the already considerable number of ecclesiastical institutions constantly swelling: nine new monasteries had been founded in Seville in the first twelve years of the seventeenth century. Velázquez was licensed to practice "in Seville or anywhere in the kingdom, and to set up a workshop of his own and take assistants and apprentices"—which he did a year later. He could have puffed out his chest and accepted congratulations, but it didn't seem to be his way. He had in any event a real reward to come from his former master. Pacheco said he so admired the young man, already a sort of son, that he gave him his daughter, Juana, in marriage.

Although this of course wasn't an uncommon happening in families of artists at this time, we can speculate about how well it matched the inclinations of those most concerned. Judging by Diego's paintings that seem to have used Juana as a model, she was a pretty girl. Over the previous five years he would have been used to seeing her, being with her, in the Pacheco house, almost like brother and sister, latterly the prize student and the boss's daughter. Young Spanish women of her sort were strictly supervised and chaperoned, and for Juana, thrown into the constant company of a good-looking, ambitious, and talented youth, praised by her father, it may have been fairly easy for interest and proximity to promote the even greater interest that might be love. She may simply have seen that among the young men in her surroundings, he was the most talented, and the best catch. Pacheco perhaps saw how things were going and encouraged it.

The marriage took place on the feast day of Saint George, April 23, 1618. It was the day on which, two years before, Miguel de Cervantes had died.* Diego was not yet nineteen, Juana was sixteen. Even by local standards, in a time when lives were shorter, it was an early marriage, but the die was cast, two hearts were one, and why wait? Pacheco's

---

*Some of Cervantes's best readers were in the Low Countries. Nineteen editions of his works were published in the Netherlands between 1607 and 1670. April 23 was also coincidentally Shakespeare's birthday. The year 1618 was by the way when a dazzling comet was seen in European skies, for many a portentous omen; the Thirty Years War began, which devastated much of central Europe.

golden circle celebrated the wedding in fitting style, with music, contests in verse, and literary debate. One of the witnesses was the poet Francisco de Rioja, the scholarly librarian of Count Olivares, who lived in Seville from 1607 to 1615, a period during which the count tried to retrench from some years of massive overspending in an as yet unsuccessful bid to get a post in the royal household. Rioja wrote poems that celebrated his patron's love life. He had immersed himself in Greek and Latin literature. In Seville's scholarly circles Tacitus and his Flemish editor Justus Lipsius were matters of frequent discussion when statecraft and classical learning came up. At the wedding of Pacheco's daughter with Diego Velázquez, there was a theatrical contest about whether Saint Teresa or Saint James made the best patron saint for Spain. A short play was performed and poems read, including an epithalamium by the poet Baltasar de Cepeda. It all sounds pretty high-flown, but there were also more down-to-earth songs and dancing, and food and drink to seal the occasion. The wedding was celebrated in the Pacheco house; the marriage papers failed to mention the parents of the groom.

Juana's unusually large dowry perhaps represented Pacheco's perception of Velázquez's potential and set up the young couple on a sound footing. Pacheco's wife, María del Páramo, was well-to-do; from her mother, Juana's grandmother, the married pair acquired a house near the Alameda de Hércules, where Velázquez and his bride first lived. Their first child, Francisca, was born just over a year later. Two years later, another daughter, Ignacia, came into the world but didn't survive childhood. (A quarter of all Spanish children died at birth or within their first year.) And that seems to have been that as far as Diego and Juana were concerned in their efforts to procreate. Velázquez was however consistently busy as an artist at this time. Pacheco provided contacts with people who would give his son-in-law commissions, and the subject matter that interested Velázquez was still close at hand. Kitchen scenes, religious pictures, or a mingling of the two genres kept him occupied. Observing his interest in drunken tavern scenes and *bodegones*, some in the Pacheco circle "remonstrated" with him, according to Palomino, for dealing so much with "low subjects." The Spanish Jesuit writer and teacher Baltasar Gracián, Velázquez's contemporary, wrote not long after in *The Hero* (1630) of a "certain able painter"—whom he doesn't name though we can guess whom he meant—"who, seeing with Grief, that *Titian, Raphael,* and several others were gone before him, and that their Reputation was increas'd since the Time of their Death, was resolv'd to raise a separate merit, and at all adventures to make himself a Compensation for the Advantage of Priority, that they had over him. He therefore set himself intirely to paint in Grotesque; and when some of his Friends blam'd him for not continuing in his soft and delicate manner, wherein he was likely to succeed, and even become *Titian*'s rival; he answer'd very briskly, *that he thought it more glorious to be first in his Way (wherein he was no mean Performer) than to be second in* Titian's, *or any others that had gone before him.*" (*The Hero,* English translation 1726, chap. 7, p. 71.)

Quite often in Velázquez's case the result was original (more original than this anecdote, whose provenance was classical) and not what we today would call grotesque. At this point, before 1620, he was dating but not signing his own work, perhaps because he didn't yet feel fully independent of his master. But the pictures themselves showed that he already was just that. One current theological battle in Seville concerned the Immaculate Conception: the belief that the mother of Christ had been born, unlike the rest of us, free from original sin. Preachers denounced one another on the subject; Dominicans (opposed to the doctrine) fought the Franciscans and Jesuits; long and learned texts pro and con were published about it, but most of the people in Seville were passionate in their devotion to the Queen of Heaven. For many she was, in a hierarchy of the faith, a step above the notional figureheads of the Trinity, Father, Son, and Holy Ghost. It was as if she were given preeminent power by the force not just of reverence but of paradox: She was both a virgin and a mother. In Seville hundreds of masses were annually said in her honor. Processions took place bearing her image, most prized being the painted statue of the Macarena Virgin by Montañés, generally kept in its own chapel at the north end of the town. Juan de Roelas, a Seville artist and contemporary of Pacheco, painted a picture commemorating the 1615 ceremony in honor of the Virgin's Immaculate Conception, a festival that went on for days, with fireworks, pageants, and masses. The doctrinal argument raged for sev-

The Virgin of the Immaculate Conception, *1618–19*,
National Gallery, London.

eral years until in 1617, under pressure from Spanish religious opinion, the Papacy decreed that no one could any longer deny *la concepción immac-ulada*. Seville once again celebrated with fireworks.

We have no knowledge of how Velázquez felt about the debate or how intensely he believed or disbelieved the doctrine, but we have evidence of his empathy with the devotion. Both Pacheco and his star pupil made representations of the young Virgin Mary. Velázquez was barely twenty when he painted *The Virgin of the Immaculate Conception*. Pacheco's painting of three years earlier in Seville Cathedral, one of three he did of the same subject, showed the Virgin standing on a moon, stars around her head, and squadrons of angels on all sides. Pacheco called the doctrine "this most lovely mystery," and he laid it down in writing that the Virgin should be painted *en fleur*, "twelve or thirteen years old, with fine and serious eyes, a most perfect nose and mouth and pink cheeks, wearing her most beautiful golden hair loose. . . . She is clothed in the sun." There was much less clutter in Velázquez's seraphim-free treatment, apparently done for an Order of Carmelite nuns in Seville. The Virgin's eyelids are demurely lowered. She seems to be levitating on a partly transparent moon, lit by the reflection from white clouds. She is, unlike Pacheco's stilted figure, a very real almost adolescent girl; Velázquez may have been inspired by Montañés and he also may have asked his sister, Juana, nine years younger than him, to be his model. Crucially the stars making a horseshoe constellation in the night sky around her head are brighter but less flamboyant than Pacheco's, diamonds in the sky rather than gaudy Christmas decorations.

What gave most support for Velázquez's reputation as the brightest young spark in Seville's art firmament was his skill in painting kitchen scenes. These would be much copied. They were done, as Palomino noted, "with most extraordinary originality and remarkable talent—animals, birds, fish-stalls and *bodegones* with perfect imitation of nature." The originality lay less in the subjects than in the boldness with which they were painted. There were predecessors for Velázquez's kitchen pictures, not from Spain but from the Low Countries, to which Velázquez early on showed an affinity. They were in particular pictures by Pieter Aertsen, the sixteenth-century artist nicknamed Lanky Peter, who worked in Antwerp and Amsterdam; his pictures figured in Seville in the collection of the Duke of Alcala and were also imported into the Andalusian city in print form by Flemish merchants. In one Aertsen tavern scene men sit at a table with food while a girl pours wine for them—just as in paintings by Pieter de Hooch and Johannes Vermeer that pictured similar scenes. But in the *bodegones* by Velázquez the tavern utensils often seem more prominent than the figures. In the painting in the Wellington Museum called *Two Young Men at Table*, for instance, the young men are turned aside, talking secretively, while the light falls on some dishes stacked upside down to dry, and our eyes focus on an orange perched on top of a jug. The turned-over dishes and jug are treated with an attention tantamount to

An Old Woman Cooking Eggs, *1618*,
National Gallery of Scotland, Edinburgh.

love. In another two of Velázquez's kitchen scenes, painted in 1618, the
same old woman appears. One wonders if she worked in the Pacheco
household or for the newly marrieds. In one picture she is cooking eggs,
holding a long-handled wooden spoon over a brown earthenware pot in
which the eggs are being fried in oil. Beneath the bottom rim of the pot
the glow of red-hot charcoal in an iron basin is just visible. In fact the
elderly woman bears a strong resemblance to another woman shown in a
double portrait Pacheco is thought to have painted of himself and his
wife, María del Páramo; we can take it that she was doing the cooking on
this occasion. A plump-faced young boy stands close by, holding in one
hand a glass flask and in the other a melon. The viewer is made to look
down on the eggs in the pot—an earthenware *cazuela*—and on the
objects on her table, a gray dish, a brass pestle and mortar, a carafe and a
jug, a red onion. The perspective is similar to that in a wonderful Zurbarán still life, a fragment of canvas showing a two-handled mug full of

Francisco Pacheco, Portrait of an Elderly Man and Woman,
Museum of Fine Arts, Seville.

water, sitting on a silver plate, with the head of a rose peeking over it. From the viewer's point of view one expects the top of the mug to reveal less of the water-filled interior than it does. Zurbarán, from Extremadura, was a year older than Velázquez but started his apprenticeship in Seville three years later; they evidently met and in later life were in touch on several crucial occasions, though, unlike Velázquez, Zurbarán spent most of his career working for monasteries and churches, painting saints and religious scenes that combined an austerity of action with the most brilliant colors.

The bony old woman we take to be Pacheco's wife was seen again, wearing the same scarf, her forehead furrowed by deeper lines, standing close behind a kitchen maid who is working with the brass pestle and mortar, evidently crushing garlic, with four fish and two eggs waiting on the table. In what has been seen by some as a religious picture on the wall to the right but is more likely a kitchen hatch into the next room are revealed three smaller figures. Christ is addressing Martha and Mary. This seems to have been Velázquez's first use of a split-screen effect—a device fairly common since the previous century and practiced in the seventeenth century in Holland by such artists as Nicolaes Maes (Maes's *The Listening Housewife* pauses to lean over the banisters,

Kitchen Scene with Christ in the House of Martha and Mary, *1618,*
National Gallery, London.

jug in hand, while downstairs in the cellar we glimpse a servant girl
being embraced by a young man). In Velázquez's *Kitchen Scene with
Christ in the House of Martha and Mary* the old woman in the left
foreground seems to be admonishing the maid to behave herself, and
the maid looks as if she is trying hard to preserve a grumpy silence.
Velázquez manages to fit a moral message about serving—even tight-
lipped—amid the pots and pans into a kitchen scene that once again
seems to have Netherlandish connections and marvelously observed
detail; in terms of quality it was on a par with the best the Low Countries painters of the time could produce. That Velázquez was thoroughly at home in the kitchen was shown in further paintings. Two
show the same maid. In these she is not an unhappy overweight
Andalusian teenager but a girl with brown skin and African features,
with flat nose, full lips, and frizzy hair. The brass bowl, pestle and
mortar, gray and blue jug, clove of garlic, and basket hanging on the
wall are items we have seen in the *Old Woman Cooking Eggs.* One of
these pictures (now in Chicago) is darkened and damaged and less
amplified than the other (now in Dublin), which once again has a religious scene partly visible through a hatch, a sort of cartoon thought

bubble, this time the Supper at Emmaus, where Christ recently risen from death has appeared in order to break bread among his astonished disciples. As Luke put it, "And their eyes were opened, and they knew him, and he vanished out of their sight." Here as well as being entranced by the wonderfully rendered *bodegón* elements, we are held by the foreground figure of the preoccupied servant girl, quite likely a slave in the Pacheco household, bending forward over the kitchen table, her face partly in shadow but revealing the most evident signs of an epiphany. (Seville had roughly six thousand slaves, mostly of North African but also of Caribbean origin.) Her turbanlike cap is more tightly pinned than the head scarf of Vermeer's *Girl with a Pearl Earring*, and she has no pearl earring. It is as if she were waiting for an angel to arrive and present her with astounding news though Velázquez no doubt meant only to show us her inner awareness of what was happening in the view through the hatch. Whatever her thought, it was one accessible, Velázquez suggested, to the humble and lowly.

Velázquez made a habit of reusing his small cast of characters as well as his store of domestic utensils. His brothers may have figured in *Two Young Men at Table*, about which Palomino described "some earthenware vessels, oranges, bread and other things," although the bread was in fact not on that table but on the table in another picture, this time of musicians, known in four versions, that in Berlin most likely the original. Here, too, the young men possibly played a part. One of them is also at a table, smiling or gesturing, eating and drinking, in several tavern scenes the young Velázquez made, for example the *bodegon* now in the Hermitage—a painting in which the plump-faced boy from *An Old Woman Cooking Eggs* appears again. Although the cast of characters Velázquez had at his disposal was limited, he reserved the right to interpose a novelty: a monkey looks around the back of the youngest musician in *The Musical Trio*. A young girl with a cap on the back of her head (similar to that worn by the Moorish servant girl in *The Kitchen Maid with the Supper at Emmaus*) pours wine, as if for the first time, with nervous concentration, in the tavern scene that now hangs in Budapest. An unseen hand in the making of these paintings was that of the Italian master Caravaggio, who died in 1610, and whose theatrical pictures, full of fierce contrasts, had an immense influence not so much on his fellow Italians as on Rubens and Rembrandt, and here in Seville. On the young painter of *bodegones*, this influence could have occurred in the reproduced form of prints, or possibly—indirectly—as a result of encountering paintings by Juseppe Ribera, the Valencian-born painter and follower of Caravaggio, sent from Naples (where Ribera worked) to Seville, or even perhaps after Velázquez saw several actual Caravaggios brought back to Seville from Rome by Prior Camillo Contreras. Caravaggio went in for painting from life with strong lighting and dramatic foreshortening. Pacheco saw Caravaggio's influence on his pupil in Velázquez's ability to evoke "force and plastic power" in order to create three-dimensional forms. And as Palomino later noted, Velázquez rivaled Caravaggio in the boldness of his painting; he was called a second Caravaggio "because he imitated nature so successfully . . . keeping it before his eyes in all things." Fortunately, the work of Velázquez wasn't generally as stagey, or as affected, as that of the Milanese painter— except nearly a decade later in a "religious" painting called *Christ After the Flagellation Contemplated by the Human Soul.*

One painting from the Seville years contains two male figures whose faces we seem to have seen before in Diego Velázquez's youthful oeuvre; it is not at all Caravaggesque and it is his masterpiece from this period. *The Waterseller of Seville*, also known as *El Corzo*, The Corsican, is remarkable for several reasons. The elderly man who dominates the picture stands mostly in shadow, his weathered, bearded face in profile, only his white-sleeved left arm brightly lit under his shabby leather poncho. The by now well-known chubby-cheeked boy stands before him, clutching the glass goblet that the water seller—perhaps the same elderly man with a beard who sat in the tavern with the girl pouring wine—holds out ready for the water to be poured into it. The goblet has either a flaw in its glass or a fig at the bottom to sweeten the water. Once again Velázquez has chosen a humble actor for a leading role. At the time water sellers were found all over Spain, and in places like Seville, in summer, they did a vital job. In a hundred-degree Fahrenheit heat, water was truly the most precious element. At the entrance to every inn in southern Spain (Richard Ford assures us) a clay waterpot or *alcarraza* hung, ready for those arriving to take a long drink from. The Corsican with his big jars of water was not so much a tramp or peddler as a bearer of blessings. For the parched, his clear cool water tasted sweeter than any wine. *"Agua muy rica,"* very tasty water, was how it was described by the sellers, and so it felt when one drank it. The *aguadores* generally carried along with their jugs a tin box for storing their glasses and biscuits in, the latter usually being *obleas*, a sort of sugar wafer. The painting also has something sacramental about it. Water had an almost religious importance in this part of Spain. The boy's contemplative look, not saying anything aloud as he presents the goblet to *El Corzo* in a way as acolyte to priest, conveys his participation in an act of communion, a mystery. Jar, water, glass, the server and the recipient—in all things are signs of God's presence.

The Waterseller evidently caused its painter considerable pains. A strip of canvas several inches wide has been added across the top. The shadows in the picture are given depth by the ground whose tone Velázquez manipulated (so the art historian Zahira Veliz tells us) "with decreasing densities of paint . . . to achieve the notable chiaroscuro evident there. The shadow on the right side of the large water jug in the foreground is achieved by scumbling over the ground with a drab tone, allowing a delicate play of light and cool tones, from which the form of the jug is brought into relief by the finely graduated lead-white based colour of the highlight." Corrections have been made to the collar of *El Corzo*'s sleeveless pancho and to his thick fingers. Some of the details are exquisitely done, the goblet that seems to have an air bubble in the glass at its bottom, the light on the boy's face reflected up from his twisted white collar, the pearls of moisture on the clay surface of the biggest jug and the glinting highlights on the glazed gray curves of the smaller, two-handled jug. Begging all manner of questions is the dim grotesque figure who can just be made out between the boy and the old water seller, perhaps the sketched suggestion for another participant who was never fully rendered, but left presenting a spectral or gnomic potency: broad faced, bearded, observant. He gives us a foretaste of Goya. Why is he there looking on? In any event, Velázquez knew this picture represented what he was capable of; it was a pearl of great price. For a young man, painted at a time when most artists would have been floundering as they tried to find "their own voice," it was astonishingly mature. He took it with him when he left Seville on the next stage of his career, gave or sold it to his patron Juan de Fonseca y Figueroa, chaplain to the king of Spain, and valued it at four hundred reales when Fonseca's collection was appraised in 1627, the highest value given any item. A number of copies of the picture were made.

The Waterseller of Seville is, apart from the heat implicit in its subject matter and the demonstrated profession of its main character, by no means a Spanish picture. In this and in the two kitchen scenes with servant girls, one detects a sympathy with the intimate and day-to-day that is positively Netherlandish. In European politics the Low Countries were tied to Spain in a relationship that, as we've already seen, was Oedipal or fratricidal, but Velázquez shows that he felt a similar tug. A large number of Spanish merchants were in the Netherlands, particularly in ports such as Antwerp, and in Seville the same was true of representatives of Dutch and Flemish businesses. Much Spanish wool went to Flemish textile makers. Diplomats and soldiers and royal officials went back and forth between the two countries. Art traveled, too. It may of course only be happenstance that eight hundred miles away and thirty-five years later we find Johannes Vermeer of Delft working in the same territory as Velázquez: a *Christ in the House of Martha and Mary*, with fewer kitchen implements but the same inspiration in Luke 10:38–42. Of the two paintings, Vermeer's now seems the more modern and more composed but Velázquez's has its depths and complications, its thought-provoking ambiguities.

His Seville years must have felt long at the time, but when he looked back, how fast they went by. Some of the work he accomplished then was less original in subject matter, more usual for the time and place, less low-life and more conventionally aspirational. "Religious Art" is a term that doesn't stir the emotions anymore and it may take an effort to shift oneself back to a period when the sea of faith was still at the full, and the patronage of the Catholic Church kept artists alive. Living up to his declared billing by the Guild of Saint Luke examiners in 1617 as "a master painter of religious images," Velázquez redressed his cargo of down-to-earth kitchen and tavern scenes with some more devout and more designedly devotional imagery. *St. John the Evangelist*, probably painted for the same Carmelite convent that had commissioned his *Immaculate Conception*, depicted John on Patmos, a young man having a vision, staring soulfully at a sign in the heavens that showed "a woman clothed with the sun, the moon under her feet, and on her head a crown of twelve stars." Thus Revelation 12:1. The saint, a man with a thin mustache, looks like an Andalusian kitchen helper but has in his lap an immense manuscript of many pages in which he has been writing. Behind him stands a heavily pollarded tree and behind it an area of background on which, with a series of almost calligraphic diagonal strokes, Velázquez seems to have cleaned the paint from his brushes, a common habit with him.

He obviously hadn't completely kicked the need for religious art that obsessed most Spanish painters. Other subjects he painted in these years included a bushy-haired and long-bearded Saint Paul and a Saint Thomas, a slightly more vigorous figure than represented by the same model in the Saint John, this time carrying an open Bible in one hand and in the other an iron-tipped lance—the weapon with which the saint would be martyred. Saint Ildefonso, the seventh-century archbishop of Toledo who defended the concept of Mary's perpetual virginity, was shown in Velázquez's painting of him receiving a chasuble from the Virgin as a reward for his good works. It was seemingly intended for a Franciscan convent in Seville, where it hung in the open atrium and even in its present damaged state makes a striking picture: Mary with a chorus of very real women stands over Ildefonso as he kneels to receive her gift, presenting a gaunt prayer-abstracted profile. The picture has, perhaps alone among Velázquez's saints, something of the power of the carved wooden figures of Juan Martínez Montañés, sometimes (as we've seen) polychromed by Pacheco. Montañés was forty-one years older than Velázquez. His crucified Christs were tormented men, rib cages evident under taut skin, muscles and tendons tense behind shoulders and knees. His *St. Hermenegild* showed the son of the Visigothic king dressed in Roman armor and holding aloft a crucifix, and it was probably carried in procession to a chapel in Seville designed for honoring the saint and opened in 1616.

Most openly attractive and perhaps most traditional of Velázquez's religious works in Seville was his *Adoration of the Magi*, apparently painted for a Jesuit chapel in the city. The novices of the order performed their devotions in this building. In this painting the Virgin of

Adoration of the Magi, *1619*,
Museo del Prado, Madrid.

Velázquez's *Immaculate Conception* has grown up. She is no longer a thirteen-year-old adolescent but a young mother, holding on her lap with big workaday hands an infant child. A wise-looking self-possessed little boy, swaddled in white cloth, is being admired—indeed adored—by a kneeling man, one of the three kings; though he and his colleagues are perhaps wise men rather than kings, for they wear no crowns as they proffer covered chalice-like containers for their gold, frankincense, and myrrh. One, his black features accentuated by a white ruff, is African. One looks rather like Pacheco. We are evidently in the countryside, at the opening to a cave. No animals can be seen and no star, but a creamy dawn light is spreading into the black sky over a nearby hilltop, and an almost theatrical brilliance passes over the magi to spotlight the mother and child before bouncing on more lightly to the upturned countenance of the woman's husband, Joseph—he seems smitten by his responsibilities. A fifth participant is a young man who bears a strong resemblance, a few years on, to the youth we've seen holding a glass before the Corsican water seller and the flask to the old woman cooking eggs. He is familiar, as if he were one of us; he is part of the family. (Some experts believe two of Velázquez's brothers served as models in this picture and for the saints, John and Thomas.) On the ground beneath the Virgin, in front of the Magi, are thorn branches, hinting at troubles to come for this serene babe. If the picture was meant to prompt the Jesuit novices to ponder their faith, one feels it did its job. The word was made flesh. It dwelled among us. The *Adoration of the Magi* also had northern European affinities, with a debt to a painting by Alejo Fernández, an artist of German origin who had worked in Seville in the first half of the previous century. Fernández's *Adoration*— which in turn was based on a print by Martin Schongauer of Colmar— was to be viewed hanging over the high altar in Seville Cathedral.

There is no doubt about the convincing nature of the last paintings of a religious person Velázquez made in Seville. They are both portraits of the same woman and one picture is more or less a replica of the other. Their subject is a sixty-six-year-old nun. Mother Jerónima de la Fuente was en route from her convent in Toledo, via Cadiz, to a posting in Manila, in the Philippines, when she stopped for twenty days in Seville in June 1620. There she posed, standing rather than sitting, for Velázquez to paint her. Manila, founded by a conquistador in 1571 (the same year as the great naval victory of the Catholic fleets over the Turks at Lepanto), was then as far away as the moon would be for us; it was a fortified city where Chinese and Japanese traders met the Spanish and money was made. A Spanish galleon brought silver from Mexico once a year to finance businesses; storms, calms, and shipwrecks were met with on the ways to and fro, and there were frequent deaths from scurvy, "the Dutch disease" as the Spanish called it. The order of Poor Clares that Mother Jerónima belonged to enjoined its members to seclusion. The Latin inscription at the head of the paintings means "It

The Venerable Mother Jerónima de la Fuente,
1620, Museo del Prado, Madrid.

is good to wait in silence for the salvation of God"—though one wonders how this admonition was put into practice alongside her role as a
missionary converting the heathen. It took Mother Jerónima over a
year to reach the Philippines, a trip broken for six months in Mexico.
In Manila she founded the first cloistered convent in that part of the
world (surrounded by a thirty-foot-high windowless wall) and perhaps
had to lead entirely by quiet example. She was known to reenact the
Crucifixion by hanging unsupported from a cross for three hours. For
Velázquez she holds her long-stemmed crucifix like a weapon. He makes
her look like a tough old bat, though the art scholars David Davies and
Enriqueta Harris more charitably describe her looks as "indomitable."

* * *

AT THE AGE of twenty anything can seem possible. But in Velázquez's case, the good fortune of being born prodigiously talented in what was still the most well-endowed city in Spain was enhanced by influential acquaintance. The word spread. Ripples from the Pacheco circle reached higher levels. Pacheco and thus his protégé had access to libraries and collections of antiquities such as that of the Duke of Alcala in his *mudejar* palace, the Casa de Pilatos, not far from Seville Cathedral, a palace with cool patios and handsomely tiled chambers full of books, paintings, sculpture, and collections of coins and jewels; the duke owned among other things two *bodegones*. Rodrigo Caro (1573–1647) was another of Pacheco's circle who was passionate about classical learning and art as was Pacheco's uncle and guardian, the cathedral canon Pacheco, who had the same Christian name as the artist Pacheco. However, the most important connection turned out to be with Gaspar de Guzmán, the Count of Olivares, whose father was at one time the honorary governor of the Seville Alcázar palace and who had lived in Seville during his twenties. The Dukes of Medina-Sidonia, one of whom commanded the ill-fated armada, were Guzmán's relatives, as was, it later transpired, a grandmother who came from a family of converted Jews. Their blood was therefore by the standards of the time "impure" and "tainted." Guzmán was born in Rome, in (so his later critics suggested) Nero's palace and was taken to Naples by his father, the viceroy there. In 1600 at age thirteen he returned to Spain to study law at Salamanca. Although the third son, his older brothers died, and he went to court (at the time in Valladolid) where his father was a counsellor. On his father's death, he inherited the title of Count of Olivares in 1607. He was a resident in Seville from 1607 to 1615. In October 1609, the twelve years' truce was signed with the troublesome Dutch (the truce, being a pacific move, didn't come naturally to him), and on the same date Olivares was presumably among those who approved the news that Philip III had signed a decree expelling the Moriscos from the country, the by now almost indigenous people of Moorish descent.

For his eight years in Seville, Olivares kept up his suit to become a member of the royal household. He competed with the Duke of Alcalá as a patron and saw a lot of people Pacheco knew well, such as the poet

Francisco de Rioja and another cathedral canon, a colleague of Pacheco's uncle, Juan de Fonseca y Figueroa. Olivares's desire to get fully taken on at court was fulfilled in 1615; he was appointed a gentleman of the chamber to Prince Philip, the heir apparent, in that year. The prince's new court servant was by no means a courtierlike figure but a big broad-shouldered man with physical and mental problems, limbs that twitched, and a propensity to throw tantrums. But he soon found that finesse and politesse were dispensable. To begin with he acted the part of a courtier prepared to be humbled—on one occasion he put up with the adolescent prince Philip telling him he was tired of his presence as he stood holding the prince's chamber pot. At that point Guzmán—biting his tongue?—dramatically kissed the pot. However, in April 1621 he was rewarded for his deference by being told to keep his hat on in Philip's company; this meant that Guzmán now had grandee status. Indeed, after the death of Philip III at the age of forty-two, Olivares quickly became the visible power behind the throne. The late king's favorite, or *valido*, the incompetent Duke of Lerma, was muscled out of the way. Nominally the chief minister was now Guzmán's uncle Baltasar de Zuniga, a former ambassador in Brussels, a tutor to the prince, and a man whose good Low Countries connections included a Flemish wife. Olivares, on the other hand, seemed to lack a natural rapport with that northern part of the Spanish empire, as would become perilously evident in time. He added the title of Duke of San Lúcar to his name in 1625, which as we will see was the year of an astonishing Spanish victory in the Netherlands. He was thenceforth called the count-duke.

In 1621, four years before that achievement, Spain was coming to an end of its twelve years' truce with the Dutch rebels. Little more than a week into Philip IV's new monarchy, the hourglass of relative peace ran out. Olivares had never backed the truce; he thought it injured Spanish trading interests and imperial expansion plans; and—one policy somewhat at cross-purposes with another—he believed a renewed war would give the insurgents pause and allow Spain time to work out an honorable way of bringing the interminable conflict to an end. A surge! And then a permanent peace! Meanwhile the southern provinces of the Low Countries had to be defended. Somehow Spain's integrity depended on it. Defending the Catholic religion and opposing Protestantism were involved. Yet many in both Madrid and Flanders thought that immediate peace should be given a chance instead. The southern provinces had prospered during the truce. The leadership on the spot was not gung ho about a renewed war—neither of the "arch-dukes" was keen, with Isabella doubtful about its long-term value and Albert, on the point of death, with his thoughts on eternity. Their senior military commander Ambrogio Spinola was a member of a dis-tinguished Genoese banking family. Lack of financial support from the Spanish crown forced him to invest his own funds in providing for the Army of Flanders; he wanted the Dutch to be given a chance to cool off. Unfortunately, the Dutch were once again feeling belligerent and ill-feeling mounted on both sides. The Spanish Council of State took the majority position that refinancing the struggle against the Dutch would be worth it if the conflict preserved Spain's glory. "A good war in Flanders" would promote peace elsewhere. It would also keep the restless Spanish army busy in the southern Netherlands. The troops needed something to do that would take their minds off their long overdue pay. And of course money would be found to pay for the renewed war, wouldn't it?

BOTH SPAIN AND Seville were at tipping points. Seville had begun to lose its luster as the golden city. Ships from the Americas were bring-ing home less bullion. The river was silting up and trade was moving down to Cádiz. The hardworking Andalusian Moriscos had been expelled or enslaved. Madrid was at last making itself felt as the real center of power, the city of the royal court. In April 1622, Diego Velázquez made his first visit to the capital, perhaps prodded by his father-in-law, who saw that it meant a way ahead.

Velázquez was nearly twenty-three. It was a time of possibilities, of all sorts of doors being suddenly open for him. He owned several houses in the Alameda de Hércules, part of Juana's dowry. He had taken on an apprentice, Diego de Melgar. He had two small children, Francisca born in 1619, and Ignacia, born in 1621. One imagines him from later self-portraits as having eyes well set apart, and with the expressive mustache of a young hidalgo or would-be hidalgo. A young man from Seville. Already a stunning painter, astonishingly mature, although in Madrid only a few, in Olivares's circle, knew his name. Before he set off on the road to that city in April 1622, he asked his father-in-law to take over the collection of rents from his properties, and his younger brother Juan, also a painter, witnessed Pacheco's acceptance of the power of attorney. (When Pacheco in turn went to Madrid for a time, Juan Rodríguez, Velázquez's father, took over the oversight of the properties, which were damaged in the floods of 1626 and sold by auction two years later.) Diego Velázquez made what is considered to be a portrait of his former master before he left Seville: it's a picture that might have been painted by only one other living artist, Frans Hals, who lived in Haarlem in Holland. Having said that, one can't be sure Hals would have left in shadow so much of the mustached and goateed face that springs out above the freely painted white ruff and the otherwise all-black background. The shadow is all Velázquez. It makes the portrait that much more brilliant. Pacheco was aware that the pupil had surpassed the master and said so, proud of the fact, in print, in his *Arte de la Pintura* in 1649. But this wonderful picture of Velázquez's teacher, identified by its resemblance to a self-portrait Pacheco had done in 1610–11, made the pupil's preeminence evident nearly thirty years earlier.

If Velázquez left this as a token of his ability, he took with him another piece of evidence when he set off for Madrid. His painting of *El Corzo* went with him. The pictures he had painted so far provide our best testimony of what sort of person he was: concerned with detail; alive to domestic circumstances; sensitive about such vital elements as water, food, the common stuff of daily existence; aware of religion, the Bible, the sacraments, all providing a structure that could shelter and insulate an individual; highly conscious of art elsewhere in Flanders and Italy and particularly influenced by the heightened realism of Caravaggio. His interest in what Palomino later called "rustic subjects" was interwoven with an interest in higher things. We are given hints that along with superrealism, Velázquez, mature at twenty-three, could already tap into a transcendent dimension.

III. MADRID: FOR THE FIRST TIME. 1622–

THE ROAD NORTH IN APRIL WOULD NOT YET HAVE BEEN BAK-
ing. Alongside it, wildflowers relieved the dry red landscape. In
bodegas and inns beside the route the bread was hard, the wine coarse if
not sour. The then recently published adventures of Guzmán de Alfarache may have come to mind, Guzmán a runaway youth of uncertain
parentage from Seville, seeking fame and fortune but finding en route to
Madrid hard knocks and con tricks, "veal" stew made of mule meat, his
clothing pilfered, beds full of fleas and lice, the innkeepers rapacious.
Bumping and shaking, the coach traversed northern Andalusia before
heading for Castile through wild and depopulated Extremadura. As a
half dozen mules pulled his conveyance across the celebrated "plains"
of Alcudia, a well-read traveler might also have recalled their recent
description by Cervantes in one of his exemplary tales. To fend off bandits, the coachmen and muleteers often formed caravan convoys, protecting scores of passengers and up to a hundred horses and mules, with
bells being dragged on the ground behind the last members to alert the
guards to attacks by thieves—no sound of bells meant something was
amiss. The caravans camped in the country at night with guards posted.

Velázquez, taking with him *The Waterseller* and a few other tangible
examples of his talent to demonstrate to future clients what he was
capable of, was going to Madrid as Seville began to seem burned out.
His father-in-law later claimed that Velázquez went in order to see the

Escorial, King Philip II's massive monastery-palace west of Madrid, though that may have been shorthand for Velázquez's hopes of getting a post near the seat of power, fame, and fortune. His ambition was not expressed too loudly. He may have had doubts. He had known no other home but Seville and despite the economic downturn he could have stayed there and carried on doing what he did so well, followed in Pacheco's steps or, like Zurbarán, gone on working for churches and convents and monastic orders. But he wanted more and felt he had the ability to achieve it.

In Madrid he was greeted by some of those who formed a Seville contingent there. Luis and Melchor del Alcázar, a Jesuit priest and a poet, were of Jewish *converso* origin, brothers who had helped put on the Immaculate Conception festivities in Seville in 1617. Juan de Fonseca, the former canon of Seville Cathedral, was now *sumiller de cortina*, a court chamberlain, and a royal chaplain who assisted the monarch at services in the chapel. Fonseca shortly became the owner of *The Water-seller.* Another Sevillian was Francisco de Rioja, the poet who had been a witness at Velázquez's marriage to Juana and brought to court by Count Olivares as his librarian. So Velázquez had plenty of connections. They worked to bring the young artist to the attention of the new king, Philip IV. However, the fourth monarch to be named Philip—and called "the planet king" because people then thought the Earth was the fourth planet in the solar system—seemed to be too busy to allow an introduction or a hoped-for sitting to take place.

Unable to paint the king or the queen, Velázquez got started on another picture. Pacheco had asked for a portrait of Luis de Góngora, poet, satirist, and a former chaplain to Philip III. Velázquez was always good at expressing determination and this painting of Góngora—useful as a calling card—was an early example of this ability. Perhaps he was helped by the fact that Góngora didn't appear to have particularly enjoyed sitting for the young Sevillian. "How much longer is this going to take?" his look seems to say. The self-consciousness imposed on the sitter by the painter may have interfered annoyingly with Góngora's hopes of using the time for thinking about other things. But Velázquez used his time brilliantly—he caught the high brow, keen eyes fixed on the artist, beak of a nose, and clenched downturned lips,

Luis de Góngora, *1622, Museum of Fine Arts, Boston.*

the head of a raptor. An unforgettable skull that rose out of the white shirt and enveloping black coat. A highbrow indeed. When Velázquez captured his look and personality, Góngora was in his early sixties, an isolated man originally from Córdoba who felt out of his time but who nevertheless managed to fit together an inherited church post with a love of gambling, philandering, and writing. He knew what it felt like to be condemned. One heartfelt poem expressed a Spanish slave's long anguish, chained to a rowing bench on a Turkish galley. Góngora endured the endless waiting-around at court with little grace and suffered in his later years from acute writer's block. He lost most of his fortune gambling at cards. A stroke caused him to lose his memory. His death in 1627 at least relieved him from knowing that his collected poems, published posthumously, were suppressed by the Inquisition.

El Corte. The court was the capital and the capital the court for those attracted to it. Under Philip III Madrid had drawn the nobility high and low, their servants and followers. The city had become crowded not least with criminals, who saw easy pickings there. But for Velázquez Madrid had at the moment no opening, and in early 1623 he was back in Seville; there he bided his time. And he didn't have to wait long. By way of Fonseca, the summons to return to the court came in the summer. Count Olivares had taken the matter in hand. A portrait Velázquez had done of Fonseca had been acclaimed at the palace. Fifty ducats was sent to Velázquez as an advance for travel money. This time the journey was a hot one but worthwhile. Pacheco went, too, sure his pupil would succeed. And by the end of August, Velázquez had his entrée and had painted a portrait of the king, the eighteen-year-old Philip; this received all-around acclaim. Count Olivares declared that the king had never been painted successfully until now. (The portrait is possibly that now in the Meadows Museum of Southern Methodist University, Dallas.) The young Sevillian was also asked to sketch Charles, the Prince of Wales, in Spain on a mission of possible matrimony, traveling incognito with his friend and mentor the Duke of Buckingham as Mr. Brown and Mr. Smith. Velázquez received a hundred escudos as a reward for his work from Prince Charles but on religious grounds the Spanish court wasn't keen on the marriage, despite Charles's claims that he would allow religious tolerance to Catholics in England. A year or so later the Stuart marital bed was occupied instead by a French princess, Henrietta Maria. Olivares confirmed Velázquez's first step up the ladder by ensuring him accommodation for Juana and the children in Madrid. He was clearly needed there; no one else was as talented. On October 6, 1623, Diego Velázquez was favored by the king and appointed a court painter.

As such, he was a member of the Royal Household—in effect a staff artist. He was put on a salary of twenty ducats or escudos a month. Extra sums would be paid for the paintings he did. Of course, his life had rarely been his own: First he had belonged to his father; then to his master; now to the king. Yet in return for what we might regard as freedom he had the security of the household, one perquisite being what today would be called a health plan, including the services of a physician, chemist, and surgeon. A further sum of three hundred ducats—more than his annual salary—was provided for living expenses.

Another three hundred was promised for a pension that would be funded by an ecclesiastical living; the church officialdom worked on this and a papal dispensation for it was granted in 1626. Velázquez's father was also remembered. In the ensuing seven years, the cathedral legal scribe was awarded three secretaryships, each worth a thousand ducats. Velázquez himself was given working quarters in the royal apartments on the ground floor of the Alcázar, the huge palace with some five hundred rooms laid out on two floors around two arcaded courtyards. The formerly Arab medieval fortress had been built overlooking the escarpment of the Manzanares Valley, on the west side of Madrid, and had been enlarged, given a new facade, and somewhat modernized after 1610. Velázquez was presumably glad that he enjoyed a private residence outside the palace. To begin with, this was a house in the Calle de Concepción Gerónima, off the Calle Toledo, but by 1625, when he and Juana were joined by her father, they were all living in a rented house in the Calle de los Convalecientes (now called Calle San Bernardo). In 1626 the king directed that Velázquez be given the right to housing worth two hundred ducats per annum. In Madrid he might have missed the thicker, more pungent odor of Seville—as Mateo Aleman had observed, taking note of the greater refinement of the capital, Seville had "the smell of a city."

However, Velázquez's route every day to the court lay through the Plaza Mayor and along fairly unclean streets. Much food was cooked in the streets and many food sellers prepared their wares outside, too; salt cod was left to soak in tubs and the smelly brine was then poured into the gutters. Many people went out each morning for their breakfast *torreznos*, bacon grilled on smoky fires and chased down by a cup of wine. The court centered in the palace was the biggest single employer in the city. Roughly 10 percent of the national income went to maintain it. Some 1,700 individuals, many glad of their sinecures, others striving for further favors, jockeyed for position within it. Their promised wages were by no means guaranteed. Velázquez was one of 350 officials at the heart of the court, whose workings depended on protocol and etiquette going back to Burgundian days. The monarch seemed buried inside a mountain of antique ceremony. Routine was sacrosanct and the king was obliged never to act in an unaccustomed manner.

The palace was—according to foreign visitors not used to the darkness of Spanish interiors—exceptionally gloomy. However, commercial shops and workshops surrounded some of the ground-floor courtyards, and the women's quarters upstairs were lighter. The king had his own set of keys to every room in the palace and was able to pass without notice through a maze of galleries and corridors. He also followed a habitual route in mannerisms, one French observer saying that he acted like an animated statue, "not moving except for the lips and the tongue." His own rooms were in the Torre Dorada in the southwestern corner of the palace from which he could look out on the woods around the Casa del Campo, where rooks nested, descendants of the colony of birds Charles V had brought from the Netherlands. Philip's apartment included a study, an oratory, the "gilded gallery," and two rooms set aside as the places where he ate his meals. The king took a private passageway from his quarters to the court painter's studio when he wanted to have a personal view of the work going on.

Hidden much of the time from the people, walled in by ceremony, Philip IV felt compelled to act with Hapsburg gravity, stiff, never smiling. He was reputed to have laughed out loud only three times in his life. This impression he gave of never being amused was one of the Hapsburg characteristics, like the protruding jaw, fleshy lips, somewhat bulging eyes, and a trapped expression that hovered between melancholy and obstinacy. It was claimed that his father Philip III looked out of a palace window on one occasion and saw a passerby laughing. He said, "That man is mad or has been reading *Don Quixote*." Professional fools and jesters, often dwarfs, were employed to create amusement at court, though when Philip IV's young second wife, Mariana, arrived in Madrid from Austria and laughed at a dwarf who was playing the fool, she was told off. Laughter was not becoming to a queen of Spain. "In that case get rid of the dwarf," she said smartly. Philip IV did not make many appearances to the people of Madrid except when receiving a foreign ambassador in public. He went to a few formal occasions such as opening performances of plays or the marriages of ladies-in-waiting, but his privacy was often theatrically enhanced. On the notable occasions when the king left the Alcázar on the west of the city for San Jerónimo church on the east, every member of the court made their way across the city in a long procession to watch him attend the service. Another rare royal appearance was on Maundy Thursday, when he went to a city church to wash the feet of a beggar. He eavesdropped on his Councils of State, listening to what was said at their meetings through small windows that kept him out of sight. He dined alone. A small army of guardsmen, ushers, stewards, and sommeliers attended him, washing his hands, pouring two glasses of wine so that it could be tasted before the king drank it, parading back and forth to the kitchens for each course, and brushing away crumbs. A martial procession of servants with soldiers as guards accompanied the arrival of and tasted each dish at his table—although from 1630 a policy of austerity dictated that lunch contain only ten dishes and supper only eight.

Olivares having insinuated his way into power brought in many reforms. The number of servants permitted was restricted as was the use of carriages and the importation of luxuries from abroad. The display of silver plate and access to brothels was meant to be controlled. Elaborate fashions were banned: Intricate lace and linen ruffs and cuffs were prohibited and the plain *golilla*—a saucer-shaped stiff collar made of cardboard sandwiched between silk and cloth—was introduced; the king took the lead in using one and in wearing plain black clothes. Yet other fancy accoutrements, such as heavy gold chains, remained fashionable. The visits of foreign dignitaries and celebrities also made for exceptions. When Charles Stuart, the Prince of Wales, turned up in Madrid to seek the princess María's hand, the reform decrees were suspended for the period he was in town. Lavish balls and theater performances took place, along with fireworks displays and bullfights. Moreover, women were less affected by the reforms in their clothing. They went on wearing the then fashionable *guardainfante*, a wide skirt on a framework of iron, willow, and whalebone; it eventually got so wide that those wearing it had trouble getting through church doors.

If impromptu laughter was in short supply at court except for those reading the bestselling adventures of Don Quixote, one reason was money. Everyone might well look dour because they all lived on credit, including the king. Philip was betrothed to Isabella of Bourbon, the sister of the French king Louis XIII, in 1615, when she was twelve and he was ten, though the marriage wasn't consummated for another five

Don Gaspar de Guzmán,
Count-Duke Olivares, *1624*,
Museo de Arte, São Paulo, Brazil.

years. As a youth he struck many as spoiled and petulant. Most Spanish children are coddled and adored, but the future king went on having his own way and unlike most Spanish men never had to take further steps to prove he could act independently, self-confidently, unless it was as a huntsman or lover. He eventually had thirty-two bastard children, of whom he acknowledged eight. One of his natural sons was another Don Juan (1629–79), the first prince of that name in this generation, who became popular. Juan's mother, the actress María Calderón, also had a turn as lover of Olivares's son-in-law, though to spare the king further embarrassing publicity she eventually withdrew to a convent in March 1642, when Philip recognized Juan as his son. Not that Philip's affairs were very secret. Olivares was believed to be the chief provider of mistresses to the king. In 1621 the count was criticized by the archbishop of Granada for accompanying Philip on his nocturnal adventures. The count-duke replied that the king shouldn't be kept in ignorance of what went on in the world. He, Olivares, would keep a close eye on him since he trusted the king with no one else.

Olivares, the king's favorite, sponsored Velázquez's assimilation into the court, and the young painter returned the favor with several portraits that conveyed the count's political clout. That Olivares found nothing to complain about in being depicted as a powerful operator seems evident by the number of portraits that showed his hulking figure. He perhaps understood that in Velázquez he had a potent weapon in public relations. The portrait, for instance, of 1624 (now in São Paulo, Brazil) was commissioned by the wealthy wife of an influential lawyer; she wanted a portrait of her husband, one of the king, and one of the count. Olivares's shape fills the canvas, his head high up in the frame and relatively small compared with the bull-like body, shoulders exaggerated by padding, a heavy gold chain draped across a chest whose black satin smock is emblazoned with the insignia of the knightly Order of Calatrava, a huge key—the key to the kingdom, one feels—tucked into his belt in one painting, showing that he was *sumiller de corps*, chief man of the household, and in another work a pair of golden spurs that symbolized his position as *caballerizo mayor*, the king's master of the horse. Holding more than one royal office was not intended to be the rule and that Olivares managed this showed how high he was above the law. As groom of the chamber he was the last to leave the king's bedroom at night and the first to come into it in the morning, pulling back the curtains. He got up at five to start the day's business. In the 1624 portrait Olivares stands with one hand on a red-velvet draped tabletop, the other hand grasping the hilt of his sword, beneath him a dark pool of his own shadow. "I am the enforcer," he seems to say.

Velázquez was gradually absorbed into the life of the court. It was a mysterious organization, another gilded cage to enclose him or a giant sponge that sucked him in. If he hadn't had his painting to worry about it might have driven him crazy. He met with some resentment at first from other court artists who were his stablemates. The Sevillian newcomer's talent immediately won him envy-provoking favors. One of his first paintings after his appointment was a life-size portrait of the king on horseback. It was hung up outside the church of San Felipe in the Calle Mayor, where fashionable crowds came to admire it, and was later displayed in the Hall of Mirrors of the Alcázar opposite an equestrian portrait of Charles V by Titian, a spot of great honor. The king soon let it be known that from now on only Velázquez should portray him, in the same way that, as it says in *Don Quixote*, "Alexander forbad all Painters to draw his Picture, except Apelles."

This of course fanned the flames of dissent. Critical voices complained that Velázquez wasn't as good as all that, or that he had limitations: He was only good at painting heads. The established court painter Vincente Carducho, a Tuscan, was thought to have made that jibe, since he was known to believe that heads were easiest to paint because you had a human likeness in front of you to work from. Velázquez may have acknowledged some truth in this, but responded that his critics were in advance of him, since he knew no one (himself included) who could paint a good head. He apparently went on working on the picture of Philip on horseback, erasing much of it, dissatisfied with the horse. To alleviate the bitter atmosphere, Philip decided to hold a painting competition. Whatever his weaknesses, the king loved art: He himself painted now and then, composed music, and wrote poetry. He attempted to build a scholarly library and often spent two hours after lunch every day in serious reading. He learned Catalán, Portuguese, French, and Italian. The subject for the competition was—rather daringly—the expulsion of the Moriscos in 1609, the punitive act that some Spaniards had thought counterproductive but which signaled for most the leading role the Spanish Hapsburgs had taken in defense of the True Faith, and the final stage in Spain's ridding itself of its Muslim invaders. Three other court painters entered the lists with Velázquez, all Italians by birth: Carducho, Eugenio Caxesi, and Angelo Nardi. All were "history painters" in their old-fashioned mannerist ways.

We don't actually know how much of a contest it was, but we do know that Velázquez's painting won. As we've noted, when ten years old he may well have seen masses of enforced emigrants being funneled toward the wharves in Seville for transport to North Africa. His prize-winning painting was apparently hung for a while in the palace's Salon Nuevo and later, according to Palomino, in the Salon Grande, where it was described as showing Philip III in armor in the center, pointing his baton at the weeping Moors. They were being led on to ships along the shore, while an allegorical figure of Hispania in Roman costume—"a majestic matron"—held up a shield and arrows, and more pacifically ears of corn. At the bottom of this picture the artist painted the representation of a parchment on which was written: "Diego Velázquez of Seville, Painter to Philip IV, King of Spain, by whose command he made this in the year 1627." The atrocity at that time was considered to be Philip III's victory for Catholic Spain and was used as propaganda to bolster the Hapsburg dynasty. Velázquez's *Expulsion* disappeared after the fire that did great damage to the Alcázar in 1734; we also have no way of knowing whether, although Palomino's description made it sound stagey, it was any more or less so than its competitors. At the time, to crown his artistic success, Velázquez was given a boost to his court career, being appointed a gentleman usher to the king. This post not only gave him an additional salary but meant that he was now a fully fledged member of the household and not just a minor official in the royal department of Works.

We don't hear very much of some fellow citizens of Seville who came with him to court: his brothers Juan and Silvestre, for example, although we know that Silvestre, who had been living with Diego and Juana and was not quite eighteen, died in Madrid in mid-May 1624. There is little further mention of Velázquez's assistant Diego de Melgar and any other studio helpers Velázquez must have had; Melgar continued his apprenticeship with Francisco López Caro. Later on we become aware of the fact that one of Velázquez's assistants was a slave, a young man possibly a bit younger than himself named Juan de Pareja. Pareja came from Antequera on the road from Seville to Málaga and was apparently of mixed Morisco or Arab descent. He seems to have been one of Velázquez's studio assistants from sometime in the 1630s. A large nonfree underclass dwelled in many Spanish cities; Seville's slaves worked as domestic servants, like the kitchen girl in Velázquez's *bode-gones*, as assistants in artisan workshops, and as laborers, fetching and carrying in small factories and markets. They often learned the trades of their masters, in the way that Juan de Pareja picked up the practice of painting from Velázquez. Some slaves were inherited, like furniture. Velázquez's maternal grandfather, Juan Velázquez Moreno (ca. 1545–99), a breeches maker and moneylender, owned a slave who was thirty years old in 1588 and who ran away. Kevin Ingram tells us that he was recaptured on the road to Granada. Identification was made easier because he had been branded on his cheeks with the letters *Ju* and *Ve*. Nevertheless, being a domestic servant was better than being a slave captured by the Berbers, as Cervantes was, or an oarsman chained to a bench like those prisoners who could be seen in many of the galleys docked in the Guadalquivir in Seville.

In Madrid Velázquez soaked up the pleasure of being in a privileged spot, and perhaps enjoyed, too, the sense that no one ever seemed absolutely sure of what was going on. The world spun around, but who knew which way? It was a world of questions but was anyone directing them at those who could answer them? In the court good news of course spread quickly. In 1623 Don Fernando Giron, one of Philip's counsellors, had declared that war in the Netherlands was causing the total ruin of the monarchy. The Council of State in Madrid believed it was the moment for defensive rather than offensive operations against the Dutch, possibly taking heed of the military maxim of the time that "One good towne well defended sufficeth to ruyn a mightie army." But now in 1625 the clouds momentarily lifted. There were smiles all around and applause as word wafted through the Alcázar that things for a change were going well in the Low Countries; the Army of Flanders was heading for Brabant; this could be the start of the recapture of all the rebel provinces and the collapse of the heretic cause. A victory would herald a new golden age for Spain. The Dutch would be under dire pressure once again. Think of all the money that would be saved! Let's not think about possible defeat. In any event, Spinola shook off the quagmire mud and first directed his forces toward the town of Grave. This was a feint. The archduchess Isabella, sole governor of the Netherlands since Albert's death in 1621, had approved an action against a town in Brabant. However, when Breda—"the right eye of Holland" as the prolific court newsletter writer Andres de Mendoza put it—was proposed for the purpose, she and her council thought it might be too hard a nut to crack; it was well fortified; it had been held by the Dutch since the peat-boat assault in 1590 and in recent years had been judged the best-manned garrison in the Dutch defensive ring. But it was at Breda that, taking the offensive, Spinola took aim.

IV. What Happened at Breda. 1625

SPINOLA AT THIS POINT WAS ALREADY KNOWN THROUGHOUT Europe. His successful siege of Ostend, his capture of towns and fortresses in Cleves-Julich, a German duchy close to the Dutch border, and his consequent control of the Rhine Valley and with it the Spanish Road, all led to him being recognized as the best army commander of the time. In 1618, the year the Thirty Years War broke out, Spinola was invoked along with the celebrated imperial general Bucquoy in an English verse inveighing against the evils of tobacco, a "dear drug" that gallants spent their gold on, but which might make—the author Thomas Pestel suggested, tongue-in-cheek or fingers holding his nose—a useful poison gas:

> 'Tis our artillery too; and armed this way
> Our English scorn Bucquoy and Spinola:
> Set but each man unto his mouth a pipe
> And—as the Jews gave Jericho a wipe,
> Raising a blast of rams' horns while it fell—
> Some ballad on a time, the truth shall tell
> How it befell, when we our foes did choke
> Like bees, and put them pell-mell to the Smoke.

For the Spanish, in the improving early 1620s, embargoes seemed to be working against the Dutch. The rebels were prevented from entering Iberian ports, while their herring boats were being sunk in the North Sea and their merchant ships blockaded. Prince Maurice had started negotiating with Brussels about a new truce but the talks were stalled. Moreover, there was now peace with England and France— France particularly had its hands full and was sundered by religious conflict. The Spanish army had been expanded to sixty thousand men, causing the Dutch to increase their forces while having difficulty raising taxes to pay for them. A butter tax of four guilders per vat, imposed by the States General in The Hague in June 1624, provoked urban riots; in Haarlem some of the town's militia—one member of which was the painter Frans Hals—fired on the angry demonstrators.

Spain's army was cosmopolitan, reflecting the fact that Spain was less a nation than an international organization: a conglomerate of kingdoms, princely territories, duchies, states, colonial possessions. The Spanish army included men of all ages. Some Spanish towns recruited by lottery, taking into the ranks males even in their sixties. Most who volunteered did so to get food and clothing. A common soldier in *Don Quixote* says, "I was driven to the wars by my necessity. If I had money I would never go." The Spanish *tercios* were units of varying size, anywhere between one thousand and five thousand men, and they included—the military historian Geoffrey Parker tells us—boys of sixteen, without hats or shoes. Many recruits never reached the Low Countries; trudging north up the Spanish Road, they vanished in the snow on Mount Cenis, in the forests of the Vosges, and the fields of Luxembourg. Some were criminals or tramps, and some were poor gentry, so-called *particulares*, gentlemen-rankers who weren't inhibited by strictures against their participating in manual labor, in trade and warfare. The king of Spain was served by Spaniards, Italians, Burgundians, Germans, Walloons, Flemings, Dutch, and English. For the moment, too, the Army of Flanders was being properly financed, and with the Dutch on the verge of revolt against their own leaders, it seemed to Brussels, if not Madrid, that the chance should be seized. Spinola had his opportunity. On July 21, 1624, he and his army set forth from Brussels as the corn ripened in Flanders fields.

Breda was defended for the United Provinces by a garrison of seven thousand armed men, also of motley origins. Since the turfship assault, the town had been reinforced with fortifications immediately outside the existing stone walls. Among the soldiers who briefly served in the town was a Frenchman, René Descartes, an expert in mathematics. On one occasion in the town's Grote Markt he got talking to a teacher from Dordrecht and helped him solve a geometry problem. Breda's people were predominantly Catholic but for 220 years the town had been the seat of the Nassau family, and hence the home of the Orange-Nassau dynasty. This made it a splendid target for the Spaniards: the hometown of the rebel chiefs; the lynchpin in the necklace of towns hung like a chain around Holland, mostly along the rivers, which impeded even if they didn't prevent the movement of armies. Capturing—recapturing!—Breda would be a coup indeed. What counted most in laying siege to such towns was the ability to get an army together that would be big enough to envelop the town and yet could be sustained with provisions and pay for the duration of the siege. Sources differ about the size of Spinola's army, Andrés de Mendoza saying it was 23,000 men, and Herman Hugo, Spinola's Jesuit chaplain, who kept an account of the siege, reckoning 18,000. On the way to the city, Spinola decided to wind up Prince Maurice, who was trying to gain advantage by dithering over the truce talks. Spinola set his troops to ravage the prince's family lands around Moers, Grave, and Breda.

In August Spinola began to establish his own ring around Breda. His troops camped in the woods and pastures and took over farm cottages; some locals were glad of the rent they were paid. Spinola's staff officers tried to convince their chief that Breda posed great difficulties with its strong walls and surroundings, which could be readily made inaccessible by inundation. Even Philip IV when he heard about his general's plans thought it a risky business. Some in the Council of State suggested withdrawing the army if this could be done without sacrificing its honor. But the captain-general—although also mocked by Dutch pamphleteers—went ahead. Spades and wheelbarrows were for the moment the chosen weapons rather than pikes and flintlocks. In less than a month Spinola's men had created a network of trenches, parapets, moats, pits, redoubts, bastions, batteries, and causeways across swampy ground. The double line of trenches didn't incorporate "saps," which would have been needed for wall-breaking cannon, because Spinola intended to take the town by starvation. The siege lines made a slightly irregular circuit of ten leagues, a distance it took three and a half hours to get around.

Prince Maurice, William the Silent's son, wasn't in the best of health and at first didn't grasp the full measure of Spinola's challenge. Maurice thought Breda was impregnable (although the turfship backed by him thirty years before had surely proved the contrary). Father Hugo believed the Dutchman should have anticipated the Spanish threat and moved his army, camped at Meede only twelve miles from Breda, to occupy the low-lying land around the city. From there he could have resupplied the garrison by boats. But Spinola's arrival outside Breda forestalled him. Spinola was ready to cope with however long the siege might take. To his men, the Genoese seemed to be everywhere at all times of day and sometimes all night, checking progress of the siege works, riding, walking, skipping meals, taking a nap in a cart or a soldier's bivouac. He was a hands-on commander. He rode constantly to call on his officers and see how things were in the lines; this kept the soldiery on their toes, never sure when he might turn up. He had a particularly good eye for spots where the enemy might attempt an attack. He seemed to need less sleep than most men and wasn't bothered by rain and wind. He sometimes went days without a proper meal. Any officer anxious to see him could gain access but he was reserved about his plans. All would be well. His serenity spread confidence through the ranks. His presence made his men think of victory, and therefore plunder. They were still short of half their proper pay. In fact, for a time there seemed to be greater danger of famine among Spinola's besieging army than in besieged Breda. But Spinola ensured that basic supplies of food and clothing were dispensed using four hundred carts, and he took care discipline and morale were maintained. The siege was soon famous. The nobility of Europe came, as it were on a grand tour, to inspect the operation and some actually to get their hands dirty by cutting turf or heaping up soil for the Spanish siege works. Among Spinola's notable visitors were the Duke of Bavaria and Prince Ladislaw Sigismund of Poland. During the latter's visit at the end of September three volleys were fired in his honor by the Spanish artillery, aimed so that the shot passed intentionally over Breda. However, by the arcane rules of sieges the firing of enemy cannon meant that the townsmen of Breda were now exempt from taxes. And the salvoes encouraged the Dutch to reply. A ball from one Dutch gun killed a local Brabant miller with what would now be called friendly fire. The Breda defenders also fired at Spinola's party as it conducted Prince Ladislaw around the siege works. Later one Dutch cannonball landed on Spinola's cabin, carrying away the canopy over his field bed and breaking two tables. (The general was out at the time.) On another occasion gunfire struck the bit of his horse's bridle, leaving the reins useless in Spinola's hands. Father Hugo wrote, "It is probable that, either Almighty God hath a peculiar care of great Generalls or that, by how much more a man adventureth himself, so much the less danger, for the most part, he incurreth." Yet actual large-scale fighting was rare. On one occasion in September 1624, during the prince of Poland's visit, the Dutch made a raid on the Spanish lines and Spinola set up a new headquarters at Terheyden to oppose them, with a small battle ensuing. The Dutch set fire to the church at Oosterhout and Spinola's troops made a counterattack. Small skirmishes were commoner, and hand-to-hand encounters now and then occurred when patrols or foraging parties ran into one another.

Maurice in his camp at Meede also had foreign visitors. Denmark and Sweden sent men to fight for the Dutch rebels, though they were unable to get into Breda itself to reinforce the garrison. Spinola squeezed the city in such a way that not even a bird could get in or out, said Andrés de Mendoza. The most effective weapon for the Spanish was inaction; then the Dutch had little to do except contemplate their grumbling stomachs. In the course of the siege more than a thousand men in Breda tried to surrender, but Spinola cannily wouldn't let them. He sent them back into the town, knowing they would do his cause more good by consuming the diminishing provisions there. When one eight-strong group of young French nobles attempted to escape, they were captured and sent back in Spinola's own carriage. But gradually attitudes hardened. Two peasants caught bringing wheat into Breda were hanged on Spinola's orders. Looters were tortured with the strappado and strung up on gibbets, although Father Hugo gives the impression that Spinola was far from severe by the standards of the day.

Both sides used water as a weapon. They dammed and diverted rivers and drains, creating flooded fields or causing navigable channels to run dry. Spinola cut the banks of the rivers Mark and Aa in crucial places; he ordered sluices to be opened to allow the tides to rise, shut to enclose a good head of water, and then reopened, with a consequent outrush, when the Dutch were at work trying something similar. Prince Maurice sent one fleet of supply boats but the high tide they expected to carry them to Breda was held back by the wind. The Dutch attempted to raise the water levels by flooding but the Spanish channeled the waters back into the city. After these inundations, a large lake formed over the Vucht polder and Spinola's men built a causeway, the Black Dike, a mile and a half long, which gave them a secure and dry route across it.

Because it was a time before regular uniforms, with soldiers on both sides wearing the same sorts of clothing, friend and foe were distinguished by scarves. The Dutch troops flaunted scarves of blue and orange, the men of the Army of Flanders wore red scarves. The flag flown by the armies of the king of Spain was the old Burgundian device, Saint Andrew's emblem, a red cross. Spanish army wagons had their canvas covers marked with such crosses. The siege lines and water wars brought both sides close together. As in other conflicts, proximity sometimes provoked not fighting but impromptu truces: Dutch and Spanish soldiers had shouted conversations and made it clear in one language or other that they would for the moment stop trying to kill one another, putting down their pikes and arquebuses. Once in a while the king of Spain's men threw bits of cheese and tobacco at the Dutch and the Dutch hurled back crusts of bread, though eventually these became too precious to give away.

It was a mild winter, which helped the Spaniards trying to keep alive in bivouacs out in the countryside. In Breda, food and fuel prices rose rapidly. Spinola's men intercepted messages passing between the governor, Justin of Nassau, and Prince Maurice and learned that scurvy and cases of plague were appearing; rape oil was running short but the stores of wheat might last till the end of April. The Breda hangman was kept busy killing stray dogs and rats, supposedly to prevent the spread of disease; however, he sold dog meat to many now willing to buy it. The tolling of church bells was proscribed at funerals. About five thousand people, a third of the city's inhabitants, died during the siege. Meanwhile out in the Spanish siege lines and their fortified camps, the troops were hard-pressed; any animals that moved were fair game; the carcasses of horses were eaten. Wanting food and forage, the Army of Flanders began to steal—"that ancient tollerable theft," Herman Hugo called it, "winked at of old in soldiers." Houses in the villages close to the lines were ransacked. Most soldiers had a bag of loot, which, their pay being as uncertain as it was, represented their savings.

The Dutch army seemed more handicapped by the long periods of nothing to do. Prince Maurice appeared to have lost his impetus, and in the final stages of his mounting illness he abandoned the camp at Meede and retired to The Hague. His last words were said to have been, "Is Breda saved?" The new stadtholder prince Frederick Henry, Maurice's older half brother, who took over the command after Maurice's death, attempted a breakthrough near Terheyden in May with his English mercenaries. Part of the Army of Flanders was encamped where a small Spanish fort—the Kleine Schans—had been built near the river Mark in the northernmost sector of the siege ring. Most of the king of Spain's troops were in fact Italians who had made the long march northward up the Spanish Road from Lombardy. Spinola's men were ready and there was a savage engagement. Father Hugo reported "a great slaughter of the enemy." The United Provinces' attacking force lost two hundred or so men, the king's defenders a mere dozen. Moreover, five hundred of the Dutch army's horses were captured, having been (said Father Hugo) "carelessly put to grass near their camp." After that there were bodies to be buried, not difficult in the Brabant ground. Anyone who had a copy of *Don Quixote* might have read of the roadside meeting of the knight from La Mancha and a young man who was going to the wars. Don Quixote tells him not to be uneasy about possible misfortune. "The worst can be but to Die, and if it be but a good Honourable Death, your Fortune's made, and you're certainly happy. . . .

As Terence says, a Soldier makes a better figure Dead in the Field of Battle, than Alive and safe in Flight."

Spinola kept the pressure on Justin of Nassau, too. Justin was sixty-six and had been the governor of Breda for more than twenty years; he didn't want to give up what he felt was his city. His mother, Eva Elincx, had been a Breda girl and William the Silent's mistress between the prince's first and second marriages. William had acknowledged Justin and raised him with his legitimate children. As a lieutenant admiral in the late 1580s Justin had captured two galleons of the Spanish Armada. Spinola wrote to the governor at Easter (March 30 that year) just before Prince Maurice died, suggesting that he surrender, but Justin politely declined. In May Spinola made further efforts to get the Dutch to treat. His men had captured letters that the new Dutch captain-general prince Frederick Henry had sent on to Justin, and Spinola now forwarded these to the Breda governor, showing him who was in control. Justin then agreed to talks that took place on the last day of May just outside the town. Articles of surrender were discussed, including a pardon for all citizens of Breda for any offenses against the king of Spain committed since 1590, the year of the turfship, more than a generation before. The Dutch were offered 1,200 wagons and sixty boats to carry away their casualties, their sick, and their household goods. Some commentators thought Spinola too generous, but the Genoese general said he regarded it as "a point of wisdom to be merciful rather than severe."

The articles were agreed upon on June 2 and the surrender took place three days later. The Dutch garrison of just less than 3,500 men marched out of the three gates of the town, colors flying, drums beating, and looking in better shape than those they were surrendering to. As Herman Hugo noted, "They had been better lodged, having had the benefit of good fires; and their bread never failed them till the day they marched away." Outside the Bosschepoort, Spinola took the salute of the assembled Dutch columns. The Dutch dipped their ensigns respectfully as they passed the Spaniards' commander. They looked cheerful, grateful to be out in the great world again, and showed no resentment about their situation. Spinola in return saluted the Dutch captains, in particular the gray-haired governor. Justin rode on horseback while his wife and children followed in a carriage. Here he may have performed the symbolic gesture of handing over to Spinola the keys to the city, but this was not made much of until later. The Dutch procession moved off northeastward toward Geertruidenberg, leaving their sick and wounded to be carried away in boats. Taking over the city again, the Spanish forces celebrated. Spinola, we are told, led the rejoicing. Bells were rung from church towers and on June 13 a victory ceremony was held: The weathered hull of the turfship, hauled out by the castle, was burned. Cannons were fired in salutes of triumph. The town records describing the surprise turfship attack were destroyed in bonfires, as though to expunge them from memory. As the news of the surrender spread, *Te Deum*s were sung throughout the empire. Philip IV wrote to say that he was bestowing on Spinola the office of *Encomienda Mayor* of Castile, a nominally profitable honor somewhat circumscribed just now by the fact that the lucrative income meant to come with the post was mortgaged for the next dozen years.

As high moments go it was splendid; but the moment of glory soon passed. In 1627, less than two years later, the Spanish government again declared bankruptcy; fortunately the bankers of Portugal picked up the baton of debt from the Genoese, and funds aplenty managed to reach the Army of Flanders. That year the king was seriously ill, and when he recovered it was whispered that he had promised to turn over a new leaf. For a while he spent less time hunting and perhaps fewer nights on the town.

IN 1628 THE big event in Velázquez's artistic life was the eight-month-long visit to Madrid of the painter Peter Paul Rubens. Rubens was a star. Both artist and ambassador, he was fifty-one at this time. His father had been a Calvinist supporter of the Reformation who had fled his hometown of Antwerp on the approach of the Duke of Alba's Spanish army and had become the lover of William of Orange's wife. Young Rubens was brought up at any rate as a proper subject of the Spanish empire, was taught by the Jesuits, and mastered seven languages. He studied painting with Adam van Noort in the Netherlands before joining the household of the Duke of Mantua. On his first trip to Madrid twenty-five years before, in 1603, Rubens had failed to be

excited by the local art scene. He had deplored "the miserable insuffi-
ciency and want of care" of Spanish artists. When he looked at contemporary Spanish paintings, he thought "there is not a single one of them
worth having." In 1609 he had been named painter to the "archdukes,"
Albert and Isabella, who had jointly ruled in Brussels on behalf of the
king, and on this present trip he came as emissary for the latter, Philip
IV's aunt, the surviving governor of the Spanish Netherlands. His mission was to help arrange a peace treaty between Spain and England,
and so he had frequent meetings with the king and Olivares. Before
Rubens got to Madrid, Olivares had written to him sympathizing with
him for the loss of his companion, Isabella Brant, a grief he understood
all the more because of his own losses—his nephew cardinal Guzmán,
who had recently died at the age of twenty-two, followed a few days later
by Olivares's only daughter, "carried off in consequence of a bad labor."

Rubens arrived with a cargo of art: eight paintings of his own for
Philip IV to consider and a pile of tapestries he had designed for a convent with royal connections. While in Spain he painted a series of
portraits for the crown, treading on the toes of the court painters,
Velázquez included, though the younger artist took no visible umbrage.
Philip had charged Velázquez with looking after Rubens, entertaining
him, and showing him the Hapsburg collections in the Escorial and
Alcázar. Pacheco said loyally that "Rubens ignored the other court
painters and kept only the company of Velázquez." Pacheco's son-in-
law had to put up with the fact that his modified portrait of the king
on horseback was taken down from its place in the Salon Nuevo and a
portrait, also equestrian, which Rubens had just done of Philip was
hung in its place. (So much for Philip's promise to have only Velázquez
as court painter.) But Velázquez saw much to admire in Rubens. The
Fleming had now been knighted in several countries. As an artist and
courtier he showed Velázquez a way ahead that could with luck be
emulated. There was no disguising the role hard work played in Rubens's
success. He sat down like a student and copied all the Titians in the
royal collection. In nine months in Madrid he painted at least thirty
pictures, many quite large. In one letter from Madrid he wrote that he
"kept to painting, as I do everywhere." The king delighted in watching
him paint, coming to visit him nearly every day in the rooms he had

been given in the palace. Rubens felt sympathy for the young monarch, who seemed to him to have been "endowed by nature with all the gifts of body and spirit. . . . He would surely be capable of governing under any conditions, were it not that he mistrusts himself and defers too much to others. But now he has to pay for his own credulity and others' folly, and feel the hatred that is not meant for him. Thus have the gods willed it." The fatalism was perhaps a by-product of life in the Hapsburg court. But it was noteworthy, too, that the great Baroque painter invoked "the gods," the pre-Christian deities, rather than any from New Testament or even Catholic times.

Being close to Rubens might have aroused jealousy in Velázquez but seems rather to have provoked sympathy and admiration. He passed on to his father-in-law the information that Rubens had gout. That Rubens returned Velázquez's high opinion of him was noted by Fuensalida, the keeper of the royal records, and Pacheco learned that Rubens "greatly favoured Velázquez's paintings because of their *modestia*," their simplicity; they certainly weren't as attention-seeking as Rubens's pictures. Rubens, albeit a Hapsburg insider and a Catholic, was not a warmonger. He had painted a series entitled *The Horrors of War*. He seemed to have felt that the continued truce in the Low Countries was good for everybody; it would not only mean less blood spilled and money wasted, it would create better conditions for the Counter-Reformation to flourish. Antwerp would become prosperous again. The two painters discussed the state of art and the way ahead, and Velázquez apparently asked Rubens what he should do next. Rubens had permission from the archduchess Isabella to visit Italy in company with Philip IV's sister, the queen of Hungary, but her departure was delayed and Rubens went off at the end of April 1629 to the London peace talks and then back to Brussels. The message Rubens left with Velázquez was "Think Italy."

Although Velázquez was clearly affected by Rubens's feelings about his great predecessors and Rubens's strong sense of his own artistic personality, the impact that Rubens had on Velázquez's style is another question. The manner of Titian and Caravaggio certainly had marked him, though as noted it isn't certain that he had seen any of Caravaggio's work in the flesh at this point. Although some have recognized "a new era," "fresh glowing tones," and a "new freedom of execution" in Velázquez's work, dating from the Rubens visit, as the late-nineteenth-century German art historian Carl Justi asked, did Velázquez need to learn his finest qualities from anyone other than himself? "Was it necessary to bring a man from the foggy Netherlands to show him the light in the torrid land of Spain?" On the other hand, the two painters shared a studio and saw each other daily with palettes and brushes in hand. Something may well have rubbed off. With Rubens Velázquez walked through the Alcázar and the Escorial palaces and stood before the Titians and other masterpieces, discussing them. Later, paintings copied from Rubens's pictures were hung in Velázquez's Alcázar studio, and Velázquez made no secret of this, as his painting *Las Meninas* was to show. Rubens's *Adoration of the Magi*, a 1609 painting that he reworked while in Madrid in 1628–29, contained a self-portrait of the artist as a gentleman with a sword, standing in the throng of figures around the mother and child; it provided a precedent for Velázquez when he came to paint *Las Meninas*. Moreover, with the help of his son-in-law Juan Bautista Martínez del Mazo, around 1645 Velázquez painted a copy of Rubens's *Equestrian Portrait of Philip IV*, florid, over-the-top, with bare-breasted heavenly creatures floating in the sky above the royal head. Seeing this example of Catholic-Baroque art at its most flamboyant, the Spaniard may well have thought that there was a less strident way of making this point, a way that might be even more eloquent. The word *baroque* is derived from *barocco*, meaning an encrusted pearl. Velázquez was a Baroque artist only in point of time.

At age twenty-nine or so, he nevertheless seems to have been pushed into fields other than court portraiture by Rubens's obvious success with mythological and liturgical subject matter. One of two pictures of this period in which scholars detect a "Rubens-effect" is *Christ after the Flagellation Contemplated by the Christian Soul* and it makes uneasy viewing for the modern museumgoer. It has the feeling of being a commissioned work, whose specifications were contractually laid out. The very title suggests the overload of religious sentiment with which the picture is infused. Although the figure of the flogged Christ is treated with restraint, a man still alert and without buckets of blood oozing from his wounds, Seville's sometimes sadomasochistic devotional

The Drinkers: Bacchus and His Companions, *c. 1629, Museo del Prado, Madrid.*

observances seem to be reappearing. The guardian angel—the Christian Soul—could be visiting from one of Velázquez's kitchen scenes. In fact, mythology makes a more comfortable bedfellow at this point. Titian and various Venetian scenes of bacchanalia provided antecedents for *Los Borrachos*, or *Bacchus and His Companions*, but this picture, Velázquez's first "history painting" since *The Expulsion of the Moriscos*, may well have been painted while Rubens was in town and may have been inspired by his presence. The light tones favored by the Fleming may also have directed Velázquez this way, albeit he was working with simpler, less lavish means than Rubens. The event takes place in a rural spot, though lit rather theatrically from one side; the revelers are for the most part common country folk. Velázquez puts the adolescent Bacchus in the center of the action, a plump young master of ceremonies perched on a wine barrel under a tree. Bacchus is crowned with a wreath of vine leaves and with a sly grin is bestowing another wreath on the head of a soldier kneeling before him, one of the crowd of drinkers in the right half of the picture. No one, not even the young god, looks anything other than human. The satisfied, inebriated air of several of the drinkers helps create an atmosphere of mockery. A vine-wreathed bagpiper makes his music in the shadowed left foreground, the gloom of the spot intensifying the soft radiance in which the god is bathed. Bacchus, now in human form, has apparently been called on by the peasants to help them drown their sorrows, but his youthful flesh is palpable, his sense of fun as he participates in the coronation proceedings is conveyed. The pleasure passes from his companions to the viewer—particularly by way of the hat-wearing drinker who bares his teeth beneath a mustache, face creased in an encouraging smile directed at the artist who had presumably just told the model to look happy, and now at us, the viewers. One feels that at any minute the whole crew will start talking mischief, maybe even talking dirty.

This is Velázquez's only "merry company" to set alongside the carousing of Steen and Teniers. It has been conjectured that the Spaniard may have read how Leonardo da Vinci now and then got some peasants together and, while they were in their cups guffawing, sketched them—Velázquez himself at Pacheco's had done something similar, paying the country youth to model various facial expressions. There's an element of parody in the performance. Velázquez seems to be making fun of a mythological event; the divine is made comic. But there is nothing academic or labored here. The balance is just right: the company leaning forward toward the viewer; the bare-chested accomplice of the young god reclining to the left; and the bearded old man crouching respectfully, like a magus before the holy infant—he has something of the proud independence of the Corsican water seller. Even in this one-off one-of-a-kind painting Velázquez seems keen to connect with his own recent past.

The picture may also be a sardonic commentary on straitened times. The court cost roughly a million escudos a year. Getting paid was often tricky for royal servants, the royal guards, and household officials. Courtiers were even asked to dip into their own pockets to help out; in 1625 Velázquez pledged a "generous" one hundred ducats toward a national call for defense funds that the Olivares regime was asking for, and he and Juana paid off this gift to the state in installments of ten ducats a month.

The word *arrears* came up often at court and complaints were vocal. A year or so after having been sworn in as a new gentleman usher on March 7, 1627, Velázquez was given a raise by the king and allowed other perquisites, including daily attendance by the palace barber, worth twelve reales a day, and a new suit of clothes every year worth ninety ducats; but we don't know what he had to go through to get his wages. (He was never a cheap painter. His first Madrid portrait of a lady, the marquesa of Montesclaro, cost the marques 900 reales.) As an usher, Velázquez was one of a dozen or so functionaries who took turns to attend to the royal antechamber at mealtimes, opening and closing doors only to permitted staff and royalty. Velázquez's daily allowance for this was twelve reales. He may have been specially fortunate in terms of actually getting paid, for the Tuscan envoy Baglioni wrote of continued hard times at the Spanish court in November 1630: "The King pays nobody. The bankers of Genoa are owed everything." However, Velázquez from the start of his court career was shown exceptional favor by the king, who evidently worked out various ways to get money to his painter, not just as painter to the King's Chamber, with allowances payable by the royal household, but as a servant of the Board of Works and Forests. The art historian José Manuel Cruz Valdovinos has shown that Velázquez—recognized early on by the king for his dedication and craftsmanship—"got two offices and several grants of payment in a continuous and almost annual way." On August 26, 1625, Velázquez was also awarded the use of a guesthouse—property given him with surprising speed, after the king royally struck out bureaucratic objections to the award. A church pension of three hundred ducats, requiring a papal dispensation, followed.

Four hundred silver ducats was the sum given to Velázquez in July 1629, Pacheco tells us, for a journey Velázquez wanted to make, and for which Philip IV gave permission, along with an advance to the painter of two years' salary. The generous king also let Velázquez keep all his perks, his rental house, his court allowances, while he was away. The 1629 sum included three hundred on account and one hundred for the *Bacchus*, and the journey represented the happy culmination of Velázquez's desire, abetted by Rubens, to see Italy and look at Italian paintings in Italian light on Italian ground. The count-duke, as Olivares was now called, gave his fellow Sevillian a further going-away present of two hundred gold ducats, a medal showing the king's head, and letters of introduction to important personages in Spain's possessions in Italy. Here was a chance for Velázquez to show how he could make out as an artist-ambassador in the Rubens manner. In the course of preparations for the journey, Velázquez was brought together with a man who would be going along to Italy as well. This was Captain-General Ambrogio Spinola, now a marqués, a title that may have made up somewhat for the loss of family funds he had put into keeping the Army of Flanders afloat. Spinola had helped persuade Philip IV to summon Rubens to his court and send him on to England as an ambassador to promote peace. We can assume that Spinola was sympathetic to Rubens's expressed opinion that the Spaniards who supported war—as a way of securing the triumph of the True Faith—were "the scourges of God." But Spinola had been in Madrid on an equally difficult effort, attempting to convince the Olivares regime that it was time to try again a less aggressive policy in the Low Countries: a new long truce or a negotiated, lasting peace. For Olivares, however, a truce was only a holding measure; the peace with England seemed for him to mean mostly a better chance of success when it came to whacking the Dutch again.

V. The Way to Italy. 1629

THE SMALL FLEET LEFT BARCELONA AND SAILED EASTWARD ON
the feast day of Saint Lawrence, August 10, 1629. Going by sea had
risks even in summer. When an aide to Infante Antonio, Lord High
Admiral of Spain, later suggested they use a boat to cross the pond in
the Retiro gardens of Madrid, the admiral-infante declined, saying,
"Since I sailed from Naples to Spain, I have never ventured on water."
There were nine galleys in the 1629 convoy and although no log of the
voyage records their exact route, they presumably steered a cautious one,
close to the shore but allowing for the southwesterly set of the currents
that prevailed along the rugged Spanish coast. Sheltering ports were
few. Sight of the snowcapped Pyrenees on the port beam meant France
was near, but by no means at this time a place for Spanish ships to seek
protection. Moorish pirates had to be considered. Ahead lay the broad
Gulf of Lion, across which they hastened hoping to be spared the attentions of either a mistral, funneling out of the mountains, or a levanter,
on the nose from the east, which could cast you on the rocks. As far as
we know Velázquez had never been to sea before—had never even seen
the sea. His home waters were the Guadalquivir, well inland, and more
recently the river in Madrid, and that occasionally just about dried up.
On board, out on the Mediterranean, the sea of seas, Velázquez had
the opportunity to take deep breaths of briny air. He must have felt suddenly on the way to somewhere new—with new opportunities—and

could cast aside some of the cares of being a courtier (the *desengaños de Palacio*, as his colleague the playwright Calderón called those concerns).

Yet he was in exalted company. With Captain-General Spinola were a number of noblemen and grandees, a high rank whose membership had been greatly multiplied since Charles V introduced it in 1520—from twenty-five at the start, there were now at least a hundred. Spinola's suite included Admiral Don Álvaro de Bazán; the Marquis of Santa Cruz; the third Duke of Lerma; and the abbot Scaglia (agent in Madrid for the Duke of Savoy). Ambrogio Spinola had been charged by the court in Madrid with resolving the problem of Mantua, a duchy whose rule had come up for grabs when the Duke of Mantua died in the last week of 1627. Cardinal Richelieu wanted to thwart Hapsburg power on every occasion and saw Mantua as an opportunity; the duchy was now threatened by French forces in support of their candidate for the vacant dukedom. (Mantua, by the way, was where Rubens had gone in 1600, at age twenty-three, to serve the Gonzaga family and to study and travel.) After Spinola had talked Philip IV into bringing Rubens to Spain and then sending him on to England to make peace, the Genoese general had clearly wanted to go on trying to sort out the situation in the Low Countries. He had been reluctant to take on the new posts of captain-general in Italy and governor of Milan. But Olivares told him that he was the only general in whom the crown had confidence, and he had certainly been granted greater powers than any so far given any Spanish official. Yet he knew from his Netherlands experience how morale and funds fluctuated. As a general, you were only as good as your last victory.

On board, in Spinola's company, Velázquez got to see the renowned general at close hand. Spinola's great success in 1625 at Breda may have been talked about. But probably little was said about the great reverse to Spanish interests that occurred in 1628, when the Dutch supremacy of the seas was reestablished in Matanzas Bay, Cuba. Dutch school-children still sing of their hero Piet Heijn (1578–1629):

> *Piet Heijn, Piet Heijn, zijn naam is klein,*
> *Zijn daden benne groot,*
> *Zijn daden benne groot,*
> *Hij heeft gewonnen de zilver vloot.*

Piet's father was a North Sea herring fisherman and Piet went to sea young, was captured by the Spaniards, and as a prisoner rowed in their galleys for four years. Freed in an exchange of captives, Heijn by 1628 was in command of a Dutch West Indies squadron that came across some ships from a scattered Spanish bullion convoy off the coast of Cuba. Four naval galleons and eleven trading ships were carrying the king's share of the biannual haul of silver. They headed for the shelter of Matanzas Bay, but their commander Juan de Benavides acted indecisively and his ships fell prey to the Dutch before the Spaniards could land and hide the treasure. The Spanish loss was estimated at four million ducats, or eleven million guilders. The West Indies Company declared a bumper dividend of 75 percent. Piet Heijn sailed home and bought a big house in Delft to retire in. But as Spinola was to find out, successful commanders are rarely allowed to rest on their laurels. Piet Heijn led the Dutch fleet again against the piratical Dunkirkers; he beat them but died in the battle.

The effect of Matanzas Bay was to throttle for the time being Spain's military efforts in the Low Countries. Madrid sent no funding between October 1628 and May 1629 for a new military campaign there. Philip and Olivares moved their troops to northern Italy to cope with the French, and any spare cash went that way, too. The very size of the Spanish empire caused problems. Cardinal Richelieu was one who thought the chief obstacles to Spain achieving universal dominance were the distance between its many dominions and lack of men on the right spot. The manpower shortage was enhanced by failures to meet the need for rations and pay. Sickness was also a factor. In 1629–31 a plague in Lombardy nicknamed the *peste di Milano*, thought to be one of the last outbreaks of bubonic plague in Europe, carried off a quarter of a million people and hundreds of possible recruits for the Army of Flanders. Many enlisted only to desert when provisions were short and their pay failed to turn up. Military commentators frequently quoted Thucydides: "War is waged not so much with arms as with money, which provides the sinews of war." The Marquis of Aytona, Spain's ambassador in Brussels, reported that the war against the Dutch rebels had been reduced to a form of commerce. "Whoever has the last escudo will win."

* * *

VELÁZQUEZ MAY HAVE been attracted to Spinola—driven to sketch him, even, or at least after this voyage to keep the look of him in his memory—because they were of similar temperament. They were both serious and undemonstrative. Both were known for their *modestia*. On the last day of their eastbound voyage the ships of their fleet steered for the 1,300-foot high peak known as the Bric del Gazo and then for the harbor of Genoa, which sheltered under it. From the sea, the town had the look of a dazzling amphitheater. How long they stayed in Spinola's hometown—Columbus's birthplace—isn't known, but Genoese hospitality would have ensured the artist an intimate view of the local palaces. Spinola's family was one of the oldest in the city, his father the Marquis de Sesto y Benafro, his mother the princess of Salerno. Genoa's ruling class, the *nobili vecchi*, had close ties with Spain, lent large sums to the monarchy, and in return got Spanish help against local opponents and rebels supported by the French. At this time Genoa's independence was being threatened by the Duke of Savoy. There were family rivalries, which, like those between the Montagues and Capulets in Verona, made for vendettas. The English diarist John Evelyn was here fifteen years later and noted how, as with "our neighbours the Hollanders," lack of ground had forced the rich merchants of Genoa to employ their money not on large estates but on pictures, hangings, ornate houses, and rich furniture. In the Strada Nova, built of polished marble, Evelyn saw the magnificent mansion of Don Carlos Doria and the gardens of the Spinola house, with huge lemons hanging on the trees. In much of the city, however, the ways were narrow, tight lanes and twisting alleyways, bringing to mind Seville; carriages couldn't negotiate them, only sedan chairs and litters. Evelyn said the place made one think of horrid acts of revenge and murder; he was told it was a "galley-matter" to carry a knife that hadn't had its point broken off.

The martial life had come easily to Spinola. His younger brother Federico (born 1571) had gone to sea as a youth, chasing corsairs, but led the way into soldiering, enlisting in Italy, serving in Flanders, and, at the age of thirty-three, meeting a hero's death on the island of Walcheren, blown to bits by Dutch cannon fire. By then his older brother Ambrogio was also serving in the king's army. Ambrogio recruited six thousand Lombards for the king of Spain and soon rose to high rank in Flanders. Banker, magistrate, and eventually captain-general, he was a modern condottiere. (The contemporaneous development of banking and artillery has been noted. David Jones, poet and artist, wrote after World War I that "Explosions are grand things, but they cost money, and the bigger they are, the more they cost.") Parting with Velázquez now, and carrying one and a half million ducats to help in the campaign to secure the Mantuan succession from the French, Spinola went on to Milan to relieve Don Gonzalo de Córdoba, whose siege of Casale had been faltering. (Casale was on the river Po, which passed through the Mantuan lands of Montferrat, and was a place held by the Duke of Nevers with French and German troops.) Although Spinola's daughter Polissena had married into the highest circles in Madrid, marrying Olivares's cousin and closest aide, the Marquis of Leganés, in the queen's apartments in the royal palace, the captain-general didn't see eye to eye with Olivares about how to sort out Hapsburg problems in the Low Countries and Italy. Spinola thought he was still needed in Flanders, where his replacement, Count Henry van den Bergh, had gone off the rails and Frederick Henry and the Dutch were gaining ground. Yet here Spinola found himself on the way to Lombardy to sort out Mantua, and was—Olivares soon thought—not putting his back into it. Spinola probably didn't know that Mantua had been infected with plague by French and German troops until he noticed corpses lying unburied along the roadsides; and he was heading into one of the hot spots of what became known as the *peste di Milano*. He would be fully stretched between his duties as the new governor of Milan, asked for help by the anxious citizenry, and as a field-marshal attempting to win a local war.

In northern Italy at least a million people died from this plague. Its lethal effects are well conveyed in chapter 31 of Alessandro Manzoni's novel *The Betrothed* of 1827.

VELÁZQUEZ, HAVING RECOVERED his land legs, journeyed across northern Italy to Venice. Comparisons were forced upon him by nearly everything: people, landscape, townscape. With fortunate timing, he seems to have arrived in Venice before the plague swept east from Lombardy. Undoubtedly there was in normal times something lighter in the Italian atmosphere and perhaps something more serene than in the Spanish air; things were less serious here, though life could be just as desperate on occasion. He was abroad for the first time and, adding to the elation, was often given entry to places where no ordinary man had access. The king of Spain's painter! Philip IV wanted him to learn about the latest trends in Italian art and bring back ideas for expanding the royal collection. Pacheco, briefed later on, tells us who received the artist and where he stayed. His first important stop was in Venice, rival to Genoa, where the Spanish ambassador put him up and gave him a guard to protect him when sightseeing. John Evelyn— there not long after—suggested that the evenings in Venice were particularly dangerous, "when the students go to their strumpets." He also noted that the city was "miraculously placed" and that the ladies, dressed as if always in masquerade, were much to be fancied. Venetians were pro-French and Spaniards weren't popular, but despite this, Palomino says, Velázquez unsurprisingly came to love the city. He drew a great deal while visiting its marvels: the palace and church of Saint Mark, the Sala de Gran Consiglio, and the Academy. He spent hours with the Titians, the Veroneses, the Tintorettos. He particularly took to the latter's *Crucifixion* and made a copy of another Tintoretto that showed Christ's last supper with his disciples.

From Venice he traveled southward. Not everyone was welcoming despite his letters of introduction. The Duchess of Parma had been warned by her ambassador in an encrypted letter that Velázquez was coming and that he was probably a spy. However, he spent two nights in Ferrara where Cardinal Guilio Sacchetti asked him to stay at his palace and dine with him. Velázquez thanked him but demurred about dinner invitations. The cardinal had been papal nuncio in Madrid, was used to Spanish ways (presumably to very late dinners), and got one of his staff, a Spaniard, to look after Velázquez and his servant and serve them when they wanted "with the same dishes as were prepared for his own table." The cardinal knew a good deal about painting and with his brother Marcello had helped persuade Pietro da Cortona to copy Raphael and Titian, learning how to fuse Raphael's design talent with Titian's color sense. Sacchetti took Velázquez seriously, sending one of his staff to guide him around Ferrara's sights and spending three hours in conversation with him before he left. Horses were provided for the travelers to journey onward next to Cento (Guercino's town), Loreto, and Bologna—and then to Rome.

Velázquez stayed a year in the eternal city. We have little documentation to go on, no letters to the king or his father-in-law; we have no idea how husband-and-wife relations were affected by his absence. But *el pintor real*'s influential connections were ever helpful. He was admitted to the papal presence and kissed Urban VIII's toe. We know that a "don Diego pintor" rented a room in Casa Mannara in Rome, agreed for sixteen months, but thanks to the pope's nephew cardinal Francesco Barberini was given an apartment in the Vatican. He had his own keys to rooms where pictures and sculptures were displayed, and he spent a good deal of time making sketches of Raphael's frescoes and Michelangelo's *Last Judgment*—though no sketchbook has survived. Then, feeling lonely and isolated in his palatial quarters, and not looking forward to the heat of Rome in summer, he asked one of his best contacts, the Spanish ambassador to the Holy See, the Count of Monterrey, to find him a new place to live. Monterrey—Manuel de Fonseca y Zúñiga—was Olivares's brother-in-law twice over, that is, they had married each other's sisters. Monterrey seems to have been involved in a roundabout request to Grand Duke Ferdinand II of Tuscany that Velázquez be allowed to move into the duke's property at the Villa Medici, though the permission came in May from Cardinal Carlo de' Medici. Another guest in the villa at the same time was the scientist Galileo Galilei, said to be an excellent conversationalist, though no record of any *conversasione* with Velázquez is preserved.

The advantages of the Villa Medici lay in its position and the antique statuary planted in its grounds. Palomino says the villa was in the "highest and most airy part of Rome" and Velázquez clearly found that the place raised his spirits. At about this time in Rome the artists Claude Lorrain and Joachim Sandrart were among those establishing a new mode, painting out of doors, and Velázquez—from something in the air, perhaps—did the same in the enchanting gardens of the Villa Medici. Here he painted two small pictures, more sketches than elaborated paintings, thinly painted observations a little over a foot square, the surfaces of the canvases visible as canvas, on which he caught the dim gray-green light that suffused the place. The colors were muted. The seemingly spontaneous, impromptu handling (which was in his preserved works something new) is marvelous. Both pictures were painted in the open air, both out-of-doors scenes showing the tumble-down buildings in the gardens of the villa. "The sketchiness is the style"—so the art historian Enriqueta Harris neatly puts it. In one of the paintings two male figures are seen meeting in front of a pillared pavilion, within which we can make out another man looking at a recumbent statue, a figure of Cleopatra with one arm thrown back over her head. In the other picture, two men in broad-brimmed hats are talking below the balustraded facade of the villa's grotto-loggia, whose entrance archway has been boarded up in a patchwork way; proper repairs and restorations are apparently going to happen one of these days. To the right a pale statue stands in front of its own shadow in a niche. Above the balustrade, a woman is hanging some white sheets out to dry. A line of cypresses fills the sky. The gardens, Henry James suggested two centuries later, are fabled, even haunted. A brief moment has been caught by Velázquez—the moment in which a crease in the sheet is pulled flat by the woman handling the laundry, and one man says something while the other listens. Neither painting is at all old-masterish. We sense a modern moment, or maybe an eternal moment brilliantly seized.

When the English diarist John Evelyn was there fourteen years after Velázquez he admired the villa's position "upon the brow of Mons Pincius" with "an incomparable prospect towards the Campo Marzo," its gardens with two huge marble lions, rare bas-reliefs, a goodly fountain that threw water fifty feet high, an obelisk with hieroglyphics, and statues of infinite price. Evelyn and Velázquez were four hundred years closer than we to classical times, and perhaps felt the proximity to that age more than we. Here what Walter Pater called the pagan world was tangible and vibrant in the bright Italian light. The statuary included the Sabines, and Niobe and her large family as big as life, in the way Pliny had described them, and (says Evelyn) "esteemed amongst the best pieces of work in the world, for the passions they express, & all other perfections of that stupendous art." Velázquez, at home among these antiques, responded in a low-key way, with his own two modest masterpieces. As far as we know, he never again painted outdoor scenes quite like these.

On the Mons Pincius Velázquez hoped to avoid not only Rome's summer heat but its malarial problems. The hope was in vain. After two months in the Villa Medici he came down with a "tertian fever." Once again the Count and Countess of Monterrey came to his aid. The victim was nursed by the countess, while the count ensured that Velázquez had everything he needed. Food was carried up daily from the count's house. Doctors and medicines were sent at the count's expense. "Sweetmeats and frequent messages" accompanied them until the artist recovered.

Perhaps this episode increased a sense of urgency. What if the fever had proved fatal; what if he hadn't been spared? What paintings would he have failed to paint? He got on with a portrait of the countess, Olivares's sister (a picture that has since disappeared). But his time in the Vatican with the Sistine ceiling gave him new ideas about conveying the human body and how to express emotions via anatomy. More than just the face was involved in this; physical animation and gesture were needed. Jusepe Martínez, a painter friend who later featured in Palomino's book *El Museo Pictorico*, declared that Velázquez's skills in perspective and composition were "much improved by his study in Rome of ancient and modern paintings, statues, and reliefs." He was thirty, a bit old for first impressions fired by careless rapture, but Rome made its own unforgettable impact on him. Dramatic action, caught at a moment that could be pictured, was involved in the two major paintings he made on this Italian stay. *Apollo at the Forge of Vulcan* and *Joseph's Bloodstained Coat Brought to Jacob* were both painted in 1630, apparently uncommisioned; in both the underlying theme was betrayal.

In the *Apollo* a young god appears, his laurel-crowned head surrounded by radiance, announcing to the amazed and rather scrawny blacksmith Vulcan, who is backed by four muscular helpers, the shocking news that the smith's wife, Venus, has been carrying on with Mars. (It is Ovid's story.) In the second painting, Joseph's bloody coat is being shown to a horror-stricken, bearded old man, who is making aghast gestures, while a small liver-and-white spaniel barks at the five new arrivals. Two of these

Apollo at the Forge of Vulcan, *1630, Museo del Prado, Madrid.*

men are evidently Joseph's brothers, and several look like those who modeled for Vulcan's helpers at the forge. The two brothers are lightly sketched
in, their unfinishedness contrasting with the clearly over-the-top behavior of the pair who clutch the coat that has been stained by the blood of a
lamb, while their colleague, torso bared, stands with his back to the
viewer, stretching his arms and shoulders in a rather too manifest demonstration of agonizing grief. The elderly, mullah-bearded Jacob is—we
realize—trying to take on board the story he has been told that Joseph
has been torn to pieces by wild animals. In *The Forge of Vulcan*, the later of
the two paintings, Velázquez also did something new with his canvas
that involved a more fundamental lightness: He began to use a lighter
ground, of gray rather than brown, and kept up this method of prepara-
tion thereafter. In both these pictures Velázquez was apparently working in a narrative manner common to artists in Rome at this period, and
it's possible that he may have been throwing down a gauntlet—or a

Joseph's Blood-stained Coat Brought to Jacob, *1629–30, El Escorial.*

paint-loaded palette—to his purported rivals in Madrid; those who claimed that he could only paint heads. With Michelangelo's example close at hand, and remembering Montañés, he was showing that he could also paint muscles, ligaments, and skin under tension. The figures in both the *Forge* and *Joseph's Coat* with their outstretched arms, bent elbows, turned heads, and feet whose toes are just touching the ground are figures almost in motion. A likeness to Juana Pacheco has also been seen in the spotlit head of the young Apollo. Was Velázquez missing her, or was there here a hint that provokes the question: Why now this theme of betrayal? There might also be a link with what a Spanish painter would consider the disloyal attitude of some Italian states to the Spanish crown.

In any event, Velázquez seems to have been measuring himself against past masters and the masters of the time: the antique makers of redis- covered sculptures and reliefs; Titian, Tintoretto, Rubens, and Cara- vaggio; and Nicolas Poussin, Claude Lorrain, Pietro da Cortona, and

Gian Lorenzo Bernini, all working in Italy. Velázquez chose to give his classical and biblical pieces an everyday look. But while striving for genre-scene realism and producing lively illustrations of animation and gesture, he doesn't seem in either the *Forge* or *Joseph's Coat* to have created pictures that have the essential stasis of great art—the sense of a moment caught without grandiloquence once and for all in a way it never would be again.

A "SERVANT OF Velázquez" was mentioned when Cardinal Sacchetti asked the painter to stay with him in Ferrara. Only later do we have a name to put to such a helper, but it makes sense to introduce here, nearly twenty years before he stepped into the limelight, again in Rome, the one "servant" of Diego Velázquez who gets into the records. If Juan de Pareja was along on this first journey to Italy, as he may well have been, he would have been about twenty at the time. Pareja, as already described, was a brown-skinned Moor, probably of mixed Arab and Berber blood, who was born about 1610 in the town of Antequera, between Seville and Málaga. In Spanish society, slaves were, as noted, members of the lowest caste and did much of the dirty work, practical and domestic, in trade establishments, workshops, farms, and private houses. As we've seen, Velázquez's grandfather Juan Velázquez Moreno had owned several. The term *slave* was used specifically by Palomino in the next century to describe Pareja's status—though one should perhaps blend with the harsh connotations of captivity a particularly Iberian form of household indenture. Slaves were generally treated no better or worse than their supposedly free workmates. In Pareja's case, the slave became a valued assistant to *el pintor real*. How Velázquez came to own Pareja isn't known, maybe as a gift from his father or as an acquisition that attended his marriage to Juana. Juan de Pareja seems to have performed for Velázquez many of the humble jobs an artist needed done, grinding pigments over and over until they made a fine powder that could be mixed with oils, and stretching canvases on their frameworks before laying on the grounds. Pareja took in much from this experience. In Velázquez's company he saw picture after picture, duds and masterpieces, and learned from Velázquez's reaction to them. Pareja had the benefit of being in close contact with a master; he was an apprentice by proximity and learned how to paint. (He may also have taken heed from Rubens, whose style seems to have influenced his own paintings, when he came to make them.)

From Rome Velázquez traveled south to Naples. The Count of Monterrey was about to do the same, taking up the post of Spanish viceroy there. In Naples that autumn Velázquez was paid 154 gold scudi by Monterrey for paintings; one on which he worked was a portrait of the Infanta María, Philip IV's sister, the woman whom Charles Stuart, when Prince of Wales, had failed to persuade to marry him in 1623. She had since been betrothed to her cousin Ferdinand, the king of Bohemia and Hungary and son of the Holy Roman emperor. The pair were married "by proxy" in Madrid in April 1629 and were now about to make the relationship real. The Tuscan ambassador diplomatically described the Infanta as having "the face of an angel," even though—like her brother's—her tastes ran to hunting as well as the theater. Velázquez intended to take the portrait back to Madrid for Philip. The queen-to-be had russet hair, tightly curled, with a latent smile on her lips above the unescapable Hapsburg chin, which rested in a high gray ruffed collar. At some point in his Italian travels Velázquez also painted, according to Pacheco, a self-portrait. His father-in-law said that he, Pacheco, had it in his possession, a painting in "Titian's manner . . . worthy of the admiration of connoisseurs and a tribute to art." The whereabouts of this picture are no longer known and we are forced to speculate whether it showed a man with an intense gaze, long black hair, a long straight nose, and a pronounced *W*-shaped mustache, all features of portraits associated with Velázquez in the following years.

Now, in Naples, Velázquez seems to have felt his time in Italy was up. He had been away from Madrid for nearly a year and a half. He took his chances on a Mediterranean voyage in winter and sailed for home. Before embarking he would have learned of the final days of the man who had been his companion on the way to Italy. The marquis Spinola had managed to surround Casale but then had failed to work his military or his diplomatic magic there. His control over the siege was threatened by plague in his army, a request for reinforcements was refused, and then a peace settlement with the French and their Savoy allies was undermined by Olivares during the summer of 1630. The regime in Madrid negotiated with the enemy behind their captain-general's back. Demoralized, feeling acutely the lack of support, and lack of men and supplies, Spinola became ill in his camp outside Casale. He had spent a fortune and a career helping the Spanish king. His morale collapsed; he felt his reputation and his honor had been taken from him. On September 25, 1630, the victor of Breda died, brokenhearted. Olivares wrote to the Marquis of Aytona in Brussels complaining that Spinola's death was inopportune, but it was too late for any crocodile tears; while the Duke of Feria was made governor of Milan in Spinola's place, in fact there were no substitutes for Spinola. Quevedo, the satirist and secretary to the king whose portrait Velázquez had painted around 1632 showing the poet wearing owlish horn-rimmed spectacles, wrote a poem expressing distress about Spinola's death—which he called a bequest of overwhelming sadness.

VI. The Good Retreat. Madrid. 1631–

I T WAS ONCE AGAIN A BAD TIME FOR SPAIN BUT IN THE CAPITAL few seemed aware of it. Brazil fell to the Dutch in 1630; Spain and Austria, the allied Hapsburg powers, were defeated at Breitenfeld in 1631 and at Lutzon in 1632. Yet in Madrid theatrical festivities and masquerade parties went on regardless. Despite the constant drain of cash into the various theaters of war, the Low Countries particularly, Olivares continued to present Philip IV as a hero of the age. A great deal of Castile's taxes was spent not only on maintaining Spain's armies abroad but on putting on a good show at home, making it seem as if everything *va bien*—still a potent political slogan today. The impression had to be given that the Spanish empire was conquering its enemies on all fronts and the forces of Catholicism were triumphing over Protestant heretics. In this, the arts had their parts to play: Playwrights created performances on stage; artists made paintings. In the gilded cage of the court, as the reality of imperial might and royal influence slipped away, some ceremonies became more conspicuous. Pageantry increased as power waned.

Velázquez was welcomed home from Italy by his unofficial patron, the count-duke Olivares. He was taken down the long corridors of the Alcázar to kiss the king's hands. Palomino adds unctuously that Velázquez thanked His Majesty for "not having allowed himself to be portrayed by any other painter during his absence"—as if this were the highest favor Philip could bestow on Velázquez. (Rubens was no longer around to muscle in on the territory.) The king commanded that Velázquez be given a studio-workshop in the palace's Del Ciezo gallery, and that a chair be placed there for the monarch's private use so that Philip could sit and watch his painter painting. This was, as noted, what Alexander was said to have done with Apelles, and what Philip's great-grandfather Charles V had done with Titian. Titian had been with difficulty lured from Venice but only twice came as far as Germany; on one occasion Charles V bent over to pick up a brush that Titian had dropped. For many courtiers Philip appeared like a royal automaton, going through the same daily motions of custom, never visibly changing his posture or expression, but Velázquez had the opportunity to stare as hard as he wanted, to note physical details and quirks as intimately as he liked. And along with this constant, personal contact came occasional rewards: extra payments for pictures; honors such as the office of Gentleman of the Wardrobe that was bestowed on Velázquez in 1636. Whether he got the full benefit in salary isn't known—most household officials had to worry about their wages actually being paid—but since Philip evidently wanted real work from his royal painter, Velázquez probably got real emoluments.

Soon after his return from Italy he was asked to paint several royal portraits. In them can be seen some of the effects of his time away. For several modern scholars, it was Italy that helped turn Velázquez from "a gifted but somewhat provincial painter into a brilliant master of the prevailing international style"—as Jonathan Brown puts it—though in fact at the time Velázquez's friend the painter Jusepe Martínez merely (and rather obliquely) observed that Velázquez came back "very much improved in perspective and architecture." But his palette was also lighter, his tones brighter than before. The significance of Titian and the Venetians had been grasped. Brown also sees the influence of Pietro da Cortona in color and composition, though admitting that Velázquez's paintings were less "animated." Cortona's were in fact a veritable sea of waving arms and conspicuously contorted bodies; by contrast Velázquez's were examples of eloquent restraint. His freer and more sumptuous way of dealing with clothes also seemed to have been influenced by Italy.

He was now thrown back into the court organization, a staff artist from whom—"by royal appointment"—portrait work was demanded. It was a busy period. Among pictures he did at this time were portraits of the king's younger brother, the cardinal-infante Don Ferdinand in hunting kit (he had been appointed a cardinal at the age of ten and in 1632 went off to Brussels where two years later he took over as governor of Flanders), and of the count-duke, showing off on horseback, almost as though he were king. A much more restrained likeness was of Don Juan Mateos, the king's master of the hunt. A *Sybil* shows a woman in profile, intently staring over the top of a wooden panel or tablet, and could be Juana Pacheco, Velázquez's wife. A *Young Woman Sewing* is a different person—though possibly the same lady who is elsewhere portrayed with a fan, a rosary, and a mantilla, looking out at the viewer. Sewing, she has her face in half shadow, eyes lowered to her handiwork, and with dark hair and black dress, which gives a feeling of still being painted, almost meant to seem unfinished. When one seeks other artists for comparison the only names that suit are those of Dutch painters, painters of masterpieces, Rembrandt, Hals, and Vermeer.

While Velázquez was in Italy, the royal family had had joyful increase. On October 17, 1629, Prince Baltasar Carlos came into the world—a son and heir! The celebrations were ecstatic. The healthy-looking infant would be the only legitimate child of the king to survive childhood. In 1629 Philip fathered two sons, one being Baltasar Carlos, the other being María Calderón's child, Don Juan, brought up in the castle at Ocana. Nights on the town, creating the likelihood of venereal disease, and years of inbreeding did great damage to the Hapsburg line, but at least Baltasar Carlos's mother, Isabella of Bourbon, had Navarre, de Valois, and de Medici blood, and there were hopes that the male heir would be healthy, as well as longer-lived than the five siblings who preceded him, all girls, and all dead within roughly eighteen months. (Baltasar Carlos reached seventeen. The surviving child was María Teresa, born in 1638—sadly, another girl.)

Soon after his return, Velázquez painted the prince, just over two years old. The painting is believed to commemorate an oath of allegiance sworn to the new heir by the Cortes of Castile on March 7, 1632. (The regime took the opportunity to prompt the cortes to approve extra funds for Spain's wars.) The little infante stands erect, richly robed, a red sash across his chest, left hand on the hilt of his sword, a small gorget rather than a bib under the beginnings of his Hapsburg chin, cheeks already looking swollen with the genes of Hapsburg majesty (though maybe he was just teething), and the baton of command clasped in his pudgy right hand. A splendid hat with a brilliant white plume rests on a nearby dark scarlet cushion. One suspects that the painter has asked his Royal Highness to put the hat there, leaving the child's face—pursed lips, apple-red cheeks—fully visible. The painter couldn't resist the chance to show off his skills in the folds of the velvet curtains, dented like bruised flesh, and in the big gold-braided tassel that hangs from the cushion—hangs, one might say in hindsight, with a suggestion that it might fall off. A step below the infante, an attendant stands, only slightly bigger than Prince Baltasar Carlos, sex indeterminate, but remarkable for his or her much-older face: The attendant is a dwarf. If we take a bead necklace as evidence of a female wearer, the dwarf holds in *her* right hand a silver rattle made to resemble a miniature royal scepter, in the other an orb, a tiny world, in the form of an apple. This is the first such small person to be painted by Velázquez: court companions, professional jesters, chamber helpers, and possibly psychological props—to be examined more closely later on. This little one looks askance at her royal playmate, as if guarding her possessions from a princely toddler who might snatch them. The look may also ask: Am I doing this correctly? Am I showing sufficient respect and making clear that I know who is really in charge here? It is a portrait in inequality. Both figures are small. But *deo volente* Baltasar Carlos will grow bigger; the dwarf will not.

Philip IV came through this period looking—in the eye of history—as Velázquez painted him. Whatever his manifest failings, Philip has to be given credit as an art lover and patron for recognizing in Velázquez a painter who might immortalize the king and his family. In these years Velázquez made a series of portraits of Philip, some of which were copied by assistants, some of which were sent abroad to royal relatives. The first that Velázquez painted after his return from Italy is probably the one now in the London National Gallery, showing Philip around 1632 standing stiff armed and stiff legged, unsmiling, indeed looking somewhat imprisoned in his rich brown and silver costume, which

Infante Baltasar Carlos with a Dwarf, *1631–32,*
Museum of Fine Arts, Boston.

Velázquez painted with seemingly impromptu brushstrokes. The flourishes of the king's extravagant mustache echo the fluent curls of his auburn hair. He is a stuffed shirt but also a human being. Philip had as a boy acted in the plays and masques put on at court; he retained for most of his life the malleability of an actor. In his brown and silver costume he was all dressed up, albeit with hints of self-knowledge in his wary gaze. The king had been seriously ill in 1627 and had tried to turn over a new leaf, with less hunting and less wenching for a time. But María Calderón and other women came along. He needed to escape into pleasure, back to the theater and actresses, to horse riding and hunting. He is not, in Velázquez's picture, a man at ease with himself. He is a man without willpower and—curious for a king—with little self-esteem.

The soubriquet "Planet King" didn't help. In this portrait he wears in badge form the Burgundian Order of the Golden Fleece and rests his left hand on the hilt of his sword. He felt bullied by Olivares, who rose at five a.m. and often told off Philip for not keeping up with the royal paperwork. Here, as if to demonstrate to the minister his concern for the duties of monarchy, he holds in his right hand a document, a petition, which began *"Señor"*—a simple salutation whose use had been decreed in 1623, along with the less fancy wearing of golillas—and was signed by Velázquez as painter to His Majesty. Philip generally signed his own correspondence *"Yo El Rey"*—I, the king. Here Velázquez's name, painted by the artist, is also his signature on the picture, though signing his works wasn't a common practice with him.

Velázquez's portraits of Philip done at this time tend to have a rather violent perspective—the floor tilted up, the king seemingly on the point of sliding down the canvas; the lighter tone Velázquez was now using also made for a more edgy atmosphere. Both father and son, Philip and Baltasar Carlos, were portrayed by Velázquez in the first half of the 1630s with batons in hand, on horseback, the horses rearing—rather stage-set paintings with Titian and Rubens among their progenitors, both father and son looking nervously human and not especially regal, but providing for all that effective images of the monarch and (with luck) the monarch-to-be as commanders whose powers were derived from God. Velázquez's royal portraits also had precursors in the works of the sixteenth-century Hapsburg court painters, Antonio Mor and Mor's pupil Alonso Sánchez Coello, in which the grave, dignified atmosphere around Philip II was well-expressed. But Velázquez's images were more human, easier to connect with, and would it was hoped stick in the minds of Spain's subjects around the world. A pamphlet published in Madrid in 1638 made Philip absolutely preeminent in a kingdom in which the Catholic religion was central: "Divine Faith provides the stability and strength of empires, so that as Faith grows, empires grow, and as Faith recedes, empires collapse." Velázquez had—as we have seen—already taken part in a contest celebrating the expulsion by Philip III of the supposedly converted Moriscos from the Iberian peninsula: A triumph for the Faith.

The equestrian portrait of Baltasar Carlos was painted to be seen by the viewer from below, hung high over a doorway in a new palace that Olivares promoted at this time in a bid to present the Spanish monarchy as still the answer to world problems. Velázquez's equestrian portrait of Philip IV was lower, to the left of the same doorway and at shoulder height. The king may have come to sit for the painter still flushed from his mistress's bed and, obeying his painter's direction, perched on a bench as on horseback (the horse would be painted in later as would the blown-back plumes of his hat). Philip, shown wearing armor and a general's sash, sat looking straight ahead with the gaze of someone thinking about what he might need to tell his father confessor when they next met. Some art historians have observed a proud confidence in this *Philip IV on Horseback* (1634–35, Prado), but Philip could be seen as someone trying hard to put out of his mind the saying "Pride cometh before a fall." His world was turning fast from certainty to question.

The new palace was the Buen Retiro. The count-duke created it to take the king's and country's mind off Spain's imperial problems, and spent money the state could ill afford in building it. The Army of Flanders at this point was costing three million ducats a year. The Retiro palace cost more than three million ducats over nine years. New funds were gathered from the sale of offices and privileges. New excise taxes on wine, meat, and oil were raised in Madrid to help fund the palace. Still, it would make a change from the immense dark fortification that was the Alcázar. The Buen Retiro expanded from small beginnings in rooms kept for the royal family in the monastery of San Jerónimo on the eastern side of the city; Olivares's wife's family also owned property in the area that provided space for the new palace, not far from the Prado, the wide avenue popular with the Madrid public for evening promenading. There the count-duke collaborated with an Italian alchemist Vincenzo Massinci in experiments that they hoped would produce gold. There he had gardens where he spent any spare time with his pet birds: swans, pheasants, prize poultry. And there he eventually made available several hundred acres for the Retiro and its grounds.

Construction of the new pleasure palace began in 1630. At its heart were two large courtyards, as at the Alcázar, but surrounded by lower buildings, outlying smaller courtyards, a chapel, a plaza for tournaments and bullfights, and a park; the grounds eventually covered an area half the size of the existing city. The park contained several hermitages, formal gardens, grottoes, ponds with fountains, orchards, and a large ornamental lake. The buildings went up in a hurry, some thought all a bit *chapuza* (a botched job or jerry-built, we might say). For those allowed inside, like the many royal guests accommodated there, the interior was more approved than the hastily finished outside, which seemed to most of the public too close to the ground and lacking any overall form or grandeur; the Retiro came to be nicknamed *El Gallinero*, the henhouse or chicken run; an ornate aviary of caged birds stood near its entrance. The Retiro's architect Giovanni Battista Crescenzi was so exhausted by building problems and the stress of dealing with Olivares, the boss, that he died in 1635. In that year Olivares was quick to defend the cost of the new palace, about which the people of Madrid were complaining and which Olivares explained was needed for the crown in case an epidemic—such as smallpox—required Philip's family to evacuate the Alcázar. By then, the Retiro had been open over a year. The inauguration party in December 1633 went on for four days of plays, bullfights, and tournaments. Despite the worries of the English ambassador that the hastily constructed buildings held together with "greene mortar" would collapse under the weight of the throng, the Retiro remained standing.

As it was, Velázquez was greatly involved in the much less criticized Retiro interior, and particularly in the large throne room called the Hall of Realms, the *Salon de los Reinos*. (The king observed, with a note of anguish, "Many kingdoms, many difficulties.") But here Philip could preside over court happenings while his family and household watched from a balcony. Here, as the Florentine envoy Serrano noted, was "a perpetual round of ceremonies, audiences, and etiquette, with devotional exercises and 'discipline,' one following the other like sleep and wakefulness." The hall had a vaulted ceiling with gilded arabesques. Above the windows were placed the emblems of the twenty-four Spanish kingdoms. And there was plenty of wall space to preoccupy Velázquez as arranger, hanger, and painter. As noted, Velázquez's equestrian portraits of the king and the infante were displayed here, and so was his portrait of Philip's queen Isabella. She, now in her early thirties, was also shown on horseback, not cutting any equestrian capers but wearing a huge pendant pearl called *La Peregrina*. This was said to have been found in an oyster in Panama and—its shell being small—nearly discarded. The pearl got to Spain by galleon and was given by Philip II to Mary Tudor. When that arrangement came to an end, the pearl was returned to Spain and worn by various queens. (During the Napoleonic invasion, it was nabbed by Joseph Bonaparte and carted off to France. In 1969 it was sold for $37,000 to the actor Richard Burton, who gave it to his wife Elizabeth Taylor, despite claims from the Duke of Alba that it wasn't the real *Peregrina* that had belonged to King Alfonso XIII's wife, Queen Victoria Eugenia. This second enormous pearl, now called Peregrina II, has since been worn by the present queen Sofia.)

The Hall of Realms was to be largely devoted to celebrating Spain's triumphs in the never-ending war against insurgents and infidels. Here Velázquez took over from Calderón as the master of ceremonies. Nine artists were invited to produce paintings for the hall. Over the doorways Velázquez's Sevillian colleague Zurbarán, known for his religious portraits, painted ten scenes from the life of the semidivine hero Hercules—scenes showing his famous labors. Hercules had succeeded in conquering Discord and was thus apparently close kin to Philip IV; both were also identified with the Sun. Five of Velázquez's equestrian portraits of the royal family were hung in the hall, and Velázquez nominated himself to paint one of the twelve pictures that were to show battles in which Philip IV's forces had been victorious around the world. A thousand craftsmen were said to have been employed at the Retiro, and painters, plasterers, and gilders were kept hard at it for a year and a half decorating the Hall of Realms. Velázquez was still occupied with his painting in late March 1635, but the *Salon de los Reinos* and its contents were ready for the inauguration ceremony soon after Easter.

Olivares conducted the Buen Retiro performance to completion and it was more successful than the Union of Arms he had been promoting since 1626, intended to bring the Spanish realms, whether far-flung or close at hand, into active solidarity against their common enemy—not least by getting them all to help pay for the conflict in the Low Countries. The twelve paintings were in part propaganda—persuasive pictures that allowed their artists to boost the Hapsburg cause in their own ways. In Velázquez's case this didn't mean his picture was not art.

The paintings, mostly by his less illustrious contemporaries, were meant to demonstrate Philip IV's staunch defense of his disparate worldwide empire and the Catholic religion, and of course show the influence of the count-duke, the power behind the throne. They were also intended to suggest the magnanimity with which Spain accompanied its victories.

Velázquez found his theme—Breda—without apparent difficulty. We don't know if he had first choice of the twelve subjects but among those that were picked to be painted were another four occasioned by 1625: the recapture of Bahia in Brazil from the Dutch; the lifting of the French and Savoyard siege of Genoa; the defeat of an English naval attack on Cádiz; and the expulsion of the Dutch from Puerto Rico. Further claimed as Spanish successes were Spinola's capture of the Rhineland town of Julich in 1622; Gonzalo de Córdoba's battle at the village of Fleurus in Brabant seven months later (which Córdoba's opponents Count Mansfeld and Christian of Brunswick thought they had won); the temporary recapture of the island of Saint Kitts in 1629; and in 1633—in its way a second year of miracles and hope for Olivares and Spain—the capture of Saint Martin, the relief of Constance and of Breisach,* and the siege of Rheinfelden. However, Breda was definitely Spain's greatest military success in the previous decade. It was one in which someone Velázquez had talked with at length had been involved as a chief protagonist. And it was a subject for which the artist came to have an almost physical imagining, and his palette would take him there. In the mix already was his voyage to Genoa with Spinola five years before. There was his contact with the Low Countries through Peter Paul Rubens and the many previous painters of the Hapsburg monarchs. Perhaps he felt that some sort of memorial to Spinola was called for, the general sidelined by the count-duke, a casualty of his policies. And perhaps there were other personal reasons for choosing to celebrate what was both a victory and a surrender.

---

*Breisach was in Lorraine on the upper Rhine, not far from Switzerland, and formed a crucial link on the supply chain of the Army of Flanders (*Palace*, pp. 176–77; Parker, p. 46).

VII. "BREDA FOR THE KING OF SPAIN!"
MADRID. 1634–35

THE SURRENDER OF BREDA TOOK PLACE DURING THE SECOND period of relative success for Spain in the long Low Countries war. This was a short span of a half dozen years—following the end of the Twelve Years Truce in 1621—when something of a *Pax Hispanica* prevailed. But it was by no means a general peace: Risings and skirmishes occurred now and then and the Dutch cleverly got others to make economic and military trouble for their Hapsburg overlords. First to celebrate in art the taking of the Brabant city in 1625 was the playwright Calderón, who is thought to have had personal experience as a soldier in the Netherlands morass. Before the end of the year his play *El Sitio de Breda* was put on at the court in Madrid under the auspices of Olivares. Calderón's output, like that of his Dutch contemporary Vondel, isn't entirely accessible today, although *Life Is a Dream* and *The Mayor of Zalamea* come to life in the boisterous modern versions of Adrian Mitchell and John Barton. *El Sitio* particularly seems to be a procession of stilted *tableaux vivants*, marshaled with antiquated dignity. Lope de Vega also took on the subject of Spanish victory in a play about the reconquest of Brazil—dealt with as well in a painting for the Hall of Realms by Juan Bautista Maino. Maino was a Dominican friar, a drawing master at the court who had given the king painting lessons. His *Recapture of Bahia* was the only other possible masterpiece among the victory paintings, and was, with Velázquez's *Breda*, among the last to be finished and hung.

Although Spinola was no longer alive, Velázquez evidently kept vivid memories of him from the voyage to Italy; he may also have seen some of the numerous portraits that now existed of the captain-general, painted by van Dyck, the Delft artist Michiel van Mierevelt, and Rubens. The latter had painted several likenesses, one in 1627. Rubens had said that although he admired Spinola's military wisdom, he thought the Genoese lacked any taste for painting—indeed, "understood no more about it than a street porter." Velázquez perhaps retained sketches he had made of the Genoese general from the voyage to Italy. As for the siege itself, which Velázquez meant to make the subject of his Hall of Realms painting, the artist had presumably heard a good deal about it from Spinola, and by the time he got around to sizing it up there were construction materials other than Calderón's flat-footed account. Even so, a siege was difficult to picture.

Among Velázquez's materials was a record of the siege written by Spinola's chaplain, Herman Hugo. *Obsidio Bredana* was published a year or two after the surrender in Latin, English, and French versions. There was also the work of Jacques Callot (1592–1635), illustrator, engraver, and war artist. Callot had been invited by the archduchess Isabella to make a map of the siege illustrated with graphic details—and this was produced in six tall sheets (measuring 1,200 × 1,410 mm, or with text 1,280 × 1,810 mm). Callot visited Breda in the summer of 1627. Spinola had paid him an advance of 550 escudos against an agreed-upon price of 850 escudos for the completed map. Callot had Hugo's text to work with and had studied siege maps of Breda, of which there were already many—special editions, as it were, of the big news of the day—including those by the cartographers Blaeu and Visscher in Amsterdam. Callot's map was published by the Plantin Press in Antwerp in 1628. In the dedication for the accompanying booklet, credit was given to Spinola's engineer at the siege, Giovanni Francesco Cantagallina, the Florentine who appeared in Callot's map at the foot of one sheet, lower left, surveyor's staff in hand and bending over the figure of the artist. Callot had shown himself seated on the ground, sketching the siege lines, carrying a gentleman's sword and dagger, and wearing a garment the art historian Simone Zurawski identifies as a *collet* of buffalo hide, "worn for parrying."

Jacques Callot, Siege of Breda, *illustrated map of the siege,
1628, Trustees of the British Museum.*

The sheets of Callot's map looked like scrolls, which could be unrolled
upward and away from the viewer. The ground and the figures on it
were displayed as if one were looking into a concave landscape—a
landscape that first sloped downhill and then out to a far, more or less
flat, horizon. Here and there Callot sketched scenes from various
moments of the siege, active and passive. He showed farm cottages,
soldiers' bivouacs, clumps of trees, a group of cavalry, some soldiers looting a farmhouse, men found guilty of such an offense being hanged
from gibbets or tortured upon a strappado, pacific flocks of sheep, soldiers playing dice or practicing with their weaponry, a man on crutches,
some Dutch supply ships on the Mark River, a field hospital catering
for the sick and wounded, and a covered stores wagon. Spanish soldiers
foraged and chopped firewood; their womenfolk washed laundry in
the streams. The conclusion of the siege figured, too. We are shown the
Dutch refugees fleeing Breda on foot and by carriage, leaving, as siege

etiquette insisted, through a breach in the city wall, their possessions heaped on wagons. We see troops marching out past the assembled Spanish pikemen, while—an event that in fact happened a week or so after the surrender—the archduchess arrives in triumph from Brussels. Her carriage is guarded by halberdiers. Spinola on horseback looks on, turned self-effacingly toward the infanta, but dressed by Callot a bit too splendidly given the commander's well-known *modestia*; he is shown in plumed hat and extravagant scarf. In the center, off-right, Callot gives us a plan of Breda. All in all there is a minimum of violence. Callot clearly brings to our attention the now moderate manner in which Spanish armies were conducting the war, thirty some years long, which had had plenty of brutal moments.

VELÁZQUEZ TOOK FROM both Callot and Calderón. The painting he made for the Hall of Realms also gave the illusion of a scene depicted from a hill, a viewpoint higher than any in the actual watery flat lowlands around Breda. The upper section of his picture, the *Surrender of Breda*, sometimes called *The Lances*, shows an overcast gray-blue sky into which smoke from fires and pyres is rising, and into it—closer to the viewer—the iron tips of a line of sixteen-foot pikes, cut from ash wood, are raised. They number twenty-nine, the Spanish infantry's basic weapon, and they make what Calderón called an "iron cornfield," here extending across the right upper half of the painting. They also remind us of the cypresses rising above and behind the balustrade in the *Gardens of the Villa Medici*. In the distance just left of center, Velázquez painted the calm surface of the flooded Vucht polder, with a faint line stretching from shore to shore, bottom to top, to indicate the causeway known as the Black Dike, which looked as if it, too, was at this moment under water.

The painting is huge, nearly eleven feet high and twelve feet wide (307 cm × 367 cm), and is packed with compressed detail. All the figures are male. By way of them, whole armies are suggested. In the immediate foreground, stage left, a half dozen members of the surrendering Dutch staff and their aides stand with their shorter pikes and pennons. They apparently include Charles Philip le Comte and a son of Prince Emmanuel of Portugal. The spotlight, or the light of history, is on the young man nearest to us who shows us his back, covered by a well-tailored, light-brown, thigh-length coat, pleated. To his left his companion bears on his shoulder an arquebus—a primitive musket—and looks at us (as he looked at the painter), as if to ask in a puzzled way, "Why are you here, too?" Next, to the right of the staff officer in the pleated coat, is a young man wearing a white blouse crossed by a sash and decorated with flowers that, first seen, might be bloodstains, but, reconsidered, look more like embroidered tulips. He is pointing with a raised finger while a companion listens. Behind the youth in the white blouse is the head of a black horse, with thick white muzzle and a disheveled mane falling between its eyes. To the right, a darker mass of figures is given density by a second, more massive horse—a battle charger, evidently the Spanish general's, which stands with its right rear leg lifted, its gleaming chestnut-brown rump presented to the viewer. Behind this beast crowd the Spanish officers, among them Albert Arenbergh (known also as the Marquis de Balancon), Wolfgang von Neuberg, Count John of Nassau, and Carlos Coloma. Henry van den Bergh had been at the siege as well but between the end of it and Velázquez's painting of it was declared a traitor and left out of the depiction of this band of honor. Behind them the pikemen jostle shoulder to shoulder to witness, close-up, the victory ceremony. They were the poor bloody infantry of the time, the *picas secas* who wore no body armor and received the lowest pay.

The actual moment in which Velázquez depicted the surrender at Breda as taking place is almost buried in the center of the picture. Squeezed in the space between the opposing forces are the main protagonists, at last in intimate contact after more than ten months of siege. In this spot our eye is attracted by the wide white lace collar and cuff of Justin of Nassau, illuminated by the morning sun; the town's governor bends forward as he presents the large iron key of Breda to the Spanish general. The key is highlighted within a hexagonal window, formed by Spinola's dark clothing. Beyond Spinola's right arm, seemingly framed as through the aperture that showed Christ with Martha and Mary through a kitchen hatch in Seville, we see farther off the banners, pikes, hats, and legs of the Dutch garrison marching forth, the surrendering army being allowed to leave the city with drums beating and their weaponry, colors, ensigns, and honor intact.

The surrender ceremony took place near Teteringen, a village just outside Breda, to the northeast of the city. It probably didn't go exactly as Velázquez—perhaps influenced by Calderón's account—described it, but the painter had things other than the event itself he wanted to convey. Most such surrender scenes showed the victorious commander on horseback, with the general he has defeated, cap in hand, in the act of kneeling or prostrating himself. Here, Velázquez shows both generals bareheaded. Spinola is remarkably on foot. Justin of Nassau is also on his feet, leaning slightly toward the Genoese general and holding out the key to the city gates. They meet as almost-equals, recent competitors who might in other circumstances have been friends. Spinola obviously wants the Dutchman who is bowing his head to feel just that. The Genoese has his right arm stretched out to clasp Justin's shoulder, a comradely touch that also prevents the Dutchman from bowing any farther. And he meets Justin's gesture of submission with a generous look—an expression that says, as Calderón put it, that "the valour of the vanquished confers honour on the victor." (In the words of Herman Hugo's English translator a year after the battle, Spinola held that they were "more wise who are more gentle in cruelty, and that the fame of clemency was to be preferred before the name of severity.") Indeed Spinola's generous thought soon traveled, being echoed in the 1706 English translation of *Don Quixote*, where the Knight of the Wood tells Don Quixote, the Knight of the Woeful Countenance, that "the reputation of the Victor rises in proportion to that of the Vanquish'd." Spinola may well have thought this stage of the conflict could have gone the other way. And Velázquez, painting as required a Spanish victory, faces up to the fact that the victory would not be a lasting one. He was a truth-teller who saw the uncertainty of things. Spinola's graceful and chivalrous pat on the shoulder gives Justin the sense that he shouldn't worry overmuch; it will be his turn, or at least the Dutch turn, next—in fact, in less than ten years, in 1637, after a shorter siege. Spinola's gesture is also as we know an elegiac one, for the captain-general by the time of the Hall of Realms and Velázquez's painting was dead at Casale.

Something similar is indicated by the presentation of the opposing soldiery. The Dutch participants look relatively clean and handsomely clothed. The Spanish rank-and-file, lined up with their lances behind their commanders, look like vagabonds, unshaved, in motley gear. They have spent months out in the countryside foraging for food and fuel. Their opponents have been housed in the city, on strict rations but until the last moment at least being fed. Don Carlos Coloma observed the decided contrast between the defeated Dutch, well turned out despite the long siege, and the victorious Spaniards, despite their success, miserable and half-dressed in torn and tattered clothing. However, their rewards should have been soon to come: Although Breda hadn't succumbed to an assault, which would have meant that it could have been sacked and plundered, it had surrendered on terms, and this generally meant the besieging troops would be paid "storm money" to make up for the loss of booty. In the shadow of the pikes there would have been cheerful expressions in the tattered Spanish ranks. Herman Hugo, the Spanish chaplain, noted how Spinola "courteously saluted all the [Dutch] captains at their going forth" and how the Dutch troops "with a modest inclining of their banners, saluted him. No ignominious voice of provoking one another was once heard, but smiles with favourable countenances." Justin of Nassau was described by Father Hugo as "venerable for his gray hairs." And Velázquez painted in a touch of gray to Justin's black hair, though less was made of it than of the gray streaking Spinola's hair. The full light shines on the Genoese general's head. It illuminates his features, his lace collar, the gold embroidery of his coat, and the silk, pale pinky-red captain-general's sash that falls like a peacock's plumage to knee level. The gilded hilt of his sword can just be seen. In his left hand, he holds his field commander's wooden baton. The plumes on his hat, which is also held in that hand, make a vivid white mark against the bottom of the sash and his boot tops. The footwear of the opposing chiefs is noticeably different. Justin of Nassau's boots arc dark brown and baggier, coming well above the knee. Spinola's lighter fawn-colored boots are more dressy, narrower up the calf to the knee. He wears gilded spurs.

Velázquez was always good with material—the Seville water seller's leather jerkin, for example. The contrast here in how Justin and Spinola are shod is perceptive reporting and brilliant painting. But *The Surrender of Breda* is splendid in many aspects: in the variety of ways the faces of the participants are shown, in light and shadow, partially, frontally, or in profile; in a composition that conveys the slow mass of military activity among the men and the thoughtful patience of the officers confronting one another. "Hurry up and wait!" has always been a rueful expression among soldiers. Velázquez might well have served, under one flag or other, such is his empathy for his subject. We recall that both Velázquez and Spinola were known for their *modestia*, their unassertiveness and "phlegm." And we feel that the very act of surrender aroused a personal response in the artist: He knew what it was to give himself up. Hadn't he done so when, putting aside the possibility of a freelance career, he quit Seville for the court? He continued to do so as he slowly mounted the court ladder of promotion and painted portrait after portrait of Philip IV and his family. Even if he had needed Olivares or the king to say, in respect of suitable subjects for the Hall of Realms, "What about Breda?," Velázquez would have recognized that he and this particular idea were meant for each other.

He started by painting a pale, off-white ground, largely of lead white, as the underlayer for his immense canvas. His materials were similar to those used by other artists at the time, but for this picture, mixing his pigments with walnut or linseed oil, he deployed the paints sparingly—so thinly in most places that the ground showed through. For the blue sky that spans the top quarter of the painting he used azurite, an expensive mineral also called copper blue, whose coarse crystals had been employed by artists as far back as the Old Kingdom in Egypt. In more recent times it had been quarried in Hungary, but because of the Turkish occupation had become hard to get. G. McKim Smith, who has studied Velázquez's materials and technique, says the painter mixed his greens for the Breda background from azurite and yellow pigment. To create Spinola's splendid sash he painted one very thick layer of red lake, with visible brushstrokes, "rather than a series of many thinner layers." His medium was drying oils, with which he achieved "greatly increased transparency and depth of colour." McKim Smith adds that in the *Surrender* "the principal figures are still solidly constructed, if perhaps more thinly painted [than before this date]; they are firmly outlined and painted with relatively thick, fluid paint. But . . . in [the] subsidiary figures but most of all in the background and details of the setting, there is a sketchiness not present in his earlier paintings. The landscape in the background of the *Surrender of Breda* is marvellously evocative, set out in a freer, economical fashion that strongly contrasts with the more labored treatment of the figures."

The term *more detailed* rather than more labored might be better suited for the treatment of the figures. Yet in general Velázquez seems to have substituted for the detailed, concentrated ways of his Seville years a more fluid technique: The luminous almost white ground was very like that used by the impressionists two centuries later. It was an economic technique but made evident his awareness of how paint could be handled to make the eye see afresh. In places you can actually note where the paint, including lumps of pigment scraped from the palette, catches the light or throws shadows, as on the rear left leg of the great horse. There the paint appears to have been allowed to run down the canvas. Long before twentieth-century action painting, Velázquez seems to have thrown himself into both the means and method of his art, medium and brushstroke fused in the crucible of eye, hand, and brain. In the course of painting the *Surrender* Velázquez made numerous changes, adding two men to the right of Spinola, altering legs and hats, lengthening the lances. He has allowed his underdrawing to be seen, for example, in the brilliantly rendered if sketchy painting of Justin's white cuff, out of which protrudes the hand holding the key. He in fact used preparatory sketches for this picture; a few survive as they do not for most other Velázquez paintings. Justi refers to several drawings in the National Library in Madrid—one "a crayon on white paper, where the outlines are rather vaguely essayed. . . . The chief figure is the groom behind Spinola's horse, and near him to the right, but only half the size, the young man listening who here raises two fingers. On the reverse of the same sheet is Spinola himself, but much smaller, in quite faint, blurred contour." Justi also mentions a drawing in the Louvre "in clean, firm outline" in which one can see Spinola's horse and the chief group of Spanish officers. The customary lack of sketch material from Velázquez suggests either that he generally did without such preparatory matter or that he or later hands assisted in a bonfire.

Most visitors to the Hall of Realms would have obtained the impression of much money having been spent on materials, decor, and artistry.

Kitchen Maid with the Supper at Emmaus, c. 1618–20. Oil on canvas.
NATIONAL GALLERY OF IRELAND, DUBLIN.

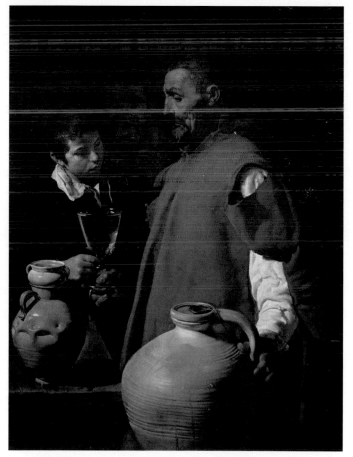

The Waterseller of Seville, 1618–22. Oil on canvas.
APSLEY HOUSE, LONDON.

Villa Medici, Rome (*Gardens with Grotto Loggia*), 1630. Oil on canvas.
MUSEO DEL PRADO, MADRID.

The Surrender of Breda, 1634–35. Oil on canvas.

MUSEO DEL PRADO, MADRID.

The Surrender of Breda (detail: Justin of Nassau and Ambrogio Spinola)

King Philip IV at Fraga (Philip IV at Fraga), 1644. Oil on canvas.

Juan de Pareja, 1650. Oil on canvas.

Pope Innocent X, 1649–50.
Oil on canvas.
GALLERIA
DORIA-PAMPHILJ,
ROME.

The Toilet of Venus (*The Rokeby Venus*), c. 1650. Oil on canvas.
NATIONAL GALLERY, LONDON.

Infanta Margarita in Pink, 1653. Oil on canvas.

The Fable of Arachne (The Spinners), c. 1656. Oil on canvas.

MUSEO DEL PRADO, MADRID.

Mercury and Argus, c. 1659. Oil on canvas.

MUSEO DEL PRADO, MADRID.

Las Meninas (*The Family of Philip IV*), 1656. Oil on canvas.
MUSEO DEL PRADO, MADRID.

The setting in the Buen Retiro's grandest space added to a spectator's feeling that due respect was being given to the monarchy. And *The Surrender of Breda* threw back at its admirers the sensation that life could indeed be noble. Partly this may have been because of the evident self-consciousness of some of the painting's figures, who catch the eye of the viewer as they would have done that of the artist, had he been right there. The composition is cinematic, and the director has signaled his involvement. But this almost contemporary participatory feeling is balanced by a skill in portraying human flesh and human emotion that was very much of that, not this, time. We are without doubt in the company of a painter who could stand alongside the masters of the age: Frans Hals and Rembrandt, say, although their soldiers and guards of the nightwatch were more often members of guilds and only part-time militiamen.

The fires burning here and there in the distance beyond Breda could be from earlier centuries. They remind us of fires and pyres burning in the landscapes of Bosch and Brueghel. As for the eye-catching motif of the *lanzas*, these pikes (a form of long-handled spear) had been the late medieval weapon of choice and a common feature in European battle paintings. They were considered to be "the queen of weapons." The Spanish pikes that helped take Breda do not quite make an evenly topped hedge; a few end slightly below the highest level; a few lean slightly to one side. (Carl Justi saw what he called the "rigid symmetry" of the pikes or *lanzas* as a symbol of the discipline that had made the Spanish infantry the terror of Europe, but the actual lack of absolute symmetry and rigidity here hints rather at a possibly waning ability to provoke terror, or at the wearying effects of a ten-month-long operation.) Pikes at this stage were still the main defensive weapons, despite the introduction of the arquebus, the predecessor of the musket. Those pikes carried by cavalry were generally called lances, hence the name lancer for the soldiers so employed. The horsemen at the Battle of San Romano, 1432, portrayed by Uccello in three paintings, were armed with lances; at the center of the action in one of these the orange-bonneted commander on his rearing white charger flourishes a broken lance while behind him a man in armor with lowered lance pierces the body of an enemy, the tip of his weapon red with blood. The foreground of Uccello's picture is lower, flatter than that shown in Velázquez's after-the-siege-ended scene at Breda. Uccello's crowded battlefield is set in a dip between two hills, with a pastoral background in which only a few skirmishes and solitary combats are taking place. The lance was a timeless weapon: A French artist known as the Master of the Cassoni Campana, working in Florence, painted *The Taking of Athens by Minos* and peopled it with warriors wearing medieval armor and carrying lances. There were lances in the *Abraham and Melchisadek* (1579) of the Antwerp painter Martin de Vos, which Velázquez might have seen in Seville. El Greco's *St. Maurice and the Theban Legion* may have provided another source though it was a picture Philip II hadn't wanted for the Escorial. And Velázquez wasn't alone in choosing the lance motif for the Hall of Realms: the painting that was hung in the hall two to the left of *The Surrender of Breda* was Jusepe Leonardo's *Relief of Breisach*, in which the tips of the pikes disappear into the sky.

On the ground, Swiss pike-squares had turned the tide against attacks of mounted Burgundian cavalry in the battles of Morat, Grandson, and Nancy in 1475–77. Pikes helped the Saxon soldiery confront the army of Charles XII of Sweden in 1706. And although the British gradually phased out the long pike in favor of the bayonet, whose hilt could be fastened to a musket, lances for a long time remained in service in British dragoon regiments. The belief endured that they could shatter the last stands of demoralized troops. Among the occasions on which lances were used in the last century was the gallant charge in October 1914 of French cavalry dragoons against the German infantry north of Bethune, in Flanders—lances versus machine guns and rifles. The British cavalry despite the often lethal impediment of barbed wire made a number of successful attacks, using the comparative speed of horses to capture German-held ground, and with their Hussars, Lancers, and Dragoons armed with swords and lances, even as late as 1918 when the final German "Kaizer's Offensive" on the Western Front splintered with cavalry help. On the Amiens road on March 30, 1918, a squadron of Lord Strathcona's Horse caught a German infantry battalion that had just left the cover of a wood: The squadron commander got his bugler to blow "charge," the men lowered their lances, the horses broke into a canter, and many Germans were killed with lance and sword. Back in the seventeenth century, Don Quixote's chivalric equipment as a knight included "a lance in the rack" and at one point, referring to his peerless Lady Dulcinea, he tells his squire Sancho Panza that she is "as tall as a lance." In Spain Velázquez's war picture still bears the preferred title *Las Lanzas*, and perhaps its most remarkable feature, those sixteen-foot pikes, do not disturb its serenity. Near Teteringen all passion is spent. Velázquez was fair—evenhanded—to both sides. We are left meditating the ideals—of loyalty to the king, religious faith, and individual honor—that impelled the warring sides.

DID VELÁZQUEZ PAINT himself into the picture? He did so in one later masterpiece and some believe he did with this one. Charles Leslie thought so, Constable's friend and a Royal Academician who in 1855 wrote a first-rate *Handbook for Young Painters*. In this work, Leslie quotes the traveler in Spain Richard Ford, who said, "Velázquez has introduced his own noble head into this picture, which is placed in the corner with a plumed hat." Portraits of Velázquez aren't numerous. Juan de Alfaro, a Córdoban who worked in Velázquez's studio for ten years or so (ca. 1650–60) and kept notes for a life of the master that he handed on to Palomino, drew one in black chalk of the artist on his deathbed. Velázquez himself according to Pacheco made a self-portrait while in Italy, a painting that is now lost although several versions of the missing original exist, including one in Munich; this is a head-and-shoulders view, dark eyes swiveled toward the viewer, pale face framed by long dark hair parted in the middle, chin resting on the tilted white top edge of a golilla collar, thick lips surmounted by a firm black *W* of a mustache. A similar head-to-waist self-portrait, also with a golilla, painted around 1636, hangs in the Uffizi in Florence: a picture of a man who looks stressed out and grumpy.

The man who attracts our attention on this score in *The Surrender of Breda* is the figure farthest to the right, squeezed into a small triangle of space between the great bulk of Spinola's horse and a drooping Spanish ensign: a mustached man in gray—gray boots, gray coat, gray hat, indeed the only man among those individually picked out who is wearing a hat. He also wears a white lace collar and a hat with a white plume, both providing highlights that catch the eye, as does his gaze.

Self-Portrait, *c. 1636, Uffizi, Florence.*

"I am a bit different from all the others here," his look suggests. "I am the one who is letting you all know what is going on." The large light blue and white checked flag that hangs above his hat makes an alleviating broad diagonal stroke across the rigid iron hedge of upright lances, interrupted only by the dark brown ears and head of the massive horse. The tilted, curled-up brim of the gray hat meets the intersecting angles of dark mane and pale flag. Full mustaches had been favored by the German-speaking Burgundian troops of Charles V and taken up by their Spanish comrades who called them *bigotes*, from the German oath *bey gott!* A fine fellow of some pretensions was *un hombre de mucho bigote*. Richard Ford claimed that "the renowned Duke of Alva, being of course in want of money, once offered one of his *bigotes* as a pledge for a loan—one only was considered to be a sufficient security." Here, in the *Breda*, it is less the mustache than the wary gaze catching the viewer's eye that seems to confirm the artist's presence. Yet he didn't have to feel shifty about it: Titian had put himself in his pictures, and so had El Greco, standing among the Toledo aristocrats attending the *Burial of Count Orgaz*. Velázquez had apparently been intending to make clear the name of the *Surrender*'s artist, for in the lower right corner of the picture, below the heavily planted right hoof of the horse, he painted a sheet of paper lying on some stones. But the blank sheet was left unsigned. Perhaps the self-portrait sufficed.

VIII. MADRID. 1632–39

THE 1630S WERE PROBABLY NO MORE DISHONEST A DECADE THAN many periods the court in Madrid had seen or the taxpayers of Castile had complained about. As the Retiro went up with its slapdash grandeur, Spain's foreign relations continued to cause worry; and as the gold-framed paintings in the Hall of Realms proclaimed the monarchy's successes, gold and silver flowed out and the structure of royal power looked increasingly rickety. The Counter-Reformation continued to promote the one true faith in its blinkered way; in Italy in 1633 the Inquisition censured Galileo—the astronomer who was also a painter—for supporting Copernicus's view that the Earth went around the Sun. (Although threatened with torture, Galileo was sentenced to three days in prison and the penalty of reciting the seven penitential psalms once a week for three years.) Only the rare Hapsburg victory of Nördlingen in Germany in 1634 gave Spinola's triumph at Breda some military backing. Philip's cousin Ferdinand II, the Holy Roman Emperor, had begged for help to hold off a force under combined Swedish-German command. His request was answered by Philip's younger brother the Infante Fernando (1609–41). Fernando had been made Cardinal-Archbishop of Toledo at the age of ten, a post to which he was then and later by no means suited. He grew up to be a man of high spirits, a good horseman, and a lover of the arts. Velázquez painted him in hunting mode. He was thinner, fitter, and less harassed-looking than his older brother Philip. He put himself at a distance from the court at Madrid and his ecclesiastical duties by accepting the problem-filled job of governor of the Spanish Netherlands.

In 1634, he was on the way north from Milan on one of the more easterly branches of the Spanish Road at the head of a twelve-thousand-strong army of Spaniards and Italians, keeping open the vital south-north supply route to Flanders, where he was about to assume the governorship. Receiving Ferdinand II's plea for assistance, Fernando hastened with his troops and combined with the emperor's Austrian force to rout the redoubtable Swedish and German Protestants at Nördlingen. The cardinal-infante and the emperor were shown in a painting by Rubens, meeting before the battle. It was a typically florid picture in which the two leaders stood beneath the wings of a huge storklike bird carrying laurel wreaths. Fernando and Ferdinand shook hands and bowed rather in the way Justin and Spinola had done in Velázquez's slightly earlier *Breda*, though the former pair were of course allies, not enemies, as the Breda combatants had been. In 1635 the Rubens painting was used to decorate an arch at the celebration of the cardinal-infante's entry into Antwerp. However, some aspects of this Hapsburg triumph rapidly proved counterproductive. Olivares had hoped Nördlingen would help force France out of Lorraine, where its troops blocked the Spanish supply route northward. When it didn't make the French budge, but rather helped push them in May 1635 to declare war on Spain in earnest, the regime in Madrid found itself fighting on several fronts. It was in 1637 that Breda was, as noted, recaptured by the Dutch and Velázquez's *Surrender* became a souvenir of former, better times. Olivares turned to trying to resupply the Army of Flanders and the Brussels government by sea. But the armada of sixty ships Spain sent with the double mission of destroying Dutch shipping and reinforcing Spanish forces in the Netherlands ran up against Admiral Marten Tromp and a thirty-strong United Provinces fleet. From the English shingle beach of Deal in Kent that looks out eastward across the some-times sheltered roadstead called the Downs, the Dutch naval victory and Spanish defeat could be seen and heard on October 21, 1639.

Nevertheless at the Retiro palace the party continued. Many thought Olivares intended it to be a place where Philip would be kept so amused and relaxed that he would give up his wild ambition to show himself as a real king, leading armies into real battles. Artists, poets, playwrights, and performers were therefore kept busy. The king, with Olivares at his elbow, was the fount of patronage, even though payment for services rendered sometimes diminished to a trickle. The display of royal magnificence was unabated. The court gave up the stuffier Alcázar for the less formal Retiro on many holidays, at the carnival of Mardi Gras, for example, at the start of Lent, and for the Feast of Saint John, and had its collective mind taken off the disasters of war and deficits in the treasury. As if to cancel out the defeat in the Battle of the Downs, there were mock naval battles on the Retiro lake. Combatants in the staged tournaments in the Retiro grounds threw eggs at one another and defended themselves with wooden swords and cork shields. The Florentine stage designer Cosimo Lotti was in his element. Among the stage performances held at the Retiro early on were several plays by the playwright Pedro Calderón de la Barca, who was also Philip's personal chaplain, and who took over from the great improviser Lope de Vega (who died in 1635) as the court's theatrical director. A theater, the Coliseo, occupied prime indoors space. Doors at the back of the stage could be opened to allow performers acting, say, as soldiery, to enter from the street. On the feast of Saint John in October 1636, the king made a point of lending the cross of the Order of Santiago for use in a Calderón comedy about the three continents in which Spain held sway. In July the year before, Calderón's proto-musical *Love, the Great Enchanter*, was held out-of-doors. Cosimo Lotti designed a floating stage for it, with three thousand lanterns, an orchestra, a shipwreck, and fireworks provided by artillery. In this the characters of Ulysses and Circe traveled by boat across the Retiro lake, while Philip and his courtiers watched from gondolas. When Ulysses finally pulled himself together and left for home and marital duty, Circe in a snit destroyed her own island home. Her palace sank below the surface of the Retiro lake while a Lotti-constructed volcano spouted flames. Viewers wondered about the theme. Was Circe the count-duke? Was Philip IV at last going to cast off the spell he was under and set about his enemies in a convincing way? Wasn't it time the king came out of his retirement—*el retiro*—and into action?

But the king and his courtiers were afloat again in 1637, the year Breda was retaken by the Dutch, in a performance to celebrate Calderón being named a knight of Santiago. While in Brabant a nail was being driven into the Spanish coffin, in Madrid, at the Retiro, heads were buried in theatrical froth if not sand. Transformation scenes, with magical effects, were a big feature of these works; in Calderón's *Perseus*, smoke and fire issued from Vulcan's smithy. From time to time the corps of professional actors could be augmented by the king and his courtiers, and even *el pintor real*. On February 16, 1638, Shrove Tuesday that year, Velázquez appeared in a romp entitled *Mojiganga de la Boda*. He played the role of the Countess of San Esteban. He was among a number of men who acted as women on this occasion though we don't know how much he threw himself into the part. There were many who thought such burlesque displays, if not the Retiro itself, showed up all that was wrong with the Olivares government. Others saw merits in the extravagance. After one lavish feast to honor the election of Philip IV's cousin Ferdinand III as Holy Roman Emperor, a banquet that allegedly cost half a million ducats and at which the emperor was not in fact present, one Madrileno declared proudly: "This great event . . . was to show our friend Cardinal Richelieu that there is plenty more money left in the world to punish his king." On the other hand, one or two may have closed their eyes in dismay and thought of the title of Calderón's play of 1635, *La Vida es Sueno*. This was a muddled play—the epithet is Gerald Brenan's—with a creaking allegorical plot; everything moved very slowly, arbitrarily, in it; but the notion that life was unreal was obviously one that people could take to. "Life Is a Dream."

THE KING'S PAINTER had his daily dose of reality in his work for the royal household, in which he kept up his gradual ascent. For a long time the would-be *hidalgo* was stuck in the working echelons, taking his seat at tournaments and festivals among the court hairdressers—who as barber surgeons did much real doctoring and were comparatively well paid. Payment for Velázquez's services came in fits and starts. In December 1632 he was paid 797 ducats for paintings. In 1634, the year he was permitted to pass on the office of Usher of the Chamber to his new son-in-law Juan Bautista Martínez del Mazo, as a dowry for his daughter Francisca, he received 74,114 reales that were owed him (a ducado or ducat was worth roughly eleven reales). In 1625 he had been granted the use of a house in the Calle de la Concepción Jerónima, a perk worth 200 ducats annually. However in 1636 he did without being paid any money. Instead, in that year he received a promotion, being given the rank of Gentleman of the Wardrobe; this was, according to Palomino, who sounded a bit smarmy about it, "one of the offices or employments of the royal household that is held in great esteem," though Velázquez actually didn't have to serve in the office, helping carry the king's clothes as he dressed and undressed, until 1645. Palomino thought the king recognized "the merits of so punctilious a vassal and so excellent an artificer." The gossip in Madrid, according to a city newsletter, was that Velázquez aspired "to become one day Gentleman of the Bedchamber and be knighted, following the example of Titian." In 1643 Olivares himself administered the oath of office to Velázquez as he was made Assistant to the Privy Chamber. Whatever the constraints of being a courtier, a punctilious vassal, an organization man, a civil servant with pay that fluctuated between high and nothing, Velázquez showed no signs of preferring the freelance life or making do as a portraitist or mostly church painter, like his fellow artist from Seville, Zurbarán. He seemed content with a system that kept him and his family comfortably fed, housed, clothed, and respected.

Things were kept in the family, as they had been at Pacheco's. In August 1633 Francisca had married one of his chief assistants, del Mazo. His younger daughter Ignacia disappeared from the records early on. But Francisca and her husband del Mazo established a firm foothold in the system. Their son Baltasar, Velázquez's grandson, later became Head of Chandlery at the Alcázar palace. Mazo himself continued to work for Velázquez, helping with and copying paintings; he may have made one of the versions of the portrait of the count-duke in armor, baton in hand, astride a rearing white horse, that Velázquez painted the original of in the 1630s: a tribute to the first minister without whose influence Velázquez might have been still in Seville. Thus one can add to the list of reasons for Velázquez to have surrendered himself to court life. He liked the proximity to the center of things and those in charge, notably such grandees as Don Gaspar de Guzmán, Count-Duke Olivares.

The big man had his opponents behind every arras, but in 1638 the critics were silenced when Richelieu sent a French army to attack northern Spain. Irun was captured. Many nobles from Madrid volunteered to carry a pike into battle against the French. Olivares—forbidden by the king to go to the front line—dispatched a force to relieve Fuenterrabía, which was besieged by the French, and when the siege was lifted and the celebratory bonfires in Madrid had died down, was rewarded by a grateful Philip with the office of hereditary governor of Fuenterrabía. Other honors included the right to dine once a year at the royal table on the date the French fled to their ships, with a victory toast being made with wine in a gold cup and the count-duke hailed as *"librador de la patria."* Velázquez's equestrian portrait of Olivares is of this time and probably celebrates the victor of Fuenterrabía.

In these years, when Velázquez was in his mid- to late thirties, he was—by his own apparently unprolific standards—a fairly productive painter. He painted portraits, including one particularly fine one in 1635 of *The Sculptor Martínez Montañés at Work*, Montañés being as we've seen another Sevillian, who had come to Madrid to make a bust of Philip IV. At this time Velázquez also painted religious pictures and classical subjects. He created not only the *Breda* for the Retiro's Hall of Realms but other pictures for a landscape gallery and for chapels in the Retiro grounds. For these a prime subject was that of saints in their retreats or hermitages. Velázquez accepted this challenge with a somewhat tentative scene showing not one but two saints in a mountainous setting. *Saint Anthony Abbot and Saint Paul the Hermit* (ca. 1633) were both depicted bearded, both praying beside a scrawny tree at the entrance to a grotto. What they are praying for is probably spiritual nourishment, but sustenance of another kind is shown coming. A crow dives toward them with a crust of bread in its beak. In an almost medieval way, other scenes from the lives of these saints are shown in smaller scale elsewhere in the picture: a lion, a winding river, and craggy mountains similar to the Guadarrama, not far from Madrid. The painting was later hung in one of the hermitages in the Retiro grounds. It has a thin translucence, with azurite—by no means a material for frugal painters—once again being used to achieve the effect Velázquez wished for.

Many of the Spanish painters gave us aspects of asceticism, the bones visible beneath the skin, though Velázquez usually did not. His people are for the most part flesh and blood, even if among the royals it is a rarified Hapsburg blood; they are visibly human beings. These two hungry saints are perhaps his major demonstration of Spanish austerity, of abnegation, and they don't make a very convincing picture, at least for the modern, post-Christian viewer. The dive-bombing bird and sweetly painted river valley are greater attractions than the saints, the purported subjects. A much more intense religious work is his *Christ on the Cross*, painted a year or so earlier. This was indeed a crucifixion, the figure radiant and marble pale. Pacheco had specified that the true cross was fifteen feet high with a crossbeam of eight feet. He said the wood should be cypress for the beam and pine for the shaft, with the block on which Christ's feet rested of cedar and the plaque giving his name of boxwood. And there should be, Pacheco decreed, four nails, not three, driven through Christ's hands and feet. This pedantry was a poor substitute for the expression of real emotion and devotion, conveyed through paint. Velázquez hung his Christ on an almost totally black background, a pitch darkness which seems lit up by the dying figure stretched over it. The details, such as the nails, are driven home. We notice the knots and the grain in the timbers. There are bloodstains below the spikes, which pierce the palms and feet. We take in the careful carpentry, the almost carved quality of a work by Montañés, the morticing of crossbeam and post, and the words—ironic or maybe heroic—inscribed on the plaque at the top, "Jesus of Nazareth, King of the Jews," in Hebrew, Greek, and Latin. Christ's head is tilted down on his chest, hair falling over his face so that we glimpse an agony that Velázquez left half-hidden, leaving much to be drawn powerfully from our imaginations. But the chaplet of thorns, a red scar where the Roman soldier's lance had pierced him, a strip of white linen knotted across his loins, and all the muscles visible beneath taut stretched skin and bones, all accumulate powerfully. Hang it next to most of the crucifixions that were turned out then, by Domenico Guidi and Pacheco, and Velázquez's is the clear winner. Even Zurbarán's crucifixions of this same period seem in comparison a touch mawkish and melodramatic. Velázquez keeps in reserve so much message and meaning, and

Christ on the Cross, *1631–32, Museo del Prado, Madrid.*

for that reason delivers a greater blow. His *Crucifixion* is also a transformation, a metamorphosis; it shows a man through the agony of execution becoming a part of God.

The darkness could be that of a Spanish church. People then seemed to live in caves and hollowed-out places, or dwellings like them, with the light entering from only one side. They prayed and worshipped their near-eastern deity in similarly occluded spaces. Velázquez may have had in mind as he painted this crucified Christ compulsory hours spent as a child and as a youth on his knees in a dimly lit church in Seville, wondering about the cross over the altar and the man nailed upon it, in some ways frightening, in other ways sublime.

* * *

THE DUTIES OF *el pintor real*, the court artist, extended beyond the Alcázar and the Retiro. Velázquez was also busy at the Torre de la Parada, a hunting lodge of Charles V's, which was being done up for the crown. A square-shaped retreat much smaller than the Retiro, it was planted amid woods on the west bank of the Manzanares River near the village of El Pardo, with a deer park, about six miles from the city. Royal hunts took place here. Philip IV was serious about hunting. He had speared a wild boar as a youth of thirteen, mounted on his favorite horse, at the time one named Guijarillo. By 1644 he was reputed to have taken out more than four hundred wolves, six hundred stags, one hundred and fifty wild boar, and a great quantity of fallow deer, breaking all records and winning many trophies. He was known, too, for his prowess at pig-sticking. One boar hunted at El Pardo was praised for defending itself like a lion, ripping up numerous horses. Philip splintered a lance while attacking it and after seeing it dispatched declared to his courtiers, "This is one of the most memorable days in the annals of the chase."

Formalized like so much else in the Hapsburg orbit, royal hunts took place three or four times a year. Velázquez painted *La Tela Real*, The Boar Hunt, to hang in the Torre de la Parada and celebrate Philip's chief hobby. The painting (now in the National Gallery, London) showed one of these elaborate spectacles, at which distinguished visitors and members of the court were privileged to observe the monarch take bloody risks and demonstrate his heroic horsemanship. By no means a sophisticated composition, *La Tela Real* depicts the event on a much broader scale than is the case in many of his pictures, save for the *Breda*. Here, however, all the figures, even those in the foreground, are relatively minute. The middle ground shows a large oval arena, fenced in by *telas*, the canvas cloths imported from Flanders that were used to pen or corral the hunted animals. (Carl Justi notes that the amount of canvas would have served to make sails for a fair-sized armada; but for the king, why not make a big thing of it?) The arena in Velázquez's painting is in fact the *contratela*, the enclosure within the main *tela* that could be several miles in circumference. As in the *Breda*, Velázquez makes the ground drop away from the viewer, in this case to the *con-*

tratela below, so that we look from a height onto the foreground spectators of the royal hunt, onto the carriage from which the queen watches in safety, and onto the hunters—mostly on horseback—at work in the enclosure. Only here the background rises in a wooded hillside with green copses and patches of sandy, yellow ground, reaching up to a thin margin of sky across the top of the picture. Among the figures one can identify are several horsemen, including the king, the count-duke (who was among other things Master of the Horse), and—on a rearing white steed—Juan de Mateos, the king's Master of the Hunt. In the immediate foreground, under the shade of a tree, a group of elegantly dressed courtiers carry on conversing, as courtiers will, and pay little attention to what's going on in the enclosure. There Philip IV is demonstrating his bravery and equestrian skills in an encounter with an enraged animal, a boar that could impale his horse, while his assistants with their fork-tipped spears called *horquillas* try to distract the boar. Once they have worn it out, the royal dogs will be able to finish it off if the king himself doesn't kill it   as he did in January 1637 at a royal hunt put on for the entertainment of his niece the princess of Carignan. The painting is not more than the sum of its parts. It seems to have the virtues of an illustration (of a hunt and Philip's hunting skills) rather than those of a more intense, self-sufficient work of art, though the self-absorbed foreground figures almost help it achieve such a status.

In Velázquez's not overlarge oeuvre, portraits of Philip and his relatives as hunters form a distinct subsection: royals on horseback, royals with guns; the king himself; Philip's brother the cardinal-infante Fernando; and the king's son Baltasar Carlos, who was being brought up properly imbued with open-air sports of this kind. The king's Master of the Hunt Juan de Mateos was granted his own separate portrait. Mateos wrote a treatise on hunting in which he lauded young Baltasar Carlos's ability to lance wild boars. Learning that skill went along with instruction in reading the lay of the land and in dog-handling and gun-handling; one portrait made when the young prince was six showed him holding an arquebus and trying not to look overwhelmed by it. Mateos declared that "the sight of the spilled blood of wild beasts . . . creates generous spirits which constantly scorn the shadows of fear." Velázquez seems to have enjoyed painting the dogs that generally accompanied their masters in these hunting portraits. He gives us mastiffs dozing, greyhounds looking alert, and retrievers patiently waiting for the command to fetch. We also of course see a number of horses in action. A mounted Baltasar Carlos figures in several pictures that Velázquez painted for the Buen Retiro in the 1630s, showing off various equestrian maneuvers. In one, possibly the earliest, the self-conscious, pale-faced little prince holds the reins lightly in one hand while the other grasps his general's baton, which is slightly smaller than full size. His pink sash billows behind him. In the background—probably painted first—the familiar foothills of the Guadarrama rise to snow-topped peaks. This stage-set scenery—like an early-twentieth-century portrait photographer's ready-made prop for all seasons—looks like the park of the Torre de la Parada once again.

The prince was a year or so older in a more complicated picture that shows him at the Retiro riding school, putting a larger and darker horse through its paces. Rather daringly unintegrated in the painting are the figures behind, sketchily rendered and in softer focus. Juan de Mateos is again in attendance. The prince's valet, Alonso Martínez de Espinar, who was also the Keeper of Arms, is handing a jousting lance (which Velázquez has painted as if it were an ornament made of transparent glass) to the count-duke, the Master of the Horse, massive as ever; Olivares was one of the prince's chief instructors in horsemanship. On a balcony watching these goings-on stand a number of spectators, apart from the event yet integral to it. They are pushed forward on the balcony rather than seen through a serving hatch, though a dark doorway behind them—as it were cutting off their escape—gives a sense of them being in their own separate world. Two of this group can be identified as the king and queen, proud parents of the boy on the prancing horse. Theirs is a cameo appearance that we will remember when we see, some twenty years later, a larger and even more intricate picture Velázquez painted with its own split-screen features.

And something else here makes one look, and look again. We get the feeling that some of the participants are on a different plane. We feel that Velázquez is disassembling the structure of things. He is playing with Art, with its conventions and its usual dimensions. One thinks of the way Cervantes amuses himself in *Don Quixote*, where

Sansón Carrasco, the "Bachelor of Arts," tells Don Quixote that his activities are already known about from a book—the book one is reading! And Cervantes gets further laughs by relating our hero's history through Carrasco, who says it was written up by the Arabian sage Cid Hamet Benengeli. In this he, Cervantes—Benengeli—mentions among Don Quixote's notable adventures those of the windmills, the two armies that proved to be flocks of sheep, the episode with the galley slaves, and the various drubbings and unhorsings the noble knight has received. Don Quixote is astounded that his biographical details are so up to date. He is amazed that the Bachelor seems to know more about what he and his squire have been up to than they themselves know. It is an inside job. And so with Velázquez: One gets the impression that he has begun to be dissatisfied with clear-cut depictions of things and people. Having put Prince Baltasar Carlos on his horse in the riding school yard, he has to alter our perception of what is real by bringing on, less concretely, the count-duke and the other retainers, and, almost on a separate stage, or royal box overlooking the stage, the royal couple, formed from a few fast brushstrokes. A fourth dimension has been created.

Another intrusion in this painting is this: Sandwiched between the thick tail of the prince's steed and a low wall below the Retiro palace is the small figure of a dwarf. He is the second such individual the painter has presented us with. We will get used somewhat to Velázquez's little people, but never entirely. They retain to the end a power to disconcert. Dwarfs were fairly common at royal courts, and had been so since Egyptian times. The Roman emperor Diocletian had a troop of tiny gladiators. Augustus's niece Julia owned several. In Saxon England a dwarf named Stratton lived at the court of King Edgar. Botticelli painted dwarfs in his *Adoration of the Magi* and they were a long-standing Burgundian appurtenance. In the fifteenth century a blond female dwarf named Madame d'Or, who belonged to Philip the Good, Duke of Burgundy, used to wrestle at court festivities with an acrobat named Hans, while during Charles the Bold's reign a woman dwarf, Madame de Beaugrant, was a feature of a wedding feast, dressed as a shepherdess; she was first seated, we are told, "on a golden lion," and then placed on the table among the plates of food and jugs of wine. Dwarfs appear

Infante Baltasar Carlos in the Riding School,
1636–39, Private Collection, Duke of Westminster.

frequently in paintings by the Hapsburg and Stuart court painters, Antonio Moro and Daniel Mytens. The kings and queens of Europe still competed to hire them as retainers and entertainers. In a court such as that of the Hapsburgs in Madrid, where those involved were hardly able to smile voluntarily, dwarfs were a straightforward way of provoking lawful amusement, "domesticated goblins," as Bernard Rudofsky called them. Some were deformed in more than size, some hydrocephalic; a few, like the English Jeffery Hudson (1619–82), whom Mytens portrayed, were small but handsome. Velázquez painted seven of them, partly perhaps because he felt they were central to court life, partly—it may be—because he received a royal suggestion that he do

The Dwarf Sebastián de Morra, *c. 1644,*
Museo del Prado, Madrid.

so, and partly one suspects because he saw them with fellow feeling.
They were small people who were also *artistes.* They seem to follow
naturally after his *bodegones* as grotesque if not rustic subjects. Velázquez
painted dwarfs without inhibition and without mawkish sympathy;
what was perhaps radical was his choice in the first place to make these
stunted creatures worthy of his undivided attention. The intense fury
in the stare of the *Dwarf Sebastián de Morra,* ca. 1644, in the Prado, is
brought to our notice by the symmetry Velázquez has thrust at us, the
dwarf's two eyes above two almost fingerless clenched fists above two
stunted legs ending in two shoes, almost by Brueghel, their soles piti-
fully facing us.

Dwarfs, fools, and jesters had the privilege of being able to speak
painful truths. Philip IV's small attendants were on hand on many

state occasions, such as the visit of Francesco, Duke of Modena. Two dwarfs dressed up to look like Castilian royalty perched beneath Philip's throne as he and the duke watched a bullfight. The twenty-eight-year-old duke was lodged at the Buen Retiro and Velázquez painted a portrait of him, wearing a golilla and a general's sash over his armor, and giving the painter a cool sidelong appraisal. Was the duke surprised at Velázquez's intensity and industry? Velázquez had by now the reputation of being a laid-back artist, not to be rushed. The duke's ambassador in Madrid, the poet Fulvio Testi, wrote to his master after the duke had set off for home that Velázquez's portrait of the duke would be marvelous—if he ever got it done. "However like other men of talent he has the defect of never finishing and of not telling the truth about how long things will take." A price of one hundred gold doubloons had been agreed upon, and Testi had given Velázquez 150 pieces of eight on account. Testi admitted, "It is expensive, but he does good work." The picture did eventually get to the duke, and according to Palomino the duke further rewarded Velázquez with a costly gold chain. As with the portraits of the huntsman Juan de Mateos and the sculptor Montañés, Velázquez's portrait of the Duke of Modena seems to have stuck at a point just before it was finished. Maybe Velázquez meant it to be so. Or was it interrupted by his famous phlegm again?

A court document of September 15, 1637 (a few weeks before Breda was taken back by the Dutch), lists the names of dwarfs, buffoons, musicians, and barbers who were authorized to receive free clothing. The document adds, "The clothes of the barbers and of Diego Velázquez should be reduced to 80 ducats." Another indicator of the court painter's matter-of-fact but necessary standing in the system is that when in 1648 places were assigned to guests at a bullfight in the Plaza Mayor in Madrid, Velázquez's seat was back in the fourth row among the barbers and servants of court influentials. Climbing the hierarchy obviously took time. And so when Velázquez painted the buffoons and dwarfs, he was painting his fellow workers at the court. Six portraits of court jesters were attributed to Velázquez in the 1701 Retiro inventory, and others of the same category at that date hung in the Torre de la Parada. Some were unlike any other representations of human beings yet painted. In Velázquez's Retiro portrait of *Pablo de Valladolid*, the

jester wore a golilla collar and struck a theatrical pose. Unlike the crucified Christ, pinned starkly against a black background, Pablo was
adrift on a white cloud. He seemed to be floating in thin air; only the
shadows of his feet and legs slightly grounded him in reality. As for his
fellows, they were saddled with nicknames. Cristobal de Pernia, at
court for thirty years from 1624 to 1654 and painted sword in hand by
Velázquez, was called *Barbaroja*, Red Beard, after a sixteenth-century
Mediterranean pirate. Another went by the title of *Don Juan of Austria*,
after the hero of Lepanto. (A painting of the sea battle was shown on
the wall behind him.) A third buffoon was given the name Juan de
Calabazas, a *calabaza* being an empty gourd, with two lying next to
him; the inference being that Juan was empty-headed. What Velázquez
also lets us know through paint is that Juan was cross-eyed, grinned in
a way that exposed uneven teeth, and enjoyed a drink or two—a wine-
glass was near at hand.

The buffoons were treated as stage players. The dwarfs were treated
as living people, albeit lives that were unfair and undignified. Some
artists might have felt uncomfortable confronting deformity so closely,
but not Velázquez. His youthful interest in grotesqueries, and in the
contorted expressions his young rural model had produced to order, was
continued at Philip's court by a fascination with what his English contemporary the writer and physician Thomas Browne called "the abnor-
malities of creation." One female dwarf is given prominence in the late
1650s in his crowded *Las Meninas*, but more than a decade before that
picture three male dwarfs received particularly powerful attention.
Their names were Francisco Lezcano, Diego de Acedo, and Sebastián
de Morra. All three were shown seated, an attitude that emphasized
their stunted forms, comparatively large heads, and abbreviated limbs.
Lezcano came from the Biscay region and had served Prince Baltasar
Carlos since 1634. In Velázquez's portrait he seems childlike, without
adult thinking power; he holds a pack of cards as if uncertain what to
do with them. His lopsided head is twisted back, tilted as though by
the greater weight of his right cheek. His mouth is open in what could
be a smile or an attempt to say something. On the other hand Acedo,
called *El Primo*, The Cousin, was a full-time civil servant, secretary of
the Council of the Signet, who later went with Philip IV on his 1644

campaign into Catalonia. There he sat for Velázquez, surrounded by writing materials and against the background of a ready-made Guadarrama mountainscape, burdened down, indeed dwarfed, by an immense volume open in his lap. His face looks like that of an ordinary if rather perplexed bureaucrat, interrupted at his work. His broad-brimmed hat is set at a pronounced angle. An auburn mustache flourishes above his upper lip. But the melancholy look in his eyes reveals one whose size sets him at odds with his capabilities. The picture is interesting also for its unfinished passages, such as the streaky areas of sky where the painter seems to have nonchalantly cleaned his brushes on the canvas.

About the third dwarf, de Morra, usually called Don Sebastián, Velázquez leaves us in little doubt. His feet stick out on puny legs, boot soles upright, facing the viewer. His short arms are seemingly without elbows or upper parts and end in two clenched fists jammed into a jerkin that covers his thighs. He looks at the viewer as he did at the artist, a look just this side of a glower—he has tired of glowering. But his resentment is deep-banked. He still wants to know how he got here. Why indeed is he like this? Don Sebastián had worked for the cardinal-infante in Flanders before coming to Madrid to attend Prince Baltasar Carlos in 1643. There is, I think, no similar look in painting where a deformed sitter gazes like this directly at the artist, with an expression as profound as any painted by Rembrandt. The brushstrokes are powerful, the broad layering of paint almost smudgy. We are told that when Prince Baltasar Carlos died in 1646, at the age of seventeen, in Zaragoza, he left de Morra some swords and daggers, souvenirs of the fighting life he would have liked but never had. The dwarf enjoyed these weapons for only three years until his own death in 1649. The dwarfs were individuals Velázquez encountered daily, accompanying the prince and the infantas about the palaces, often sane and intelligent people exposed to lifelong ridicule, and they drew from the royal painter a melancholy camaraderie, just as Justin and Spinola had done in their own way on a grander stage. In both cases Velázquez's fast-thinking originality seemed matched by that part of him that was grounded in fellow feeling.

In a study of Velázquez written forty years ago, Jon Manchip White compared the dwarfs of Velázquez to the clownlike *graciosos* in Spanish literature; he compared Velázquez's paintings of little men to the comic characters in Calderón's plays. Gerald Brenan tells us: "Calderón took to relegating all the humour of his plays into a single person, usually a servant and always of lower-class origin, who fulfills much the same function as the fool in Shakespeare. This was necessary because the increasing decorum of the age was making it difficult to allow men of the upper classes to show any sense of humour, much less appear ridiculous." When Philip's niece the Austrian princess Mariana, age fourteen, was on her way to Madrid to become Philip's second queen, she stopped for a rest and had the dwarfs in her entourage amuse her. She went into shrieks of laughter. Her ladies-in-waiting reminded her that laughing out loud was no longer a proper form of behavior for her. Despite these constraints, members of the Madrid court went on keeping dwarfs as retainers even if it meant having to smother their own giggles.

WITH NO PERSONAL record, we have to imagine how Velázquez felt when news reached the court, a few weeks after the event on October 10, 1637, that Breda had fallen again to the forces of the Stadholder, the Dutch prince Frederick Henry. Perhaps he congratulated himself on his foresight in having shown in the *Surrender* Spinola and Justin on a nearly equal footing and not as victor and victim. Certainly he had been smart in not painting a total celebration of Spanish military triumph at a time when Spanish military prowess was once again being questioned. There are other signs that Velázquez thought of war with skepticism, without tunes of glory heard in the background. In or around 1638 he painted a less than militant warrior. His ironic picture of the god Mars was hung in the Torre de la Parada rather than among the scenes of Spanish success in the Retiro's Hall of Realms. At the Torre Philip IV was meant to take time out of the court routine to enjoy himself, to hunt animals not fight men. Velázquez's portrait of the god of war showed him seated on the edge of a rumpled bed, naked except for the folds of a blue sheet wrapped around his loins. The bedspread is pink, as pink as the drapes in a painting of a naked Venus we will encounter later on. Mars although improperly dressed has his helmet on and holds one end of his field-commander's baton under a fold of the bedspread. But his shield and his sword have been dumped on the floor below his

Mars at Rest, *c. 1638, Museo del Prado, Madrid.*

bare feet, and his chin rests on his left hand, left arm propped on a knee. The pose is, once again, melancholy, and despite what would later be called the handlebar mustache, not at all gung ho. His nude torso shows bones beneath the skin and surplus flesh above the waist. He looks like an out-of-shape ex-pinup, exhausted after an overlong, penitential gym session. For a god, he seems all too human.

Scholars have argued about our artist's intentions here. Classical statues provide precedents for an inactive Mars. Michelangelo had sculpted in marble a seated Lorenzo de' Medici in the same pose, chin on hand. Did Velázquez mean to remind us of Spain's military troubles—its defeats rather than its victories? Some experts say no, no criticism or ridicule would be allowed here, at a site for royal recreation. But this Mars has evidently had enough of fighting, which was surely meant to be his divine *metier*. One recalls Cervantes paraphrasing Terence when he has Don Quixote say, "A Soldier makes a better figure dead in the Field of Battle, than Alive and Safe in Flight"—and we can add, better even than alive and safe in bed. There will be plenty of men from the Army of Flanders soon retired, with scars, lame, and maimed. There will be soldiers enough who have had it with war, and wonder if they will ever again have a cushy billet, dry and warm, let alone one like this with silk and satin sheets to lounge upon. From here, they ask themselves in the same way this soldier seems to be doing, will it be downhill all the way?

IX. MADRID AND ARAGÓN. 1640–48

LIFE SQUEEZES IN, RELAXES THE PRESSURE, AND THEN TIGHT-ens its grip again. In the first two years of the 1640s Velázquez would not have been alone in feeling a growing nervousness as the fortunes of Spain fell apart. It became increasingly clear that the Hapsburg empire was an attempt to hold together too many disparate political organisms, with little in common save for their ancestral, genealogical, or religious ties with Spain. The weight of Olivares and his ambitions continued to overbalance the court. Philip IV showed fitful signs of taking the reins and being a king. When the monarch acted up in that manner, Olivares shuddered, tried to distract him with theatrical occasions and women, and hoped for the best. The "victory" at Fuenterrabia in September 1638, when the Spanish recaptured the border town from the French, was a flourish for which the count-duke took the credit, but it was not one to be widely repeated.

Velázquez's mother had died on March 29, 1640, and his father some three years later. We haven't heard much of them since Velázquez became an apprentice with Pacheco—a substitute father for him as well as a future father-in-law—and we know little of contact between Velázquez's parents and their most distinguished child. However, Pacheco tells us that over seven years the king gave Juan Rodríguez de Silva three secretarial posts in Seville, each worth an annual thousand ducats. After his father's death, Velázquez's brother-in-law (the husband of his sister Francisca) took over the management of the Velázquez and Pacheco properties in Seville. It looks as if Velázquez went on trying to help his father, as he had done his brothers Juan and Silvestre when they followed him to Madrid. When writing of Velázquez's first trip to Italy, Pacheco (who also died in 1644) said he had a Velázquez self-portrait—which was painted in Rome—hanging in his house in Seville. Meanwhile the court went on keeping the royal painter busy in the household bureaucracy. Justi reminds us that in the fifteenth century the great painter Jan van Eyck had been *varlet de chambre* to the Duke of Burgundy, Philip the Good. In 1642 Velázquez was also made Gentleman of the Bedchamber—*Ayuda de camara sin ejercicio*—an office as honorary valet normally held only by noblemen. Palomino says he took up this post in the year 1643. He was sworn in on the Feast of the Three Kings, January 6, in the presence of Olivares, still head of the chamber, and a year later the king presented Velázquez with an actual key to his chambers, "a thing which many knights of military orders covet," according to Palomino, though the job didn't involve any real duties. In the same year he was appointed Superintendent of Works in the Alcázar Palace. His job can perhaps best be described as combining those of arranger, decorator, and curator of collections. As such, he had to assist the Marquis of Malpica, who was officially in charge of the works, though office politics occasionally turned nasty. Velázquez was meant to be paid sixty ducats a month but the Board of Works and Forests didn't have the funds to pay him. The marquis and his bookkeeper Bartolomé de Legasa frequently got in the way of payment and Velázquez had to petition the king for the receipt of his salary. In 1646 and 1647 several other posts fell into his hands, one being that of Inspector and Treasurer of Works in the palace's Octagonal Room—this reduced de Legasa's sphere of authority. When and how Velázquez got paid remained uncertain. In 1647, when the government once again went through one of its periodic declarations of bankruptcy, he had to ask for monies he was due for two years past. The following year he requested salary owed him as *el pintor real* for as far back as 1630–34, together with payment for pictures he had delivered between 1628 and 1640. Philip ordered that Velázquez be paid via the *Dispensa*, a court office that seems to have handled royal household accounts, rather than via the hard-up Board of

Works. Other sums seemed to have reached him under the counter, or via what the Spaniards called "the hidden pocket."

After Seville and the first years in Madrid, Velázquez was never the most full-time of painters. He seems to have had long periods when he was happy to wander around palaces, in Madrid, in Italy, absorbing the presence of pictures and statues, and giving his opinion about what he wanted to take home for the king or about the location where an object should be placed or hung. It was as if he knew that one day he might need to deny the fact that he had ever been a professional artist who made things for money. But his preferred role was that of a gentleman, an *hidalgo*, who was trusted to advise the monarch about his art. So he helped decide what should go in the Retiro, or the Torre de la Parada, or what should be shoehorned into the Alcázar. In the late 1630s more paintings arrived from Flanders, sent by the cardinal-infante. Philip IV had commissioned, among other things, 112 works based on Ovid's *Metamorphoses*. Rubens made many of the preparatory sketches for these but left the actual painting work to assistants. Philip's passion was pictures; the constant expansion of the royal collection aroused amazement, for example from Sir Arthur Hopton, the English ambassador, in 1638, when Titian's *Bacchanals* and many Rubenses were acquired. Velázquez saw that the finished pictures by Rubens shared the walls of the Torre de la Parada with ten works of his own. But during the following decade, the 1640s, his own creativity lost momentum. He became more than ever a part-time painter. Altogether his surviving works are believed to amount to 120, painted over some forty years, but in the last half of that time, a period of twenty years, just forty paintings came into being—about two per year.

In 1643, when he was promoted to the post of Gentleman of the Bedchamber, he was distracted as many in the household were by matters arising from a long-running political crisis in the court. The troubles abroad had resulted in big trouble at home. The centralizing policies of the count-duke had had a contrary effect, and Olivares's efforts to maintain Spain's position as a great power were blowing up in his face. As we've seen, Tromp's warships had devastated the Spanish fleet at the Battle of the Downs in 1639. In Spain's many realms, both close by and far-flung, dissent was brewing, from Sicily to Portugal, from Navarre to Peru. One of the least tractable parts of the empire was Catalonia, and the Cataláns, keen on their own autonomy, boiled over. It was a bad omen when, in late February 1640, as the court residing at the Retiro got ready for Philip IV to visit Catalonia and stiffen the authorities' attempts to keep control, fire broke out in the Retiro's royal apartments. Paintings were dropped from windows to save them from the conflagration. Olivares himself took charge of the firefighters. Next day the show went on: Theater productions went ahead as planned while workmen set about repairing the damage. Meanwhile in Barcelona armed insurgents murdered the viceroy and declared an independent state. French troops arrived to protect Catalonia and neighboring Aragón. The French king, Louis XIII, was proclaimed Count of Barcelona, a title Philip IV thought belonged to himself. And then it was time for Portugal to join the house of cards. The Duke of Braganza took only three hours to throw the Spanish out of Lisbon and get himself crowned king of Portugal. Philip IV heard about this when returning from a bullfight; Olivares called it "good news"—the Duke of Braganza had gone crazy, and this would give Philip the chance to confiscate all his possessions! As for the king, 1641 ended with the news of the death from smallpox of his brother Fernando, the cardinal-infante, just thirty-two, in the Low Countries. Philip lost his famous composure and shook with sobs.

Meanwhile money was even harder to come by at the court in Madrid. Olivares imposed new taxes and retained for the crown interest payments on government bonds. Treasure from the Americas and gold and silver items belonging to churches and the well-to-do were seized. Inflation and crime were rising. Courtiers were leaving the court for the country. The poet, satirist, and critic of the regime Don Francisco de Quevedo, who had been portrayed in his famous circular spectacles by Velázquez, was arrested by court officials and confined in a convent cell for four years, the first two solitarily. Quevedo was by now paranoiac; he believed that Spain was in a state of decline because of foreigners, Jews, and heretics. Among the country's mounting problems, the army in Catalonia needed forty thousand men and had trouble recruiting them. Troops also had to be found to suppress the Duke of Medina Sidonia's rebellion in Andalusia. It was time—as the count-duke

Pieter Snaeyers, The Capture of Aire-sur-le-Lys, *1641,*
Museo del Prado, Madrid.

recognized—to sink or swim. But his buoyancy was going. For some
years people had wondered about the pictures he had hung in the antechamber to his apartment in the palace, pictures of madmen. It was a
puzzling art collection. Yet now it suddenly seemed appropriate. At the
end of 1642 the count-duke was having severe dizzy spells and head-
aches. He couldn't sleep. He was coming apart, and Philip finally recognized that it was time to take some control. On January 17, 1643,
Olivares was "given permission" to leave the court. The sacked grandee
was ordered to retire, first to Loeches, eighteen miles east of Madrid,
and then to his estate at Toro, near Valladolid. There, not unlike his
former captain-general Ambrogio Spinola, he found the shame of dishonor and the suppressed outrage too much to bear. Madness engulfed
him. Within three years he was dead.

When troubles come they come aplenty: In May 1643 the once
great Army of Flanders, now commanded by Don Francisco de Melo,
was attempting to besiege the small town of Rocroi on the western
edge of the Ardennes when a French relief force arrived outside of the

town. The armies were equally matched, some twenty thousand on each side, though the Spanish were veterans. But the French cavalry under Condé routed the Spanish pikemen, whose slaughter was hastened by French artillery. Six thousand died, four thousand surrendered. De Melo was captured and the Spanish army's working cash was taken. It was a total disaster for Spain. The discipline that had carried the Spanish *tercios* to victory in so many battles seemed to have been exposed as hollow—a single push was apparently all it took to bring down the whole jerry-built imperial affair.

Although Olivares had been told not to leave Toro "without the king's express permission," the order did not prevent his dead body from being taken to Madrid, where Velázquez was among the mourners. For us, it is noteworthy that the royal painter, a fellow Sevillian, survived unscathed the fall of the count-duke, despite having been his protégé. How was this? Other courtiers-cum-men of the arts such as Quevedo, as we've seen, weren't spared. Jerónimo de Villanueva, who had admitted to Jewish ancestors, managed Philip's secret expense account, and commissioned twelve large silver lions for the Hall of Realms from Juan Calvo, a silversmith, fell with Olivares, and was put on trial before the Inquisition. The silver lions were melted down to mark extravagance overstepped. The Retiro, critics claimed, had been built by Olivares with the blood of the poor; Velázquez had played an intimate part in the palace's decoration. The painter was not simply a propagandist for the regime, despite being a royal portraitist whose pictures were at once complicated and honest—but this didn't harm him either. What it apparently came down to was that Velázquez and Philip got along. Unlike Olivares, Velázquez didn't boss Philip around. That was all that mattered.

Without Olivares, the king had to "grasp the reins" to a greater degree. Philip sought counsel from the count-duke's nephew Don Luis de Haro and—this was new—from the queen, Isabella. Spiritual advice came regularly from a respected nun in Aragón, Sister María Magdalena de Agreda (1602–65), who wrote to him often. She told him to shape up, trust in the Lord, and set a good example to the people of Spain. (She also suggested he govern *alone*, that is, without favorites, and told him that he'd be better off not acting like King David and keeping a harem.)

Sister María was known for going into trances; in one she claimed to have been carried bodily by angels to preach to the Indians in New Mexico. In 1643 the French had advanced almost to Zaragoza and to counter them Philip, shaping up, led his army into Aragón, achieving a victory at Monzon in early December. The king spent a sober Christmas at the Alcázar, not the Retiro, buoyed by the news that the silver fleet had arrived with nearly ten million ducats of treasure from the New World; he then returned to Aragón. Velázquez went with him. Also on hand was Philip's military chaplain Baltasar Gracián, the Jesuit writer of popular homilies whose 1630 book *The Hero* had favorably alluded to Velázquez.

In the frontier town of Fraga, between Aragón and Catalonia, while his army besieged the French in Lérida, Philip got Velázquez to paint his portrait. Three days of sittings took place in June. The studio was a simple room with an earth floor covered in rushes and so dark that workmen were hastily brought in to hack two windows in the outside wall. An easel had to be constructed for the painter. The doorway was enlarged, and this enabled curious members of the court—some five hundred had been brought along—to peek at the artist at work. (This didn't seem to bother Velázquez.) Philip, now thirty-nine, wore for the occasion a scarlet red and silver suit with a wide Walloon collar made of lace, a *valona*, not a golilla. The silver-sleeved jacket was gleamingly rendered, the paint splayed on the canvas in many small silver blobs that made it look like needlework. The background was a featureless, top-to-bottom expanse of olive brown. Philip held his baton with one hand at the end of a silver-sleeved arm, the base of the baton resting against one thigh and sticking upward as if it were the jib of a crane, capable of lifting heavy weights. Philip did in fact look like a man much burdened by care, even if in full field marshal's kit. The picture took Velázquez four weeks to paint, and was then carried down to Madrid as a present for the queen, who had it exhibited outside the church of Saint Martin in the capital during August, when celebrations were being held to mark the capture of Lérida. Other copies were made of the picture, obviously useful for public relations. One other portrait Velázquez made on the Aragón journey in Zaragoza had a less satisfactory outcome. According to Jusepe Martínez, appointed an honorary painter to the king that April with Velázquez's approval, a young Zaragozan woman asked Velázquez to paint her portrait while he was in the town. After painting her head, he told her he would finish it without her, so as not to tire her. But he apparently rendered her valuable lace collar—specially worn for the occasion—in a sketchy, "impressionistic" way, and this displeased her.

Isabella's display to the people of Madrid of Velázquez's portrait of her husband as the heroic commander-in-chief was among her last acts of kindness to Philip. In the early spring of 1644 she had miscarried, and serious illness followed. Although a Bourbon, a daughter of Henry IV of France, Isabella had stoutly taken the Spanish side in the war between the two powers. She was struck by what seems to have been diphtheria and despite being bled and allowed to touch relics from the body of Saint Isidore, patron saint of Madrid, she died in October, before Philip managed to reach Madrid. He left town again to mourn on his own, first at the Torre de la Parada, and then, drawn back to Madrid, at the Hermitage of Saint Jerónimo in the Retiro Park. The queen's body was clothed in the vestments of a Franciscan nun and interred in the royal crypt at the Escorial. Her husband went on writing disconsolately to Sister María de Agreda, telling her that he had "lost in one person everything that can be lost in this world." He felt God was punishing him for his many sins. Sister María replied that her nuns were praying for him seven times a day, seven days a week.

When the king went back north to lead the fight against the French the following year, Velázquez stayed in Madrid. He had had his own loss in 1644 with the passing of his father-in-law. Francisco Pacheco hadn't become a notability at court as he had hoped, but vicariously, through his apprentice, he had achieved much, and he felt honored on that account. "I consider it no crime for a pupil to surpass the master," he wrote in his *Arte de la Pintura*, which was published in Seville five years after his death. The pupil was kept busy: There were building problems at the Alcázar and a quarrel with the architect, who thought that Velázquez—the assistant superintendent of these particular works—was ignoring the plans in a way that would cause structural weaknesses. Velázquez pleaded his case but was overruled by the king. Velázquez then objected that he hadn't received his salary for the post for the last two years. Velázquez was paid. Even a genius needs a streak of visible and voluble obstinacy.

Knocked back by his queen's death, Philip was then further shattered by the loss of his cherished son and heir, seventeen-year-old Prince Baltasar Carlos, from smallpox. This happened in Zaragoza, without much warning, in October 1646. The king said, "I have lost my only son, whose presence alone comforted me in my sorrows. . . . It has broken my heart." The infante had only recently been betrothed to his cousin, Princess Mariana, the emperor of Austria's daughter. Although she was but twelve, the marriage arrangement was thought helpful for improving the links between the two Hapsburg monarchies; the downside, the consanguinity, was not taken into account. Philip IV was not only the cousin of Mariana's father, Ferdinand III, but his brother-in-law and son-in-law. The results of the inbreeding were beginning to appear—and did so with a vengeance in the next generation. It became visible, as it does with the exaggerated mutations of so-called pedigree dogs, in jowls, lips, chins.

As it was, father took the place of son; at age forty-four uncle married niece age fifteen a few years later in 1649. Mariana was to come to Madrid to be Philip IV's second wife and maintain the dynasty "for the greater good of the Spanish kingdoms." By then, Philip may have felt he at last had a breathing space. The year 1648 had seen the final stages of prolonged peace negotiations in The Hague and in Munster and Osnabruck to bring the Thirty Years War to an end. (The Catholic delegations met at Munster, the Protestants in Osnabruck, and negotiators traveled between them.) In the United Provinces, Zeeland and Utrecht held out in opposition to peace, but eventually went along with those who wanted the long Low Countries conflict ended. There were seventy-nine articles to be ratified. Among them was one that finally ceded Breda—as noted, in Dutch hands since 1637—to the United Provinces. For the occasion, the Dutch artist Gerard Terborch made a rather fussy painting of the treaty for the Peace of Westphalia being signed, although this sort of public event wasn't the kind of intimate, one-to-one occasion he was so good at depicting. On May 5, celebrations were held all through the northern Netherlands and in Breda a large candelabra-like bonfire was lit outside the east gate of the castle. Rejoicing in Spain and the Spanish Netherlands was a good deal more muted.

* * *

MANY OF VELÁZQUEZ'S paintings in his late thirties and forties—
which came to be seen as his middle period—show signs of being commissioned work that didn't wholly engage the artist and therefore skate
over the attention of the viewer. Some of these paintings seem illustra-
tional. He was always interested in theatrical effects—in what would
now be regarded as cinematic effects. Several of these pictures are of
actors taking the parts of antique characters in plays by his colleague
Calderón, for example *Aesop* and *Menippus*, both canvases that carry
painted inscriptions of those names. They were probably made for the
Torre de la Parada. There paintings by Rubens of the classical philoso-
phers Democritus and Heraclitus, and of gods such as Vulcan, were
hung, along with Velázquez's *Mars*. As in that picture, so in the *Aesop*
and *Menippus*, we get a hint of sarcasm, certainly of satire, but little
profundity. However, our response is quite different with the *Portrait
of a Man* who is thought to be the court official José Nieto. Here a fellow
denizen of the royal household clearly arouses strong feelings in
Velázquez. He sits facing left, head turned toward the artist, all black
below, his head separated from his shoulders by the slanting upward
slash of the white golilla, with black beard, black mustache, black eye-
brows, and black hair. His light-skinned hollow cheeks, straight nose,
and high forehead provide a powerful focal point against the dark
brown background. His eyes pierce us. Only Rembrandt was up to this
sort of rapport with his sitter and thereby his viewers. There is an immediate connection, one human being seen by another up close. And therefore reverberations.

Nieto, assuming it is he, is the pick of the bunch of male subjects for
the king's painter during this period. Among other establishment figures who weren't necessarily in favor were Quevedo, already noted, whose
picaresque novel *El Buscón* had been a success in 1626. The writer, who
had fallen foul of the count-duke, gave his name to the circular eye-
glasses he wore that were thereafter commonly called *quevedos*. Quevedo collected paintings and applauded Velázquez's "distant blobs of
colour," with which the artist "achieved truth rather than likeness." Less
irksomely owlish but rather aloof was Fernando de Valdés, archbishop of
Granada and President of the Council of Castile, who lived in Madrid

Portrait of a Man, perhaps José Nieto, *1635–45, Trustees of the Victoria and Albert Museum, Apsley House, London.*

for seven years in the 1630s. Once again the sitter was placed facing half-left, head turned toward the artist. For those aware of what Velázquez would a few years later be most celebrated for in ecclesiastical portraits, the archbishop's picture acts as a tantalizing forecast of things to come. For the moment, it is perhaps enough to say that it is an honest description of a somewhat suspicious man—a portrait that might have interested his contemporaries and colleagues but that for us has a somewhat indirect attraction, less involved with the realistic presentation of a personality who means little to us and more with how Velázquez arranged the spaces and colors on his canvas: black; faded scarlet; gray (Velázquez gray); pink and silver; and black again. The painting is portioned abstractly. The archbishop himself seems skeptically withdrawn from the situation he has been dropped into. We are told that Velázquez's picture was probably part of a larger painting, painted after Valdes's death in 1639. And a writer in the London National Gallery 2006 exhibition catalogue believes that "the extremely drawn expression, the flattening of the moustache and the unnatural pressure of the lips suggest the use of a death mask." In other words Valdés wasn't on hand for the sitting. In more ways than one Velázquez re-created him.

Other male portraits of this time include Cardinal Borja of Toledo; Don Juan de Pimentel; and an unnamed *Knight of Santiago*. They help put Velázquez high in a distinguished list of Hapsburg portraitists that included Titian and Antonio Mor. But none of them have quite the stern tangibility of the *Luis de Góngora*, which Velázquez had painted some twenty years before. And none provoke the reactions we feel at viewing the women he painted during this period.

The picture that sets off possibly the lowest charge in this category, *The Coronation of the Virgin by the Trinity*, seems—as do several of Velázquez's religious works—in some ways routinely Old Masterish, to be compared with Raphael's *Sistine Madonna* of 1512–13 (now in Dresden), also cloud-borne, with its famous pair of small pesky-looking angels at its base. But Velázquez's *Coronation* has a sumptuous Venetian feeling, without Spanish agonizing. It was meant for Queen Isabella's prayer room in her Alcázar apartment, and it showed God the Father together with Christ, the Son of God, holding a crown of rose petals over the Virgin's head while a white dove hovered in a burst of radiant light above the crown. Mary is more like a Rubens than a Raphael, a plump young woman whose downturned eyelids and hands modestly suggest "Why me?"—yet with a slight implication of demure complacency, of acting the role of Virgin. Velázquez has a flock of angels here, four of them heads-only, with wings under their chins, disporting among the celestial clouds. God the Father, God the Son, and the Virgin are richly gowned, all sitting on invisible chairs in space. Both the first and second persons of the Trinity are sallow faced and hirsute; the balding, elderly God the Father with a bushy white Papa Noel beard, and God the Son with long, matted hair and much stubble. Mary herself is a rosy-cheeked, down-to-earth beauty, Miss Madrid 1640. Pacheco had decreed that the Virgin be shown flawless, without illness or injury. She was presumed on her Assumption to be under thirty years of age. The whole *Coronation* picture is conspicuously more panoply than prayer, but must have made a sight the queen could easily rest her eyes on while getting through her liturgical chores each day.

Who was Velázquez's model for his Queen of Heaven? Wives and daughters are generally close at hand for painting purposes, as Vermeer among many artists shows us. Velázquez's Virgin bears a close family resemblance to Velázquez's granddaughter María Teresa Martínez del Mazo, painted by del Mazo in his *Portrait of the Artist's Family*, and this suggests that María Teresa's mother, Velázquez's daughter Francisca, may have been the model for the Virgin. A somewhat older and slightly more careworn woman appears in the *Lady with a Fan* of 1638–39. Despite carrying a rosary with a cross over one wrist, sheathed in a fine kid glove and lace cuff, this is not a woman primarily intent on religious experience. She holds her open fan in her other hand, wears a garnet necklace, and has a well-exposed décolletage, with a few bits of lace peeking above it. "A lady of quality," one surmises. How much more Velázquez invests in her than in his pious Virgin! Low-necked revelations of this kind were proscribed by royal decree in April 1639, Enriqueta Harris tells us, "except in the case of licensed whores." This lady clearly wasn't one of those and must just predate the proscription. She in turn looks a lot like the *Young Woman Sewing*, an unfinished but luminous work that has a lot in common with Vermeer's pictures of young women at household tasks or their toilette: the same downturned eyes, the same absorption in their thoughts. However, it is Velázquez of the two who here seems more modern, with sketchy brushstrokes, and restrained coloring—black, white, gray, flesh, and a small crescent of pale red in the tied head scarf of the woman who is sewing. An impression is brilliantly put together, and we don't mind the lack of completion.

Two women next who have been called sibyls, classical prophetesses who let us know their profession by carrying blank tablets or books in which their invisible predictions were mysteriously to be found. In the early 1630s Velázquez had painted one such, a woman who looked as if she were presenting her profile for a design of a medallion, with a thick clump of black hair hanging at the back of her head. His second sibyl,

A Sibyl with Tabula Rasa, *c. 1648, Southern Methodist
University, Dallas, Texas.*

painted around 1648, is altogether less rigid and much more freely rendered. She is also more skimpily dressed, with a gauzy sweep of stuff, a
sort of muslin wrap, across her shoulders and revealing the soft fullness
of one breast. Her head is inclined forward and just a touch to one side,
eyes mostly closed, lips just parted, as she traces with one finger the
unseen writing on the tablet. She seems to be about to tell us what it
says. Her black hair is charmingly messy. She looks as if she has just
risen from her bed. The model for Velázquez's first sibyl was perhaps
Juana Pacheco, and some have suggested that this second may have
been his daughter Francisca, although the name is also mentioned of
Flaminia Triva, an "excellent" woman painter whom Palomino tells us
Velázquez painted a portrait of in Italy at the end of this decade.
Whatever, this sibyl was a real woman. Her tangibly, even seductively
rendered femininity seems to make it more likely that she wasn't a

member of his immediate family. She makes it clear how between Seville and now, between the *Waterseller* and the *Woman Sewing*, Velázquez's work had become soft-edged, the brushstrokes fluid. Despite the refrain of "Titian, Titian" that often accompanies Velázquez, this *Sibyl with Tabula Rasa* prompts a looking forward rather than a looking back. It will be "Goya, Goya," or even "Manet, Manet."

X. ROME AGAIN. 1649–50

H E WAS FIFTY—IN THOSE DAYS, LATE MIDDLE-AGED. HE WAS
painting rarely and sparsely. A portrait of royalty as expected still
came forth now and then. Velázquez had let himself be preoccupied
with the making-over of certain areas of the Alcázar and Escorial. It
was necessary to give the king what he wanted in the way of Italian
glamor and Baroque splendor. Many of the eighty-two Rubenses Philip
had bought in the last four years were still to be hung, as were some
acquired earlier on. (Rubens had died in May 1640.) In some royal apartments, such as the Octagonal Room in the south wing of the Alcázar,
built over the entrance near the former Old Tower, Velázquez had things
very much his own way, but other areas were more contentious. The
court architect Juan Gómez de Mora as project manager had to be dealt
with, and senior to him the Marquis de Malpica. When Velázquez
made a fuss about one particular problem, Malpica asked the king to
intervene because Velázquez could be "troublesome." Malpica explained
that, knowing Velázquez, "I always try to avoid debating with him."
Perhaps Philip thought it would be a good idea to reduce friction in the
court now by letting Velázquez do what he wanted, which was to travel
to Italy again. The king may well have been persuaded that the redeco-
ration of the Octagonal Room would proceed faster if the king's painter
was permitted to go shopping for works of art on the Italian peninsula.
Velázquez intended to obtain pictures by Titian and Veronese, Raphael

and Parmigianino. He told the king that few princes possessed paintings by these masters, and even fewer possessed them in the numbers he could acquire for His Majesty. Antique statuary was also on the wanted list.

Velázquez said good-bye to Juana once again in November 1648. On the twenty-fourth of that month he signed a power of attorney so that she could look after his affairs while he was away. For travel money, Velázquez was given two thousand ducats, together with a carriage, "due him because of his position" as Usher of the Chamber, and a mule to carry extra stuff, such as the gifts he was taking Pope Innocent X from the king. A great plague was sweeping Spain, devastating Castile and Andalusia; Seville was said to have lost half its people to the disease. Famine was everywhere. The French had recently occupied Barcelona so Velázquez joined a convoy in Málaga to carry him eastward to Genoa across a sea infested by pirates, privateers, and French warships. No Spinola for company this time, of course, but the Duke of Nájera, who was on important business for the crown, heading for Trento in Austria to collect Princess Mariana, intended bride of King Philip. Velázquez was stuck in Málaga for nearly six weeks, either waiting for favorable weather or further passengers. They sailed on January 21, and after a protracted voyage arrived in Genoa in early March. When John Evelyn, the English diarist, had arrived here by sea four years before on a bark that had been storm-tossed by a mistral, he saw the villas and orchards of the Ligurian coast and gratefully "smelt the peculiar joys of Italy, in the natural perfumes of Orange, Citron, and Jassmine flowers." His vessel steered finally for the high lighthouse that marked the way into the harbor of Genoa. The town struck Evelyn as jammed full of merchants' palaces. He greatly admired the street, "built of polish'd marbles, in which stood the house of the old Marquis Spinola."

In Genoa—Palomino tells us—Velázquez gazed again at the statue of the renowned admiral Andrea Doria in armor, standing on a high pedestal, with Turks at his feet. The artist journeyed on through a country of olive groves to Milan, where he went to see Leonardo's *Last Supper*. Then by way of Padua to Venice, where since his last visit nearly twenty years before, the Santa Maria della Salute church had begun to rise next to the Grand Canal in an act of thanksgiving for the end of their great plague. Venice was home to the painters he most admired. The Marquis de la Fuente, the Spanish ambassador there, arranged for him to see works by Titian, Tintoretto, and Veronese, and Velázquez bought several paintings by these artists for his king. However, it wasn't always easy for Velázquez to prize loose some of the masterpieces Philip may have hoped for; in any event, in Velázquez's opinion, few worthwhile pictures were being offered for sale. He next traveled westward again and south to Parma, Modena, Bologna, and Florence. He ran into a mixed reception, staying with some who couldn't do enough for him and with others who, knowing he was coming, locked up not their daughters but their pictures. Velázquez's hopes of acquiring a Correggio *Nativity* in Modena were thwarted, although the duke had been a friendly enough patron in Madrid twelve years before. In Bologna the Count of Siena rode out to meet him and opened the doors of his palace to accommodate him. He arrived in Rome in time to be told "Don't stop, you're wanted in Naples." There he had to present his papers to Count de Onate, the Spanish viceroy, and the count handed over funds the king had ordered be paid by the Council of Italy for Velázquez's subsistence and expenses, together with sums owing Velázquez since 1642, when the king in Zaragoza had arranged a further settlement on the painter. In Naples on his previous Italian trip Velázquez had met the Valencian painter José de Ribera, *Il Spagnoletto*, who had become a Neapolitan resident. Ribera was—along with Zurbarán—among the most celebrated of Velázquez's Spanish contemporaries, although his paintings were more strenuous in their realism than the works of Velázquez. The artists shared a similar range of subjects although Ribera was more regularly a painter of religious subjects, whether altarpieces, holy families, or martyrdoms. Ribera already preferred Naples to Madrid but at the time of Velázquez's second visit was probably in no Hispanophile mood. His younger daughter María had modeled for Ribera's 1646 painting of *The Immaculate Conception*. A visitor to Ribera's house, sitting for his portrait, had been Don Juan II, natural son of Philip IV and María Calderón, and like father, like son, the young Don Juan seduced María Ribera. Ribera's daughter was now sheltering in a Palermo convent at her lover's behest, hoping that her furious father wouldn't prevent Don Juan from continuing to have his way with her. Ribera had painted many religious agonies but he also had personal experience of grief. He and Velázquez must have had plenty to talk about.

It was then back to Rome for a lengthy stay. Velázquez had many pictures and sculptures to collect. He had many letters of introductions to present to churchmen such as the pope's nephew Cardinal Pamphili and Cardinal Barberini, and to artists such as Nicolas Poussin and Gian Lorenzo Bernini. It was presumably almost by rote that Philip IV or his secretary of state Fernando Ruíz de Contreras told Spain's ambassador in Rome, the Duke of Infantado, to see that Velázquez got on with his mission to collect classical objects. "He should be roused from the *flema*, which they say he has." But Velázquez also had paintings to paint. Being in Rome seemed to fire him up again and the *flema*—the phlegmatic attitude he was often accused of—was discarded.*

At that moment Rome was getting ready to celebrate a Year of Universal Jubilee and nearly three-quarters of a million pilgrims were heading for the city called Eternal. Palomino gives us much detail about the casts and statues Velázquez collected for the king on this second Italian journey, and about the portraits he made of distinguished papal officials, but he says nothing about where Velázquez stayed. One may hazard that his lodgings were once again close to the Duke of Florence's Villa Medici, where he had painted those two small seemingly impromptu oil sketches of the garden buildings and statuary in 1630. He intended now to have molds and then casts made of statues in the villa's grounds, one being *The Wrestlers*. From other sites in the city copies were made of the *Laocoon*, the *Hércules*, the *Hermaphrodite*, and the *Dying Gladiator* (which had recently been dug up); all those—thirty or so—were antique, and they were joined by a cast of the head of Michelangelo's relatively modern *Moses*.

Palomino says that in Rome Velázquez was befriended by some of the best artists there; they included the painters Pietro da Cortona, Nicolas Poussin, and Salvator Rosa, and the sculptors Algardi and Bernini. He spent a day with the Neapolitan painter Salvator Rosa,

*In 1639 the cardinal-infante Ferdinand wrote from Brussels that he would be sending to Madrid a portrait of himself although it wasn't yet ready, since "the painters here are more phlegmatic than Señor Velázquez."

whose wild and supposedly savage paintings had made him a celebrity. Rosa asked Velázquez what he thought of Raphael. Now that the Spaniard had seen all the fine things Italy had to offer, didn't he think Raphael was the very best? Velázquez replied, "To tell you the truth, I have to say I don't like him at all." A shocked Rosa said, "Then there can't be anyone in Italy who suits you, for we grant Raphael the crown." Velázquez answered that he thought the top Italian paintings were in Venice. "There, in my view, is the finest brushwork. And Titian is the one who stands above them all."

Velázquez found evidence in Rome of the truth of the old saw, work made for more work. He was swamped with commissions from high ecclesiastics and papal officials. However, not all in the Vatican approved of the king of Spain's painter; for example, Cardinal Alonso de la Cueva, "an old diplomatic hand" and sometime aide to the Spanish ambassador to the papacy, regarded Velázquez as an upstart, calling him (in letters to his brother the Marquis of Bedmar) "a certain Velázquez, Usher of the King's Chamber." The cardinal didn't take at face value Velázquez's claim to be looking for art for Philip IV and regarded what was being called his royal mission as some sort of "swindle." Despite this, others in papal circles clamored for Velázquez to paint their portraits. Palomino tells us these pictures were painted "with long-handled brushes"— which allowed Velázquez to work well back from the canvas, without having to keep stopping to contemplate what he was doing—"in the vigorous manner of the great Titian; nor were they inferior to Titian's heads." The pope since 1644 had been Innocent X, and those wanting Velázquez to paint them included Cardinal Pamphili, the pope's adopted nephew; Donna Olimpia Pamphili, Innocent's widowed sister-in-law; Monsignor Abbot Hippoliti, one of his chamberlains; Monsignor Cristoforo Segni, a majordomo to His Holiness; Ferdinando Brandano, chief executive in the papal secretariat; a Roman gentleman named Girolamo Bibaldo; the "excellent" woman painter Flaminia Triva, who assisted her artist brother Antonio Triva and whom we have encountered in respect of the *Sibyl with Tabula Rasa*; and not least Monsignor Camillo Massimi, another papal chamberlain and *camariere segreto*. Massimi was himself a painter, a celebrated and learned patron of artists and a collector of paintings; he took a great interest in Velázquez and eventually owned six portraits by him. (Among Velázquez's few surviving letters is one welcoming Massimi to Spain in 1654. In the four years after that, when Massimi was in Madrid, he saw a lot of Velázquez.)

Whether all this hackwork had an ulterior purpose or not, an invitation from the top soon came. Velázquez's backup plan for gaining entrée to the pope involved gifts that Philip IV had asked him to deliver to the pontiff, but he was glad to be given a direct summons to come to the Vatican with brushes, paints, and palette. According to Palomino, Velázquez still didn't regard himself as fully prepared for this task, and beforehand decided to get into shape for it by painting a portrait "from the life." For his model, he chose his slave, Juan de Pareja. The term *slave* is shirked by some writers on Velázquez; they instead use the words *servant* and *assistant*, or put the word *slave* in quotation marks, as if the condition came about by fanciful choice. Slave, we remember, is what in Shakespeare's *The Tempest* the exiled Duke of Milan, Prospero, calls both his servants Ariel and Caliban. Toward the end of the play Prospero sets Ariel free, albeit with a few strings attached or chores to complete. (Poor Caliban, who has some of the best lines in the play, is left pondering merely the idea of liberty: "Freedom, high day! High day, freedom!") But there is no doubt that Pareja was a slave. Palomino calls him that, and not long after this Velázquez took legal measures to give Pareja his freedom, as Prospero in his ad hoc way gave it to Ariel. Velázquez wouldn't have needed to do this if Pareja hadn't been a slave. Pareja at this time was apparently in his late thirties. As noted, he was a Morisco, a half-caste with Arab and Berber blood, born in the Andalusian hill-town of Antequera, which was a place containing many people of Moorish origin. Who his parents were we don't know, or how he got to Seville and into Velázquez's ownership.

The wars in north Africa between Spain and the Ottoman Turks, who were allied with Berber tribes, had created a supply of slaves, as did the expulsion of the Moriscos in 1609–10 and the colonization of parts of the Americas. Slaves were both an investment and a source of cheap labor, providing people who worked as house servants, cooks, employees in forges and tanneries, and laborers on farms. They were members of an underclass, like apprentices indentured with no possibility of becoming journeymen unless freed. Some, as we've seen, were branded on the cheek with their owner's initials, as was a slave of Velázquez's maternal grandfather the trouser and stocking maker Juan Velázquez Moreno. A painter in Cádiz named Francisco Núñez owned a Morisco slave whom he got to peddle his works around the streets—and Núñez was upbraided by his guild for this. The Dutch also had black house servants. Frans Hals painted around 1645 a portrait of a Haarlem family complete with an attendant black boy (Thyssen Museum, Madrid). In the southern Netherlands, the Antwerp-born artist Gaspar de Crayer painted a fine *Portrait of a Young Moor Boy* in the early 1630s (Ghent Museum of Fine Arts). Many Spanish slaves were also treated as part of the family, baptized and turned into "proper" Christians.

The very fact that Velázquez painted Juan de Pareja on a fairly large canvas (32 × 27.5 inches), wearing a white lace-trimmed collar, meeting the gaze of the painter with a serious man-to-man look, and in a dignified attitude, one arm across his chest, the right hand hidden in the folds of his cloak, seems to indicate the terms on which master and slave existed. It was a pose similar to that shown in Raphael's portrait of Baldassare Castiglione, author of *The Courtier*, a book we assume Velázquez knew well, and a pose also echoed in a work by Titian—a portrait then thought to be of the poet Ariosto—and in a self-portrait by Rembrandt, a decade before Velázquez painted Juan de Pareja. In the Pareja picture there was evidently respect on both sides, between the painter and the person being painted. There was trust. Velázquez had presumably taken Pareja along on the second Italian journey because he was an indispensable studio assistant, helping prepare canvases and pigments—doing the donkey work of background painting and copying. Attending Velázquez, Pareja would have had plenty of opportunity to study the masters. Pareja was also a witness for two legal contracts to do with the making of casts that Velázquez had ordered for the king (the slave had obviously been taught to read and write).

The ancients, Palomino assures us, reserved for "free men" the practice of such liberal arts as painting. The traditional story about Pareja is that, because slaves were not allowed to be painters, he secretly taught himself to paint while working for Velázquez. (This seems unlikely;

more likely that Velázquez turned a blind eye.) The story continued that the king, wandering around the Alcázar one day and taking a look in Velázquez's studio there, examined some stacked-up canvases. Pareja had left one of his own paintings against the wall. As the king reached down to turn it around, Pareja prostrated himself before Philip, begging forgiveness, and pleading not to be punished for committing the forbidden act for a slave of putting paint on a canvas of his own. And the stratagem worked, we are told. Philip admired the painting and said Velázquez should give Pareja his freedom. In Italy, that hadn't yet happened, but it is perhaps relevant that Velázquez had by then painted his pictures of two men from classical times who were in fact former slaves, Aesop the writer of fables and Menippus the cynic philosopher.

It is unclear exactly why Velázquez chose to decide to free Juan de Pareja now in Rome. Was the painter feeling particularly good about things? Did Rome give him a sense of empowerment, of potential, of his own freedom, of being out from under court necessities? Whatever the reason, the portrait of Juan de Pareja may have been in part an act commemorating not the manumission but the decision to arrange it. On November 23, 1650, Velázquez signed a legal document in Latin whereby he granted Pareja his freedom "in view of the good and faithful service the slave has given him, and considering that nothing could be more pleasing to the slave than the gift of liberty." ("High day, freedom!") One qualification was that Pareja had to go on serving Velázquez for four more years; this was, it seems, a clause commonly appended to such acts of liberation, and it apparently caused no great problems for the slave concerned in this case. But as a testimony to how Velázquez felt about him, he could have asked for no better document than the portrait his master did of him. It makes much of black—and of several shades of olive gray. Only the broad white collar gives vivid relief and (as Svetlana Alpers has pointed out) creates a splendid riposte to the young lady in Zaragoza who was upset about Velázquez's inability, as she saw it, to do justice to her lace collar when he painted her portrait. Pareja's collar sets off his bushy black hair, wide nostrils, and broad-lipped mouth between thick mustache and bearded chin. His eyes are also black. There is no hint of servitude in his look or stance. His attitude is rather one of pride and curiosity about what Velázquez would make of him in this picture. The brushstrokes flow strongly. For Jon Manchip White they seem "to carry the light with them, determining its direction and the depth of its penetration."

The slave not only achieved freedom but immortality. *Juan de Pareja* was exhibited at the Pantheon, where Raphael was buried, in March 1650. Velázquez had been made a member of the Rome painters' guild two months before and was then elected to the *Virtuosi al Pantheon* in time for its annual exhibition. There the portrait's spontaneity was acclaimed. Palomino recorded, "It was the opinion of all the painters [in Rome], of whatever nationality, that everything else seemed like mere painting, but this alone like truth."

BY QUICK STEPS now we get to the pontiff himself. In July Velázquez painted Donna Olimpia Maidalchini, the widow of Innocent's brother, and an ambitious woman whom scandalmongers accused of being the pope's mistress. A month later, on August 13, Innocent granted Velázquez a one-day audience. Velázquez came as one in a noble succession of painters: Raphael and Titian had portrayed popes before him. Velázquez had met Giovanni Pamphili when he was papal nuncio in Madrid in 1626; it was Pamphili who sent on to Rome Olivares's request that Velázquez be given an ecclesiastical benefice to increase his income as court painter. Pamphili—now seventy-five—was a member of a well-established Roman family, an effective operator of the system, and a skilled diplomat who had caused papal policy to switch from being largely pro-French to decidedly pro-Hapsburg. He had a reputation for being taciturn in private but in public a speaker for whom big audiences were no trial. Many contemporaries thought him ugly if not evil looking, and his allegedly satanic expression had been cited at the papal conclave in 1644 as a reason he should not be elected pope— which he nevertheless was.

Velázquez's portrait of Innocent X was immediately famous. There are nearly twenty versions, on some of which assistants such as Juan de Pareja probably worked. As with the portrait of Pareja, that of the pope gives us an immediate sense not just of what he looked like but of his personality. Velázquez has almost caught the pope in flagrante: Innocent seems to be suddenly, guiltily, remembering something he would rather have not widely known. In the painting believed to be the original (now in the Galleria Doria-Pamphilj in Rome), he sits in a high-backed, gold-decorated papal chair. The immediate impact is of red-on-red, with big drifting areas of white and crimson delimited by gold. The pose is three-quarter length, head-to-knees, taking up almost all of the canvas, a format that had earlier received the imprimatur of Titian and El Greco in ecclesiastical portraits. But whereas Titian's painting of Pope Paul III (of 1543) looks out of the canvas a bit abstractedly, and El Greco's Cardinal Niño de Guevara (1596–1601) is wearing Quevedo-type spectacles that seem to be helping him focus, Velázquez's Innocent arrests the viewer (as he presumably did the artist who had dared to rumble him) with a challenging gaze. It is a look of utter suspicion; they are the cleverest, most untrusting eyes that were ever painted. How Velázquez created that look was masterful. The technique involved only a few barely perceptible brushstrokes, a few rough dabs of paint, but the result was a pair of eyes, swiveling to the pope's right, a gleam of light on the dark pupils, two blue-gray irises, the whites of the eyes moist and a little bloodshot. The Roman summer heat is perhaps responsible for the gleam of sweat on Innocent's brow. His thin lips are sealed in a straight line above a wispy gray beard, below a big nose, between florid cheeks that tug downward. Holy Father! But the Vicar of Christ is less a dictator than a headmaster wondering what to say to an unsatisfactory junior schoolteacher, and giving him a baleful glare as he does so.

Among Velázquez's portraits, one of those he made of himself presents the gaze most similar to that which the pope displays here, the dark-eyed, doubt-filled self-portrait painted around 1636 and now in the Uffizi. And if some of Velázquez's purportedly religious works give the impression of having been done with only half his mind on his job, this papal picture seems to have been painted with every nerve in his perceptive faculties awake and vibrant. It is the creation of an artist who was fully possessed by art's power, even if by no means a full believer in the divine authority of the Roman church or its benevolence. The intimidating shadow on the scarlet damask curtain behind Innocent's left shoulder—is there a Polonius behind the arras?—hints at something nasty lurking close at hand. Nevertheless Innocent was apparently not upset by Velázquez's perception. It is claimed that he said, on first looking at it, *"Troppo vero"*—too true. He may have liked the fact that Velázquez made him look younger than his age. The pope tried to pay the Spaniard for his work, but Velázquez told Innocent no money was needed; the king, his master, always paid him from his own purse. So the pope gave Velázquez a gold chain and medallion bearing the papal image to honor the artist's "extraordinary achievements." The painting was discreetly signed by Velázquez on a piece of paper that the pope is shown holding rather tentatively between the thumb and bent index finger of his left hand—as if he were about to drop it on the floor. This is probably a petition, inscribed as it is "from Diego de Silva Velázquez of the Court of his Catholic Majesty." And what was Velázquez petitioning about? The subject may well have been the artist's ambition to become a knight in one of the Spanish military orders. The Vatican signed up for this notion in December 1650 with a letter from Cardinal Panciroli to the nuncio in Madrid, citing Velázquez's merits (once again described as "extraordinary") as was shown in the portrait of His Holiness, and supporting his hopes of gaining the habit of a knight in a military order.

Meanwhile, His Catholic Majesty was beginning to fret about not having Velázquez at court. Frequent letters went from Don Fernando Ruíz de Contreras, the secretary of state, ordering the painter to return to Madrid. (These letters were sent "repeatedly," Palomino tells us.) In February 1650 Philip wrote to the Duke of Infantado, the Spanish ambassador in Rome, about Velázquez's assignments: "Since you know his phlegmatic temperament, it would be well for you to see that he does not indulge it but hastens the conclusion of the work and his departure as much as possible." The king also wanted Velázquez to bring back with him the Italian painter Pietro da Cortona, a specialist in fresco, to work on decorations at the Alcázar. But Cortona couldn't come and Velázquez, perhaps spinning things out, said he had to look for a substitute. More royal commands followed, and so did more evasions. His statue-collecting and cast-making gave him some excuses, but there may have been other factors. For one thing, Velázquez wanted to return via Paris, the capital of a hostile power, and had to obtain a passport for the purpose; but Philip seemed to think this would lead to further delays and insisted that his painter come back by sea. Even so, Velázquez stretched out his time in Italy as long as he could, for nearly another year.

It now seems likely that at the heart of this procrastination was not "phlegm" at all. Part of the cause may have been pleasure in his freer life in Rome, away from court protocol and irksome duties. And it may have been an actual affair of the heart. Around this time, amid the spurt in Velázquez's portrait painting and evidence of his disinclination to leave Italy, we find one of his most astonishing works. Whether it was painted just before this second trip to Italy, just afterward, or in Rome itself is a matter on which the experts disagree. *The Toilet of Venus* or *Venus at Her Mirror* are the titles art history gives the painting generally known as *The Rokeby Venus*, from its ownership in the early nineteenth century by John Morritt of Rokeby Hall, Yorkshire. It was earlier listed in an inventory of the collection of Olivares's great-nephew Gaspar Mendez de Haro, who bought it in 1652 from the estate of a Madrid painter and art dealer named Domingo Guerra Coronel, where it had been the most highly valued work at 1,000 reales. How long before that Velázquez painted it is unclear. The scholar Dawson Carr writes (in a recent catalogue of the National Gallery in London) that the painting could have been "executed at any time during the 1640s or early 50s, in Spain or in Italy." If in Italy, a location he seems to favor, he asks, "Was it perhaps given to a middle man [such as Guerra Coronel] to distance its creation by Velázquez?"

But why did it need to be so distanced? It was the first painting of a nude woman by a Spanish painter that we know about—and remained so for the next century and a half. When the Italian connoisseur Cavaliere Cassiano del Pozzo was in Madrid in 1626, he noted in his diary that the Venuses and other nude goddesses in the Alcázar had to be shielded from view when the queen passed by. In 1640 the church censorship authority, the *Indice expurgatorio*, prohibited the importation of paintings of nudes; their artists could be excommunicated and exiled. And as late as 1673, priests and professors at the universities of Alcala and Salamanca were opposed to pictures showing nude women, regarding "the abuse of lascivious and indecent figures in painting as a mortal sin." Although the Inquisition would have been concerned by the display of this sort of subject, and de Haro in his youth had had the reputation of wenching and extravagant loose living, he was now a member of the court and went along with the king to the fighting in Aragón. (De Haro's father Luis had been the king's friend since childhood and had taken over some of Olivares's steering role after the count-duke got the sack.) Philip himself was said to possess paintings of nudes, one or two possibly by Velázquez. And there was precedence to be invoked in the form of Titian and Rubens, both of whom had painted nudes. If *el pintor de rey* needed to hide his part in the making of this *Venus*, in Rome, was it possibly for a very private reason?

XI. ROME: VENUS OBSERVED. 1650–51

WE KNOW SO LITTLE OF VELÁZQUEZ'S PERSONAL LIFE THAT anything that draws him out of the close surroundings of his court career takes on a disproportionate vividness and scale. Thus the small episode documented in the Roman archives in the autumn of 1652 becomes something startling. The documents were, I believe, first discussed in print, almost as a footnote, by Jennifer Montagu, in the *Burlington Magazine*, in 1983. Giovanni Garzia Valentino—the same lawyer who had witnessed the deed giving Juan de Pareja his freedom and put his name on the contracts for the casts of statues Velázquez had commissioned for the king—drew up a legal document regarding a baby boy, Antonio. The papers refer to him as "the natural son" of Don Diego de Silva Velázquez. A nurse, Marta Vedova, presumed to be the infant's wet nurse, a widow living in the parish of Santa Maria-in-Via, had been paid by attorneys acting for Velázquez to "release" the babe-in-arms at the end of October 1652. This Marta did two weeks later—though she seems to have done so reluctantly. The amount she received was seven scudi and thirty baciocchi. The name of Antonio's mother wasn't given. We don't know if it was Marta herself or whether Velázquez ever saw his son—his only son. Nor has anything further been found concerning Antonio's baptism or fate. He remains what Jennifer Montagu calls "a marginal note."

It may not be coincidental that, around this time, Velázquez painted the picture that is exceptional among his extant paintings. Exactly when *The Toilet of Venus* was painted is—as we've noted—unclear; some experts (such as Jonathan Brown) believe it came into being before Velázquez's second trip to Italy, while others feel the same woman modeled for it, for the *Coronation of the Virgin*, and for the woman holding the skein of wool in *The Fable of Arachne*, a painting made around 1656. But the *Venus* seems to reflect the freedom he felt in Italy, out from under both court and family life, and it is easily associated with his time in Rome. The presence in the picture of Cupid, holding a mirror, is indicative of a love interest. The picture may have been shipped home to Madrid from Rome before Velázquez—at last—made his departure. De Haro went on in time to become Spain's ambassador in Rome, viceroy in Naples, and a prodigious art collector. The *Venus* would have been one of the stars of the collection. It is only a mythological painting in title. It is a divinely human painting in all else. A woman "at her toilet," and not very busily so, Venus is recumbent. Velázquez may have been making up for the lack of similar living models in Spain, a lack that forced artists to find substitutes, the way Angelo Michele Colonna, the Bolognese painter, used a cast of an antique statue of Venus to paint a *Pandora*. Velázquez had of course looked at many naked women painted by Titian and Rubens. A similarly recumbent form was the *Hermaphrodite Asleep*, lying stomach down, head on crossed arms, in the Villa Borghese; it was one of the statues that Velázquez had had cast in bronze to take to Madrid. In the Greek myths the ambisexual Hermaphrodite was the result of a getting-together between Hermes and Aphrodite; but for his *Venus* Velázquez clearly had a real woman model for him, lying on her right side, with her back to him.

No woman's back has ever been more sweetly painted. She is completely without clothing. Her outstretched left foot is pressed into the slate-gray satin sheet and a well-shaped left calf partly covers her right foot, which is poking out enticingly from under the left knee. That the perfection of physiognomy did not come easily was shown when the painting was cleaned and alterations to one of the left toes were found. The back of the most visible thigh casts a shadow on the sheet and then vanishes into a dark declivity molded by the complex curves of her buttocks. One's eyes make this journey from left to right, from toe to top, while at the same time following the outline of pale flesh silhouetted against the bedclothes. It is a soft ridge of upward slopes and downward valleys that suddenly over the top of her left hip sweeps vertiginously down to her waist—the most audacious hip ever. Then upward again, ascending to her shoulder. Here let us pause at the recess, barely a dimple, under her right shoulder blade; it is a spot the eyes fondly linger on before moving to her neck—such a neck!—and the back of her head, chin turned away, just a hint of eyelash visible, her auburn hair piled up in a ruffled chignon, right arm bent with the hand holding up the head. The scene has horizontal divisions with diagonal accents: pale crimson curtain; flesh colors of the Cupid and Venus; gray of sheet and off-white of the crumpled and creased undersheet. The curtain looks like that seen in the portrait Velázquez had painted of Archbishop Fernando de Valdes, and the bedcover that Velázquez's melancholy *Mars* was sitting on. The painter was obviously fond of that color, nearly pink. The viewer—not to say voyeur—is then diverted by the woman's gaze directed toward a heavily framed mirror being held just beyond her hips by the Cupid: a cherubic small boy, with a pair of seemingly stuck-on white-gray wings borrowed from a pigeon, and naked apart from a blue-gray ribbon looped over one shoulder and a pink ribbon leading from the mirror to his wrist. Cupid used such items to bind those in love. The presence of Cupid makes it clear that the unclothed woman is Venus.

But having given us those clues to her identity, Velázquez gives us a shock. In the mirror, as in one of his scenes within a scene, we are in ambiguous territory; we observe the face, a bit foggily reflected, and it isn't at all the face we've expected. From early on Velázquez had not taken the easy way with his pictures—doubt not certainty is what we expect from him—and here the mirrored face doesn't seem at all right for the woman whose back and backside we are now almost besotted with. It is a plain, even pudgy face. It is, surely, one we have seen before. There is at least a chaste, sisterly resemblance to the Virgin being crowned by the Trinity, or a likeness to that of several of his earlier sitters, one of whom may well have been Juana Pacheco. If he was in Rome at the time, an artist-husband at some distance, might this be a semi-guilty gesture, disguising the looks of the woman who was his model by planting an echo of his wife's features on his *Venus*? Velázquez has deliberately created something unexpected, possibly suggesting that beautiful women can be partly plain, or that a fairly ordinary face can coexist with a wonderful body. The situation is further complicated by those experts who have looked at the pictured arrangement scientifically and decided that the reflected image isn't in the correct spot—a mirror held just there at that angle wouldn't have shown her head in quite that way. Velázquez at any rate has heightened our interest by this complication and by concealing the woman's identity. Body and face are separated, perhaps deliberately. The device may also render this woman a love interest for all men. No specific woman can be connected with this adorable (at least from the rear) creature; she is therefore a love object open for the admiration of any contender.

Far more subtly and powerfully than Rubens, whose thick-thighed Flemish females furnished a standard for the age, Velázquez concentrated his suggestions of the sensuous on the skin and the fabrics: the crimson drapery; what looks like a white chemise lying on the bed under the mirror; a hint of the folds of a transparent chiffony green garment beyond her waist; the cover, now slate gray, which was perhaps as originally painted a mauve or ultramarine; and the white sheet curving away on the mattress below. The painting is not confrontationally erotic; it is touchingly beautiful. Softness is evoked by the brushwork, loaded here, thin there. The colors let us visualize and almost feel her flesh and the surroundings in which it is most perceptible. At first sight the painting isn't at all "sexy." Indeed, some viewers have looked at this picture and found it dispassionate. *Cool* is a word that has been used to describe it, and as a term of temperature-based criticism (i.e., not warm enough) rather than of modish compliment. But Kenneth Clark has recognized one hold this *Venus* has on admirers. He writes, a bit gingerly, "It might be argued that the back view of the female body is more satisfactory than the front." ("Satisfactory"! Doesn't he mean "arousing"?) The back view, he goes on, might also be "considered symbolic of lust," although Velázquez was somewhat out of place in his time. "The bottom is a baroque form."

Art historians! We need them but now and then we shudder at them.

Here we have what is convincingly the most erogenous female rear ever depicted. Where one's eye ultimately falls is on what's called the "small" of this woman's back. Between the curving cleft of the pressed-together buttocks and the longer and shallower curve of skin covering her spine is a zone painted with such skill that words fall away, useless. What we retain are sensations from a gentle gloss of light and lightly modulated shade, the slope of flesh above the spine, the dimple where the left buttock folds into the top of the thigh at the waist. As said, our response to this creature is not altogether an erotic one. Walter Pater somewhere talks of the "sexless beauty" of Greek statues; it was a quality that conveyed serenity, "a negative quality . . . the absence of any sense of want, of corruption, or shame." A sort of indifference or coolness.

I wonder what Velázquez's master, father-in-law Pacheco, would have had to say about this Venus, remembering his strictures that an artist should have before him only the hands and faces of chaste women when he painted the female form. Velázquez in any event dared to disagree. Compare his full-length wonderfully human *Venus* to the nudes by Rubens in his *Three Graces*—flabby, cellulite-packed. Or the Rubens *Toilet of Venus* (1606–11) in the Thyssen Museum in Madrid, an upright painting showing only half the goddess's face, albeit clearly, and wearing a chemise or cloak that leaves just one breast exposed. Velázquez made numerous modifications as he painted his *Venus*. Her right arm and shoulder were moved in the course of his work. He changed the color of the bedcover. He painted many areas of fabric *alla prima*, quickly, lightly. He left some passages seemingly unfinished, almost out of focus, with the grain of the canvas visible and tangible, for example in his Venus's left sole and right hand and in the back foot of the Cupid—who was also an afterthought. Yet on that peerless back the brushstrokes are unnoticeable.

VELÁZQUEZ FINALLY STARTED his journey back to Spain in the early winter of 1650. That December he was again in Modena, chivvied by suggestions from Philip that he get a move on. At the duke's court he tried unsuccessfully to liberate a few masterpieces, among them a Tintoretto and a Correggio. The duke himself was "not at home"—genuinely or because he wanted to avoid being talked into giving up some of his best pictures; a court official was delegated to tell Velázquez that they were unable to get hold of the keys to the rooms where the paintings were hung. The duke's ambassador to Madrid, Ottonelli, passed on the word that the duke regarded his ownership of Correggio's *Night* as one of trusteeship. The duke had vowed never to let it leave his family. "I had the impression," said Ottonelli, "that this gave Diego pause." Many had the impression that when Velázquez came calling, it was best to keep him away from your pictures. But Velázquez managed to squeeze in a stop in Venice and there succeeded in buying two Veroneses and a number of Tintorettos; these included some canvases meant for a ceiling and a *Paradisio* that the poet Marco Boschini thought would assure Tintoretto's immortality. Once again Velázquez seems to have been dawdling on purpose and he took his time catching a boat from Genoa. The return voyage to Barcelona was boisterous; Palomino tells us they ran into severe storms. He was back in Madrid just after the middle of June 1651.* But Italy remained in his thoughts—perhaps a recumbent woman modeling Venus, and perhaps an infant named Antonio, remained there, too. When Velázquez asked Philip IV if he could go to Italy again in 1657, the king said no.

---

*"Velázquez returned to Madrid in late June 1651, perhaps with *The Rokeby Venus* in his baggage" (Dawson W. Carr, *Velázquez*, National Gallery Publications, p. 46).

XII. Transformations. Madrid. 1651–59

VELÁZQUEZ WAS AWARDED A NEW JOB NOT LONG AFTER HIS return to court. It may have been a reward for finally coming home—for doing what he had been asked to do. And it may have reflected the king's greater cheerfulness. Philip now had a second wife, his niece Mariana of Austria, young and bouncy, whom he had married in 1649 while Velázquez was away on his Italian journey. At that point she was fifteen, a good-humored teenager, to be overheard actually laughing out loud in the Alcázar palace, and she soon proved herself at least capable of motherhood, if not yet of producing an heir, by giving birth to a daughter—Margarita—in July 1651. There were for Velázquez new portrait candidates for his brush and much work to do with all the art objects from Italy that were at last arriving and being unpacked. He oversaw the casting of statues in bronze or plaster by Girolamo Ferrer, a craftsman who had been brought from Rome, and Domingo de la Rioja, a Madrid sculptor. And as for the new job, it aroused among the royal painter's colleagues either envy (why weren't they given the post?) or possibly—with a more perceptive few—a sympathetic or malicious feeling that Velázquez was going to have less time for his own painting.

There had been six candidates for the post of *aposentador mayor del palacio*, chamberlain of the palace. The job involved looking after the royal quarters in the Alcázar and organizing royal journeys. The chamberlain had to see that staff opened the windows at certain times and that in winter rush mats covered the floors, and fires were lit. He supervised the king's sitting down at dinner and scheduled his attendance at various diversions, at plays, balls, hunts. He had to arrange places for the king and his courtiers to stay when they traveled, and this meant seeing there were wagons to move chairs, tables, and beds, often across country, on difficult roads. A committee from the *Bureo* of the royal household duly considered the candidates, who included the ladies' guardian and queen's chamberlain, José Nieto, and cast their votes for them in order from most- to least-favored. Only one candidate had the backing of the entire committee, but did not win all the first-place votes. One of the *Bureo*, the Count de Montalban, said the desired candidate should be of graceful appearance and capable of making journeys; he thought Simon Rodríguez, the oldest competitor, was disqualified by not being able to count. In these circles "seniority" figured large, often judged by dates the courtiers had been sworn in. Velázquez was not the first choice of any. But it was Velázquez who got the crucial backing of the king. On February 16, 1652, Philip IV cut through the discord and wrote in his own hand a note to the effect that Velázquez was to be the new chamberlain: *"Nombro a Velázquez."* "I appoint Velázquez." He had gone extremely far in the king's favor.

Real work, real time, went into being *aposentador mayor.* Despite the implications of consequence in the title, much of the job required him to look after very ordinary tasks, seeing that sheets were washed and aired, making sure that the carpets were shaken out and floors swept. It was up to him to ensure the servants on the staff did their jobs properly. He took the oath of office on March 8, 1652; his salary according to one source was to be 3,300 reales per annum, though one wonders if he was also given for the occasion the words "Good luck getting it." It was more than the average income of most of the nobles at the court. He also hypothetically did well with the annual sum out of which he was expected to pay his assistants. By 1660, for instance, he was notionally 3,200 ducats to the good, twice what he was owed. In a country where the crown was often bankrupt (as it was again in 1653) it was important to keep oneself in the black, ahead of the bailiffs. He was working in a time of constant financial crisis. Things were particularly bleak in September 1656, a time with a great shortage of food in the palace. In October 1659 there was no money for firewood, and next the sweepers and cleaners went on strike since they hadn't been paid. As chamberlain, Velázquez had overall charge of renting out shops on the ground floor of the palace, around the courtyards, another source of income for him. When his granddaughter Inés married an Italian in 1654, as a special favor for her dowry the king gave Velázquez a post with the Naples city council, valued at twelve thousand silver ducats. Another perquisite for the painter was a large four-story apartment in the Casa del Tesoro, the Royal Treasury, in the eastern wing of the Alcázar, that the king told him to move into in August 1655. Given all the pesky anxieties his chamberlainship involved—the juggling with cash, the overdrafts, the staff management, the marshaling of what would now be called "human resources," and the need for blandishments and for a frequent firm line—it's amazing that he even remembered what his first office at court had been, *el pintor real*. He was buried in the system, a mole—albeit one with an important title—burrowing along the corridors and passageways to rooms for which he had the official keys. Palomino recognized the good and the bad aspects of Velázquez's rise in the household and saw that the office of chamberlain, while honorable, was "such an onerous one that it needs a whole man."

In many respects, as Palomino noted, the job of *aposentador* was a restriction of his talents, "more of a punishment than a reward." The artist/art historian/curator shared the pride of those in the Spanish art world a generation later who were pleased Velázquez had been elevated to such a position, but regretted that they thereby lost "so many proofs of his rare ability that would have multiplied his gifts to posterity." He painted fewer pictures in the 1650s than in any of the previous three decades. Nonetheless pictures did get painted, and were mostly of Philip's family. Soon after getting back from Italy he made a portrait of the young queen Mariana (1634–96), the daughter of the emperor, Ferdinand III of Austria, and a replica was sent to Vienna for her father and mother (Philip's sister Maria). Mariana wasn't smiling. Did she suspect that these almost incestuous Hapsburg marriages of close relations weren't for the best? She looks unhappy, standing rigidly, as Velázquez had told her to, in what seems to have been the agreed mode for these portraits, the body facing slightly right, the head turned slightly left, eyes fixed on the painter (why won't he talk to her?), red-cheeked, right hand resting on a fabric-covered side table, left hand gripping a lace scarf or shawl that is draped over her voluminous skirt. The skirt is like a tent, round-topped, stretched over the frame of a farthingale. She was homesick for Vienna. The laughing teenager was soon borrowing her uncle-husband's gloomy looks.

Indeed, as time passed, Philip—no longer fired up by his energetic young wife—seemed to regard her more as niece than lover, or as soul mate, "whose affection I would be unable to deserve even if I were to live a thousand years." She had the Hapsburg chin and quite a lot of puppy fat. He referred to Mariana and his daughters collectively as "the girls," and he went on seeing ladies of the town. As one courtier noted, Philip had better luck in siring bastards than in begetting legitimate heirs. In a portrait now in the Prado that Velázquez painted of the king at this time, circa 1654–55, when Philip wasn't yet fifty years old, he looks washed out, unhappy, and sorry for himself: a hollow man. The points of his mustache are still upturned, though one doubts if much else is. Although they may make him appear more ridiculous to the modern viewer than they did to contemporaries, the waxed tips of the mustache call attention to the pronounced bags under his watery, lonely eyes, the lined jowls, and the lips he keeps clenched as though to stop himself from bursting into tears. He wears the Order of the Golden Fleece, which his ancestor Philip the Good, Duke of Burgundy, had founded in 1429, and whose members were sworn to protect the Christian faith and defend the Catholic Church. How good a job had he so far done of that? It was all downhill, he seems to think, downhill all the way. Philip prayed more frequently, and wrote again to Sister María Magdalena de Agreda. In July 1653 he had apologized to her for his inability to send a portrait of himself and seemed to blame Velázquez and his phlegmatic temperament for this, although he admitted he wasn't desperate for new portraits of himself; he didn't like seeing the evidence of growing older. The nun wrote back, but Philip's prayers were only fitfully answered. The fact that Velázquez also painted the king several years after the Prado portrait (a picture now in the London National Gallery), showed that Philip could put aside his worries about his aging looks. Velázquez did not go in for flattery. His deft brushstrokes limned the king honestly and brilliantly.

Philip IV, *1656–57, National Gallery, London.*

The "girls," dressed in their court finery, put Velázquez to tests that he passed with somnambulistic ease. He couldn't do this with his eyes shut, but he could, consummately, brush in hand, with his eyes open. The portraits he painted of Mariana, her younger cousin the infanta María Teresa (daughter of Philip's first marriage to Isabella of Bourbon), and eventually of Philip and Mariana's daughter Margarita, were remarkably similar, save for the faces. There were numerous copies for Brussels, Vienna, and even Paris, where Philip's sister Anne was getting over their long coolness and Richelieu's successor Mazarin was thinking of the usefulness to France of a marriage of young Louis XIV to the infanta María Teresa. Velázquez, and his workshop assistants, were kept busy. His professional skills were demonstrated in the portrait he painted around 1653 of *The Infanta Margarita in Pink*, a painting still in Vienna, where it was sent to the imperial court for the benefit of her cousin Leopold, to whom Margarita had been promised from the start. She was about two years old when Velázquez first painted her, evidently with more pleasure than she got from being painted. The little girl looks very serious as she stands very still, as instructed—how did she remain unmoving long enough for him to complete even a rough sketch to work from? She has a closed fan in her left hand and rests her right hand on a low sideboard covered with blue damask, next to a small glass vase containing flowers, pink and pale blue, roses and irises, and next to the clump of white rose petals that have fallen out of the vase onto the cloth. It could be a symbolic touch—"many a fair has oft declined, by nature's changing course untrimmed." (Margarita married Leopold in 1666 and died in 1673, at age twenty-two.) Or it could just be Velázquez painting flowers as no one else could at that point, so lightly and freely you might say, "Here is the birth of impressionism."

The flowers in their living and fallen state are in contrast to the little girl who is almost imprisoned in her attitude and overstuffed costume. She stands on a slightly raised, carpeted dais. Velázquez, having painted the button eyes and plump red cheeks and an outline of the body, would have been able to let the infanta go off with her attendants and take his time on the dress—hung on a lay figure—and the background and pudgy hands. She already has the unsmiling family hauteur and looks at the painter and therefore at us with only a modicum of curiosity; she is, after all, a princess! We think "How pretty she is—what a lovely dress—so brilliantly painted!" and at the same time "Poor little thing."

Velázquez in these years more than earned his keep as royal painter. His own life was not very visible but surfaced in his portraits of the royal young women that appeared every year or so. The stance was fairly uniform: standing facing half left; tightly bodiced; arms stiffly held over the elaborate farthingale; the hair ringletted or teased out in a massive headdress; and pearly white and blush red makeup accentuating a sense of make-believe, though fully believed in by the participants. In the 1650s Velázquez portrayed the young queen Mariana like this on several occasions, looking bored or sulky. (The original formal portrait is that in the Prado, but there were several workshop copies.) Perhaps we can be pardoned for thinking "spoiled cow" and concentrating

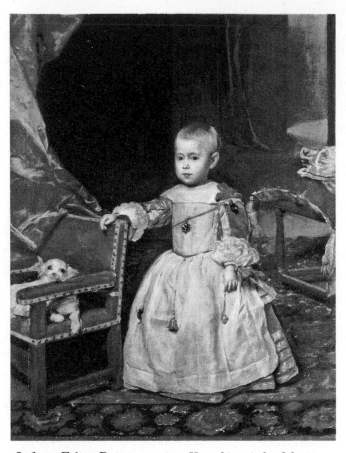

Infante Felipe Próspero, *1659, Kunsthistorisches Museum, Vienna.*

instead on the magically rendered accoutrements: for instance, the scarf that she holds in her be-ringed left hand, a piece of soft white lace that the artist has conjured into reality by rough white and pearl-gray paint strokes. Mariana's younger cousin María Teresa, the only child surviving from Philip's first marriage, had been about ten when Velázquez first painted her in 1648, and he painted her again, twice, in the early 1650s, when she was fourteen or so. Margarita, Mariana's daughter, went on looking like a Dresden doll (or an overstuffed small sofa with a sweet curly-haired head on top) in a portrait Velázquez made in 1659 showing her wearing a blue dress—a similar portrait of the infanta wearing a green dress was probably (some experts think) by his son-in-law Martínez del Mazo. The blue dress painting was sent to Vienna, to join its predecessors in the emperor Leopold's collection and keep him in touch with the girl he was going to marry, and the green dress went an imperial farther step on to Budapest.

Sent with the Vienna shipment was a portrait Velázquez had painted of Philip and Mariana's son, Infante Felipe Próspero—not yet two, pasty pale, wearing over his white pinafore a number of charms. They include an amulet against the evil eye, an amber ornament in the shape of an apple to ward off infections, and several little bells, which helped his carers keep track of his whereabouts if he wandered off in the maze of the palace. A crimson infant-sized armchair is right there for him to rest a small white hand on. And making itself at home on the chair is a white puppy, its head leaning on the arm. (Palomino tells us that the dog looks like "one for which Velázquez felt great affection.") Despite the hopes expressed in the infante's name, the child did not prosper. The Venetian ambassador to the Madrid court reported on the prince's delicate condition a year or two after this, mentioning his sluggish movements and colorless skin, the head large, the mouth hanging open, and "no bounce in the knees." Infante Felipe Próspero was guarded rather precariously by an elderly Franciscan, Father Antonio de Castilla, who was charged with carrying him in his arms. The ambassador added that although Father Antonio's "inexperience put him frequently in danger of dropping the Infante, the priest was not allowed to leave him alone."

Velázquez may have been as kind as he could be in this portrait— the child stands, his mouth doesn't hang open, the blue eyes are limpidly alert—but the suggestion of fragility and a very short future comes through. One might have thought that with the arrival of the new heir to the throne Philip and his advisers would have reflected seriously about the Hapsburg line and how best to maintain it, and this didn't mean marrying your niece. Genetic imperatives may still have been in the distance, but biblical prohibitions were well known. And although they knew how family characteristics showed up in each generation, with the chins and lips clear signs of Hapsburg blood, there was less recognition of the cumulative effect of consanguinity. "My word, he looks a lot like you!" was a congratulatory remark that should have been taken as a fatal warning. Half of the Hapsburg royal children died before the age of ten, twice the rate of deaths among the children in the common *pueblos* of Spain. The king's daughters tended to live longer than the sons, but were by no means of vigorous health. (Queen Mariana had a second daughter in 1656 who died soon after her birth.) The sickliness of Infante Felipe Próspero had no cure; the amulets didn't help; he died when not yet four. After him, things went from bad to worse. Philip and Mariana's next production was the infante Carlos, born in 1661. He made it to the age of thirty-nine, becoming king, but was nicknamed *El Hechizado*, the Hexed or Cursed, and suffered from all sorts of problems, mental and physical, including rickets, blood in the urine, what seems to have been inherited syphilis, and—as would become clear (and because of all this clearly a good thing)—impotence. This brought about the end of the dynasty.

Meanwhile, aided by his assistants, in the setting light of the Hapsburg sun, Velázquez rearranged the royal art collection and redecorated the gloomy rooms of the Alcázar and Escorial in which much of it was to be found. The Escorial hadn't suited the king's mood in his man-about-town years but did fit in with his more religiously inclined days following the dismissal of Olivares. The Escorial also contained the burial place of the Hapsburgs, the Pantheon crypt. When Philip had the bodies of his ancestors reinterred he was amazed to find that the corpse of Charles V, dead ninety-six years, was still whole, and in consequence he wrote to Sister María de Agreda begging her to not allow him to forget this sight. He wanted her to help him attain salvation. Philip put Velázquez in charge of the decorating and furnishing of the Pantheon with its side chambers, a sacristy, study, and prior's chapter room, as he got rid of many bad pieces and replaced them with good ones and put them in gold frames: pictures by Titian, Raphael, Veronese, Tintoretto, Van Dyck, among others. And the Alcázar was similarly transformed into a space, both real and potent with illusion, full of "precious and admirable paintings and statues of bronze and marble," so Velázquez's friend the court musician Lázaro Díaz del Valle wrote. In the Escorial and the Alcázar the king, despite the less attractive reality of things, looked like a great monarch: No other prince in the world, thought Díaz, had palaces so adorned. Philip actually spent a lot of time with the collection; he loved paintings and he seems to have loved being with the royal painter while he supervised the decorating. Camillo Massimi, the papal nuncio whom Velázquez had come to know and had portrayed on his second trip to Rome, noted that the king had caught a fever in February 1658 "by having spent a long time the previous day watching pictures being hung in the summer apartments." Philip liked discussing attributions, for example, with Michelangelo Colonna, the Italian fresco painter Velázquez had had a hand in bringing from Bologna with his colleague Agostino Mitelli and housing in the Casa del Tesoro, while they painted trompe l'oeil images on the walls and ceilings of several apartments in the palace. Velázquez helped plan a series of paintings to illustrate the fable of Pandora, which they helped execute. When Colonna and Mitelli were working in the Salon Grande, above the main entrance to the Alcázar, the king (according to Palomino) "went up every day to see how the work was progressing," sometimes with Queen Mariana and the infantas, and asked the artists many questions.

Not many who worked in Velázquez's studio-cum-workshop left their names on a roll of honor. We know of Diego de Melgar, apprenticed in 1620, but he is here one second and then gone, somewhere in Seville. Juan de Pareja's celebrity is helped by Velázquez's masterful portrait of him. It was a time requiring many hand-painted copies, reproductions well before the age when they could be turned out mechanically or chemically, and possibly involved in painting them were Francisco de Palacios and three well-born assistants, Diego de Lucena, Francisco de Burgos Mantilla, and Nicolas de Villacis—all "dons" so Palomino tells us, though one recalls Cervantes's remark in *Don Quixote* that the title "don," which belonged properly to families of note, had grown "very common." More is known about Juan de Alfaro, Velázquez's pupil, who was permitted to copy masterworks by Titian and Rubens in the Alcázar. After Velázquez's death Alfaro wrote an admiring account in Latin of Velázquez's career that Palomino incorporated in his *Life*. Apart from Pareja, who had the good fortune to be immortalized by Velázquez, the assistant who came out best was probably his son-in-law. He achieved an independent reputation for his hunting scenes and city views, and contemporaries admired his skill in painting small figures. Velázquez turned to him often for copies of royal portraits and he took over from his father-in-law as painter to the king. Del Mazo had been drawing master to Prince Baltasar Carlos and he succeeded to some of Velázquez's duties in the royal household, taking on the post of Usher of the Chamber and the job of making an inventory of the royal artworks. But the artistic family suffered the dire loss in 1654 of Velázquez's only surviving daughter Francisca, del Mazo's wife, and mother of several Velázquez grandchildren. Her death may have given Velázquez cause to brood about families, their successes, their disasters—one of his most intricate pictures of this period bears witness to such thought. After Velázquez's granddaughter Inés was widowed, his son-in-law del Mazo was allowed in 1657 to go to Italy to reclaim her dowry, which had been partly subsumed we gather in the valuable city council post that had been given to her husband, Onofre di Lifrangi. We recall that Philip had refused to allow Velázquez to make a similar trip at this time. Velázquez's only child at that point was presumably Antonio, in Rome, if he had survived infancy. Since Velázquez's Italian lawyers seemed to keep good records of transactions to do with him, we should know of any maintenance payments he sent for Antonio.

Some of the pictures del Mazo had been copying were those that Rubens had painted on subjects from Ovid's *Metamorphoses* and that were hung in Velázquez's studio in the palace. The royal painter owned two copies of Ovid's work, one in Spanish, one in Italian. "Transformations" were bestselling subjects in the classical world and they struck responsive notes with Velázquez; perhaps the Rubens paintings had their subliminal effect as well. He had already used Ovid material in *The Forge of Vulcan* and the classical scholar in him came again to the fore in several complicated paintings he did at this time that make evident his brilliance as a painter who thought as profoundly as he felt. Jon Manchip White has wondered whether Velázquez was drawn to the *Metamorphoses* by his "interest in the dualities of human existence: mortal and immortal, earthly and divine, sacred and profane, reality and illusion." It's remarkable that as Spain's power declined and the Madrid court seemed held captive by its own ceremonies, the king's painter struck out independently and boldly with paintings that fused (in Denys Sutton's description of the process) "different fields of vision in one composition."

One such picture was *Las Hilanderas, The Spinners,* or *The Fable of Arachne.* Scholars have set various dates on this painting: Dieter Beaujean follows J. López-Rez in suggesting circa 1644 to 1648. Enriqueta Harris and the catalogue of the 2006 exhibition at the London National Gallery edited by Dawson W. Carr go for a decade later, ca. 1656–58. The story as Ovid tells it was that of a Lydian girl named Arachne, a talented weaver, who made the mistake of claiming to be as skilled in working with wool as Minerva, known to the Greeks as Pallas Athena, the gray-eyed goddess of wisdom. Arachne was proud and conceited. Nymphs came to admire her handiwork as she shaped the wool into threads for embroidering a picture. Arachne then dared Minerva to a weaving contest. She didn't recognize the goddess when she first appeared disguised as a hag, "with hoary looks," and hobbling with a stick. Arachne stuck to her guns when Minerva suggested that the girl might be the best of all humankind but should modestly yield the palm to a deity, the goddess of wisdom—indeed, should beg the forgiveness of Minerva for boasting in the way she had done. Arachne said even more rashly, "Leave me alone, you stupid old woman!" At that point Minerva dropped her disguise. Faced with the goddess, Arachne was taken aback enough to blush, but nevertheless continued to claim that she, Arachne, was the best. The contest went ahead. Minerva wove scenes illustrating the troubles that befell those who dared to compete with the gods—for example, the pickle that Antigone, the Trojan king's daughter, got into, and as a result was punished by Juno and turned into a white-feathered stork. But Arachne wasn't to be thwarted by these warnings. Insolent to the end, she created a tapestry that showed the gods at their worst, particularly the father of the gods himself— Jove as a bull stealing Europa, Leda carried off by Jove who had taken the shape of a swan, and Danae being seduced by Jove in the form of a shower of gold. Minerva was so upset by this lèse-majesté that she struck Arachne on the head, cursing her but not killing her. Instead she sprinkled on her the poisonous juice of a plant that turned her into a spider. Thus Arachne went on spinning and weaving though no longer in human form.

Velázquez gave us for the occasion one of his split-screen performances. He shows us a stage in this drama before the final transformation of Arachne, and also a scene in "real life" that was somewhat removed from her metamorphosis. We see in the foreground of his painting a room in which five women—the spinners—are at work making wool. Through the central archway behind them, on a sort of dais in a large alcove, is an atelier, or what looks like a stage set for a studio in which an immense tapestry is hanging. There Arachne is to be seen, attended by several elegantly costumed women, with a musician ready to play a viola da gamba to keep them entertained. And there, too, in a beam of light that streams in from a high unseen window on the left, Minerva— Pallas Athena—stands, helmeted, with a raised spear, preparing to belabor the uppity misguided weaving girl. Arachne assumes a suddenly suppliant pose before her tapestry, for which Velázquez has borrowed much from Titian's *Rape of Europa*, a painting he had access to in the Spanish royal collection. In the immediate foreground a woman in a white scarf sits behind a spinning wheel that whirrs, spokes invisible, in a brilliantly rendered blur. In another wonderfully homely touch, one of the young women on the right, black-haired and wearing a white blouse and black skirt, reminds us of the young woman with a white scarf over her shoulders shown sewing fifteen years or so earlier (1635– 43). This woman is at work wrapping wool from a frame onto a ball; she leans sideways, steadying herself with an outstretched left foot whose heel is lifted off the floor just sufficiently to bring this part of the picture to vibrant life.

Velázquez painted *The Fable of Arachne* in the late 1650s, using the silver-gray ground that he was fond of at that stage in his career. It was the same time in which, in Holland, Rembrandt, who after his first years in the Uylenburg workshop in Amsterdam remained a true freelance throughout the rest of his life, fell into debt because he had been tempted into overextending, ambitiously buying a big house that soon needed expensive repiling, and was forced to have an insolvency sale. The Arachne story may have intrigued Velázquez—who, with his court posts, was more financially secure than Rembrandt—for its aspirational theme: Arachne aimed high, too high as far as Minerva was concerned, setting herself up as equal to an immortal being, but her weaving skills were displayed in the background tapestry and gave evidence of not just craftsmanship but great artistry. Velázquez doesn't seem to have come up against Rembrandt or his work and his competitive streak would have been exercised not against the great Dutchman but against Michelangelo, Titian, and Rubens. If Minerva won the competition with Arachne, Velázquez—painting a picture that presents the tussle between the contestants and the actual toil of spinning and weaving—puts himself forward as the master artist.

One moral of the story seems to be that human beings shouldn't get too big for their boots, or sandals: especially when you're up against a deity, pride comes before a fall. Dawson Carr also notes that Velázquez owned a copy of Pliny's *Natural History*, a sourcebook for ancient art that "lauds two painters for capturing movement." Aristides had managed to show cart wheels turning and Antiphilus had depicted a room in which women were occupied in spinning. So Velázquez, illustrating movement, "achieved something not realised since antiquity, surpassing Titian, and fulfilling a quest that began forty years before when he tried to capture the transformation of an egg in hot oil." And the Spanish painter may also have been aware of the suggestion made by Viana, a translator of Ovid, that the Arachne story was a parable: It showed an artist frustrated by nonrecognition. Velázquez, this theory supposes, wanted celebrity and honors he hadn't yet obtained.

Velázquez painted *The Spinners* for Pedro de Arce. Was the king feeling too poor? Or did he not take to the subject matter? De Arce was a courtier, too, the Master of the Hounds, and a picture collector; he was *aposentador normal*, a rank below Velázquez's *aposentador mayor.* De Arce was to be one of the executors of Juan de Alfaro, Velázquez's pupil, who along with Palomino provided much of our early information about Velázquez. *The Spinners* in some ways harks back to the artist as a realist painter of *bodegones*, of kitchen scenes and taverns. Here in the foreground we see depicted what may well have been a local tapestry workshop—the Saint Isabel workshop in Madrid—with the blur of the fast-rotating spinning wheel taking the place of the bubbling cooking pan and the moisture-covered water jar. There are other details to linger on: the cat; the scraps of wool on the floor; the girl on the left holding aside the curtain. . . . A lot is wonderfully going on, and one should perhaps resist the urge to complain about a possible lack of cohesion. Velázquez often dared to disrespect the unities. The right questions rather than the right answers were his prime goal. Here he evades the conclusion and leaves us wondering about the final scary moment of Arachne's story. What happens next? We remember Minerva's threats. Is Arachne really going to be turned into a spider?

The Spinners was hung first in the Buen Retiro and then moved to the Alcázar palace, where it was damaged in the fire of 1734. The painting was restored with additional canvas on all sides. In the late nineteenth century its animation attracted the approval of Carl Justi, the German art historian and Velázquez biographer; he thought it "a picture in which the representation of motion in the motionless could scarcely be carried further." But he also noted the unsightly condition of its paint surface, unusual for such a prescient painter as Velázquez, that was perhaps the result of the Alcázar blaze and displayed a network of cracks and welts through which the priming seemed to have welled up. Raphael Mengs, the somewhat earlier German writer on art who had come across Velázquez's genius in the late eighteenth century, described *The Spinners* as a work less of the hand than of the will.

STAYING AT THE Casa del Tesoro while his son-in-law del Mazo went to Italy produced some pangs, one supposes, but it gave Velázquez more time to make paintings as well as arrange and hang them. Classical subjects remained big with him; he had started with a sibyl and moved on via Bacchus, Apollo and Vulcan, and then Venus, to Arachne and Minerva. *Mercury and Argus* featured as well in Ovid's *Metamorphoses* and was also a tale with suspenseful ramifications. The lord of the sky, Jove or Jupiter, was once again up to no good. Playing away from home as he often did, he ravished the nymph Io. Then, scared of how his wife Juno would handle news of this, he turned Io into a heifer. Juno wasn't fooled but, suspecting the worst, put many-eyed Argus in charge of the transformed nymph. Jove then commissioned his son Mercury, messenger of the gods, to murder Argus. Mercury donned his winged sandals and wide-brimmed hat and flew down to play his pipe music to Argus to make him drowsy; and, when asleep, to behead him with his sword. Velázquez condensed this story into a single image, which he painted with thick broad strokes. The rough impasto resulted in shimmering effects, both free and fluid.

The painting contains more inherent violence even than the *Portrait of Innocent X*. The viewer naturally finds himself or herself taking the part of Argus, the sleeping sentry beside the dormant heifer; Argus sits with head drooping and a raised right knee, and his reputedly observant eyes, a hundred strong, not visible. (Carel Fabritius's *Sentry* of possibly a year or two earlier, showing a soldier who was similarly neglecting his watch outside a gate in Delft, in Holland, comes to mind.) One wants to shake Argus by the shoulder—why doesn't he *wake up* and notice the figure crouching just beyond his right leg? The figure is obscure, though one can make out the feathers in his hat that indicate the ability to fly, and then in the shadows a sword grasped in one hand. The light that falls on Argus's bent right leg, knee, and thigh accentuates his vulnerability. Murder is in the air.

The *Mercury and Argus* was painted for the Hall of Mirrors in the Alcázar, where it was to hang along with three other mythological narrative pictures by Velázquez that perished in the fire of 1734. It was placed over a window, in Velázquez's own arrangement, in the ongoing attempts by the crown to show off its artistic wealth—or mask from itself its decline as a power in the world. The painting's brooding force and rich coloring withstood the effect of the light from the window that radiated from beneath it, light that was also reflected from the hall's many mirrors. Palomino failed to mention the *Mercury and Argus* among "the marvellous paintings made by Don Diego Velázquez" he lists at this time though it was surely among the most marvelous. That it had the luck to survive the 1734 fire was fortunate, and we should place in the same category of good news the lines of Ovid that provided for Io, if not Argus, a happy ending. Jove placated Juno with caresses. He promised her that she would have no more vexation caused by his desire for the young nymph. Io herself was returned to human shape. She was thrilled to be able to stand on just two feet again, with hooves dissolved and replaced by toenails. But she was at first frightened to speak in case what came forth from her mouth was the lowing of a heifer. In a while she got the hang of her lost language and eventually she gave birth to a son who was assumed to have sprung from the seed of the sun god.

XIII. MAIDS OF HONOR. MADRID. 1656

WHICH SEVENTEENTH-CENTURY ARTIST WAS THE GREATEST
deceiver? A number of painters of the time vie for this role. Vermeer, the grandson of a man who had been charged with making false coinage, seemed to delight in exercising the counterfeiting genes in his system—*conterfeitsel* being the Dutch word for a portrait. Trompe l'oeil was an illusionist skill that contemporary artists in various parts of Europe enjoyed practicing. Puzzle pictures—works of art that posed for the viewer hard-to-answer questions—were common. "What's it all about?" Velázquez rose to this challenge, too.

Questions! Velázquez's painting now known as *Las Meninas*, the Maids of Honor, begs many of them. The picture has a Kafka-esque clutter in which we can easily get lost. It is a claustrophobic maze with possibly no way out. "*La Familia*"—that is, the family of Philip IV— was the name the painting had for many years before it acquired its *Las Meninas* appelation. There are ten living creatures in it and the reflections of two others. Palomino described it in part three of his 1724 *El Museo Pictorico* as a "large picture with the portrait of the Empress [then infanta of Spain] Doña Margarita María of Austria, when she was very young. There are no words to describe her great charm, liveliness, and beauty, but her portrait itself is the best panegyric. At her feet kneels Doña María Agustina, the queen's *menina*, daughter of Don Diego Sarmiento, serving her with water from an earthenware jug." Palomino goes on, diligently and respectfully, to describe the various figures in the painting. In fact, the "royal family" seems at first to consist of just one person, the small blond princess Margarita, spot-lit and stage front. However, as Palomino observes, Velázquez "showed his indisputable talent by revealing . . . what he was painting" and showing us at the back of the room he is concerned with a mirror that reflects the heads of that family, the king and the queen. They have apparently just walked into the room to see what's going on. They seem to be standing where we are, the viewers of this painting, and thus immediately incorporate us, too, in what's going on. That includes Velázquez himself—the painter at work on a very large canvas, which may or not be this same painting, which is in fact about ten feet tall by nine feet wide. Wheels within wheels!

This unseen picture Velázquez is at work on within the picture pro-vokes our decided curiosity. We can't see the front of the canvas on which Velázquez is painting. Velázquez portrays himself working on it with a long-handled brush in his right hand, one of the round brushes which Beruete says the artist favored, whose hair was "mounted in goose quills fixed to wooden handles." Part of the back of the canvas he is painting on is visible, a big slice of it, fastened to its stretcher-framework of bare wood and resting on an easel, also made of bare wood. One leg of the easel is shown to us together with the shadows the easel throws on the back of the canvas. The self-consciousness of the artist seems to be one part of Velázquez's subject here. That long upright edge of the stretcher, fencing off the crowded scene to the right of it, brilliantly delimits things while drawing attention to the fact that this is a painting about painting. The leg of the easel makes us think of the easel Vermeer shows his artist sitting before in his *Art of Painting*, painted in Delft about ten years after Velázquez's picture. The rear view of a picture being worked on was also very much Rembrandt's subject in his rather clodhopping early *The Artist in his Studio* (ca. 1629, Museum of Fine Arts, Boston), where the young painter stands gawk-ily at the far side of his bare painting room. Between Rembrandt and us is a strange foreground gap dominated by his easel. We see the dark back of the canvas or panel on it. The edge of the picture that is under way is indicated by a long bright gleam of paint remarkably similar in aesthetic function to the upright edge of Velázquez's stretcher in *Las Meninas*.

There are three girls in this painting: center stage, the small infanta, about seven years old; immediately to her right (our left) is Doña María Agustina Sarmiento, kneeling so as to bring her head to the height of the infanta's blond hair and handing her water in a red *bucaro* mug, made of a soft Portuguese clay; and, on the other side of the princess Margarita, the second *menina* Doña Isabel de Velasco, the Count of Fuensalida's young daughter, who is curtsying and apparently about to speak. All three are illuminated by sun from the right, where a window is hinted at. Above and behind Doña María's head is the painter, holding his palette in his left hand. He is mostly in shadow though we can see his head tipped a little to one side as he focuses on his subjects. Behind Doña Isabel two figures stand watching while they have what looks like a private conversation: a woman in a nunlike habit, Doña Marcela de Ulloa, who had the title of a Lady of Honor, and a man, nameless and even more deeply shadowed, who appears to be a *Guarda Damas*, his job being to keep a protective eye on the ladies of the royal household. Coming farther forward, at the right before the unseen window, stand two attendants, both dwarfs. One—the bulkiest—is Mari Barbola, a German, short and stocky, with a heavy middle-aged face that speaks of many sorrows, a servant and sometime plaything of the darling infanta who is two steps away. Mari stares directly at the viewer, as if daring him to judgment. Beauty and the Beast, but don't say it aloud. Her gaze and the infanta's gaze, directed the same way, form a sort of crossfire, beneath which we may well feel like ducking. The second dwarf is sprightlier, even good-looking. More midget than dwarf, Nicolas Pertusato had the looks of a rosy-cheeked, well-formed small boy and served the king as a valet. Here he has one hand raised and one small foot resting on the uncomplaining back of a dog—one of the royal mastiffs, familiar from portraits Velázquez painted of the king as huntsman. The dog lies drowsing, with head erect, front paws stretched out, and obviously no threat to Nicolas, who seems to be good-humoredly trying to get some sort of reaction from it, with a tap from his foot that the dog ignores. At the back of the room, standing a few steps up and silhouetted in an open doorway against the lightness coming from the room behind, is José Nieto, chamberlain to the queen and presumed subject of the intense portrait (now in Apsley House) painted by Velázquez some years before. In *Las Meninas* Nieto is also apparently struck motionless by the arrival in the studio of their majesties, who have perhaps called in while taking a stroll through the palace. On his way out, Nieto turns, pausing, to look at them, and at the picture Velázquez is at work on, perhaps comparing the reality and the painted image for likeness.

Between Nieto in the doorway and the painter himself our gaze passes to a mirror hanging on the studio's back wall. The dark-framed mirror is surrounded by murky representations of paintings. The mirror, researchers tell us, was not listed in inventories of this room, and was most likely an invention of Velázquez, put there to enable him to get the king and the queen discreetly into the picture. (The king, we remember, was at that point a reluctant sitter for his own portrait.) Velázquez shows the royal pair side by side in dim focus, upper halves only, with a splash of red curtain reflected above them. Their images aren't clear, are in fact as foggy as that of the woman we have taken for Venus regarding herself in her mirror as she lies on her couch. The wall-hung mirror again prompts thoughts of a voyeur king. The arrival of Margarita's parents on the scene hasn't led Velázquez to budge from his stance at the easel; he goes on painting, thinking, brush in midair, though his eyes have undoubtedly taken in the royal presence. He is used to Philip coming in to see what he's up to. He doesn't have to bow or depart from his routine. After all, he is *el pintor real*.

The room we are looking at had been part of the apartment of Prince Baltasar Carlos, who died ten years before. Known as the Cierzo room, it had been latterly used as a storeroom in which various objects of the royal collection were kept, including many portraits of the kings of Portugal. Since 1646 it had been Velázquez's atelier in the Alcázar. It was dark, like most of the rooms in the Alcázar, and rather dark for its present purpose, with gloomy walls and deep-shadowed ceiling. Perhaps it felt cooler that way. It was made darker by the obscure shapes of some of the forty paintings that now hung on its walls, black frame close to black frame as high as the ceiling. Most were copies del Mazo had made of Rubens's paintings from stories in the *Metamorphoses*.

Velázquez cleverly uses this darkness to squeeze the action in his picture forward, as it were to the front of the stage. The conductor/director stands in half shadow, his brush poised like a baton. What light reaches him does so in the course of falling dimly on his forehead, nose, and left cheek, and on his right brush-holding hand, seeming to bounce off the slanting palette and the maulstick on which he rested his hand when painting details. From these the light passes to the face and right shoulder of the kneeling María Sarmiento before falling on the center of attraction, the small infanta.

Velázquez's presence here shows us what footing he was on with the royal couple, a senior servant who was almost an old friend of the family. At his waist hangs his chamberlain's key. The red cross of the Order of Santiago on his chest was a later addition, painted at the royal command. Is he thinking about acquiring this honor, still to come, even as he paints—the knighthood that he seems to have coveted above all else? Is he thinking about representing this picture with as much reality as he can muster or is he wondering what more to invent, in a work in which ambiguity and artifice are conspicuously consummate? Palomino wavered on this score, saying one thing, then the other, in fact saying both. Velázquez's picture, he wrote, is "no lesser [a] work of artifice than that of Phidias, the renowned [classical Greek] sculptor and painter, who placed his portrait on the shield of the statue he made of the goddess Minerva." And then, a paragraph farther on, Palomino declared that Velázquez's painting was "truth, not painting." In which case, what about the artifice? Palomino thought the real subject of Velázquez's picture was to be seen in the mirror hanging on the back wall, "with its reflection showing our Catholic King Philip and Queen Mariana." (In the mirror, the royal pair look like a very ordinary couple sitting side by side in the back of a carriage.)

Other viewers are less sure about the subject. What was the picture he was painting within this picture, the painting being painted on the other unseen side of the tall canvas he is working on? Is it a portrait simply of the little princess, like the portrait of the infanta Margarita—now in Vienna—that is ascribed to this same year? (Margarita here has a self-regarding look, as if she were taking note of her own reflection in a mirror.) Or was the picture he was painting this very picture—*Las*

Meninas? A painting of what he was painting? A mirror image of what he could see in a second larger mirror, showing this whole small crowd of fellow creatures and the king and queen who were visible twice, out front in person and reflected in the mirror on the back wall? At this point dizziness possibly sets in.

Another mirror Velázquez would have known well was that in *The Arnolfini Marriage* from the Netherlands, then in the royal collection in the Alcázar, and again a picture in which a mirror, a round one, hangs on a back wall. Jan van Eyck's painting of 1434 has only two human figures, though his couple fill much more of the painted space than Velázquez's royal pair. Both pictures contain a dog. Both have a rather cramped effect, a feeling of the walls and ceiling closing in and the light coming from only one side. Another court painter of the next generation after Velázquez, the Neapolitan Luca Giordano, when brought into the king's private apartments to look at *Las Meninas*, was asked for his opinion for it and said he thought it represented "the theology of painting," meaning—so Palomino assures us—that just as theology was superior to all other branches of knowledge, so this picture was the greatest example of the art of painting. Theology was also of course the study of religion and Giordano may have meant to suggest that *Las Meninas* furnished the material for a profound study of art by a believer in the power of art. In our time, the French thinker Michel Foucault has said, in 1966, that the painting could be "a representation, as it were, of classical representation," and therefore a worthy subject for students of philosophy to wrestle with. Jonathan Brown echoed this when he wrote even more recently that the painting was "in part a meditation on the nature of representation and reality." It was an attempt "to create art without apparent artifice and thus reduce the gap between what the eye sees in nature and what the eye sees in art." Or was it in fact the greatest achievement in naturalism made in the seventeenth century? The jury will probably always remain out, but for now, the theory of choice has come to be that in *Las Meninas* Velázquez intended to create a work that would symbolize the nobility of the art he was practicing, the art of painting. This would fit in with the ceremonial proclivities of the court and the aspirations of a man who was both painter and courtier.

There are other possibilities about its origins. One is that it could
have been a chance arrangement, all these people coming together by
accident in Velázquez's studio, and someone, the king maybe, saying
"That's a picture." The light might then have been adjusted to help with
a scene decreed by circumstance. A mirror may have been brought and
hung in the crucial spot in place of a painting. Or it may have been
Velázquez himself who looked around the room at this unique collection of individuals—the infanta, her parents, the royal retainers, dwarfs,
dog, and a painter at his easel—and suddenly thought, *Hola! This is my
life!* Here I am, one of this collection of curiosities. In some ways it was
a snapshot, a seizure of a moment in a form that still lay in the future.
It was also, as Carl Justi noted, a *tableau vivant*, in which "the figures
might . . . have been more naturally and effectively grouped in a semi-
circle about the canvas on the easel." But that's not how Velázquez
found them and saw them when the shutter of his mind's camera clicked.

The painting pushes at its own borders. It not only asks why this
strange coming together has taken place in the way it has, but *why* so
many things. Why beauty, why deformity? Why man, why God? Let
me quote Milan Kundera, who was prompted to say, after reading
Cervantes: "When Don Quixote went out into the world, that world
turned into a mystery before his eyes. . . . The novelist teaches its reader
to comprehend the world as a question." As does our artist. And the-
world-turned-into-a-mystery in turn provokes another question: Is *Las
Meninas* the painting of a dream? Possibly a workplace dream, in
which subconscious concerns about one's working life coalesce in a surreal pattern? A not uncommon concept then was that life itself was an
"insubstantial pageant," to use Shakespeare's phrase in *The Tempest*.
Human beings were "such stuff as dreams are made on, and our little
life / is rounded with a sleep." Shakespeare's Spanish contemporary the
playwright Calderón de la Barca played with the same notion. Calderón was roughly the same age as Velázquez. He was a court official's
son who is said to have been a soldier in Flanders in the mid-1620s, an
experience that gave little authentic grist to his masquelike play *El Sitio
de Breda*, performed soon after the siege ended; he became a colleague
of Velázquez at the palace, serving the court as director of theatrical
events. Calderón had been made a knight of Santiago after the *zarzu-*

ela he arranged for the grand opening of the Buen Retiro, an honor the painter presumably envied him for. Knights were still required to perform military service, and Calderón went with Philip's army to suppress the revolt in Catalonia in the 1640s. After resigning from the court he joined the priesthood, but continued prolifically writing plays, often several a month, until his death in 1681. His *La Vida es Sueno*, Life Is a Dream, written in the 1630s at about the time Velázquez was painting his *Surrender of Breda*, featured a heroine—Rosario—who disguises herself as a man, and a hero, Sigismundo, an imprisoned Polish prince who threatens to dishonor Rosario but in the end helps her out.

For the modern reader Calderón's work is overweighted with allegories. The play's design is unclear, its meanings incomplete, its actions—such as they are—set largely in the past or in the wings. (Rape, abandonment, acts of vengeance, and even murder are talked about rather than seen.) The language often seems stilted for the great emotions it is meant to convey. Drugged with opium, Sigismundo dreams of freedom and believes he is free—or is this just a dream? He wonders if it will be worthwhile to try to get back his rightful title. Later Sigismundo is a captive in chains once again and (at the end of act 2 in the English version by Adrian Mitchell and John Barton) reflects:

> *The King dreams he's a King,*
> *Lives, orders, governs in a royal illusion,*
> *Because his fame is written in the wind.*
> *For every King that rules men in his King-dream*
> *Must wake at last in the cold sleep of death,*
> *The rich man dreams his riches which are cares,*
> *The poor man dreams his penury and pain. . . .*
> *All dream. So what's this life? A fraud, a frenzy,*
> *A trick, a tale, a shadow, an illusion.*
> *And all our life is nothing but a dream. . . .*

Scholars have been forced into complex contortions by *Las Meninas*. E. L. Ferrari wrote: "The subject of the picture is not on the canvas but in the space where the beholder stands. The figures themselves are looking at what is presumably the subject, whose place we ourselves occupy as we look at them." As for the canvas that the painter in the picture is seen to be working on, though only the back of it is revealed to us, that—the philosopher John Searle believed—is this very painting, *Las Meninas*. Kenneth Clark took special note of the fact that, "as we step back and forth between the casual brushwork closely viewed and the real appearance of the painted world, distantly viewed, it is impossible to locate the art in *Las Meninas*." Clark had walked to and fro in front of *Las Meninas*, seeing it from various angles and distances, trying to grasp how it hung together and work out at what point "a salad of beautiful brush strokes turned into an illusion of hands, ribbons, pieces of velvet. . . . I thought I might learn something if I could catch the moment at which this transformation took place, but it proved to be as elusive as the moment between waking and sleeping." (Note the word *transformation*.) J. M. White has compared *Las Meninas* to the small stage scenes one can see, as through the glass of a telescope, in one of Samuel van Hoogstraten's peep-show boxes (Dutch, of course, and of this time). In the nineteenth century, Théophile Gautier had tried to put his finger on this "blurring of the boundaries between subject and object" when he asked "Where, then, is the picture?" Estrella de Diego has commented, astutely, "Everything in the painting is slippery, every action is suspended: it is *about* to happen or it has *just* happened." (Once again, how like Vermeer.) As I stand before *Las Meninas* I find a need to pinch myself. Am I awake? Have I got here by walking in my sleep?

And who is to blame for all this? Velázquez, the dreamer and artist, was fifty-seven at this point. He pictures himself among *La Familia*, not in the front rank but in the half light, half a pace behind. His long hair, parted in the middle, falls on either side of his face in dark brown waves. He is dressed like a gentleman, a proud *hidalgo*, certainly not as an artisan in overalls or even as a painter who gets paint on his hands and clothes. But the poised brush and sidelong look toward the second, unseen mirror or toward the king and queen positioned where we are, suggest that he is pulling the strings. He is why all this is happening. If it is a dream, it is *his* dream. He is happy in it. Everyone and everything in this picture is at his beck and call. His contemplative stare is that of a man absorbed in his task, thinking about the color and placing of his next brushstroke. Dawson W. Carr has authoritatively described the "minimum means" Velázquez used here: "The ground colour serves as a mid-tone and broad washes are broken up with strokes and dabs, some long and gestural, others short and staccato. The delicate hand gestures emerge from the barest suggestion of form and the hazy definition of features increases in the darkness behind." As noted, the red cross of the Order of Santiago must have been painted in several years later, perhaps by Velázquez himself, for he hadn't yet been honored with it. His moment of hesitant contemplation prompts us to a similar act, pausing and inviting the spectator (as Enriqueta Harris has written) to "put himself in the position of the King and Queen, the position from which they could see themselves dimly reflected in the mirror in the background, and from which they could take in the whole scene before them."

XIV. KNIGHT ERRANT. MADRID. 1658–59

THE KNIGHT WHO FIRST COMES TO OUR MIND IN EARLY-seventeenth-century Spain is that most learned proponent of chivalry, Don Quixote de la Mancha, known also as the Knight of the Woeful Countenance. Don Quixote was a self-created knight whose ambition was to be a hero, achieving noble deeds; his enchanted story has frequent correspondences with that of Diego Velázquez—though that of Don Quixote is leavened with greater humor. And Diego Velázquez, one suspects, wouldn't have been amused by the comparison. Don Quixote's creator Miguel de Cervantes had a problematic past; his obituarists and biographers tried but failed to uncover an illustrious genealogy; and although the novel was still young as a literary form, Cervantes was already pulling it about in 1605, when the first part of his masterpiece was published, stretching its dimensions, playing with its structure, teasing the reader, much as Laurence Sterne would with *Tristram Shandy*. So his character Carrasco (as we've seen) at one juncture seems to know more about what Don Quixote and Sancho Panza have been up to than they do themselves; so Cervantes's duchess disputes with Don Quixote the fact of his lady Dulcinea's existence, citing what she knows from the history of Don Quixote's life, "lately publish'd"; and so his Scholar, who helps Don Quixote find Montesino's Cave, claims to be a great admirer of books on Knight Errantry, Don Quixote's subject, and is writing a *Metamorphosis* or

Spanish Ovid. Often in Spain today one finds that the history of the La Manchan knight still serves as a guidebook. In the course of puzzling away at the subject of Velázquez one comes on serendipitous fragments in this first great novel that blend the real and the dreamlike. Here are metamorphoses, such as the transformation of the barber's brass washbasin into the golden helmet of Manbrino. Here are lances aplenty, used against many enemies, real and imaginary, and occasionally even against Quixote's now and then stalwart squire Sancho Panza. On one occasion, when the squire appears to belittle Dulcinea's peerless beauty, Sancho is hit by Don Quixote with two blows of his lance.

A good deal of scene shifting goes on in Cervantes's book. We also find the Spain where purity of blood comes foremost in a man's estimation of other men and himself, as in Sancho's claim to have a soul covered "four fingers thick with good Old Christian fat"—in other words, with pork fat and without any taint of Jewish or Moorish blood, which was considered to be black blood. (Cervantes would have felt this closely, since he is reckoned now by several scholars to have come from a *converso* background.) It was a Spain, moreover, where the ambition for higher rank was common. The desire to be considered of high status was such that Cervantes's translator into English, P. A. Motteux (born in France), noted in a wry footnote circa 1700–1703 that "In Spain all the gentry are call'd Noble." This was also the case in England. Shakespeare ensured that his father was granted the right to a coat of arms by the College of Heralds in 1596, so that he, his son William, could be called "gentleman." In Spain the court was a destination devoutly wished for, though it helped to have achieved fame in other places first, and Don Quixote recognized that not all knights could be courtiers, nor all courtiers knights-errant. But he believed it was a world in which the son of the meanest water-carrier could rise "to the very Top of human Greatness."

Velázquez (as outlined earlier) seems to have been brought up with a sense that he was born under a high star. Palomino asserted that the artist's origins were noble on both his father's and his mother's sides, "although his circumstances were modest. . . . From his earliest years [he] showed signs of his good disposition and of the good blood which flowed in his veins." The little preposition "de" in his full name, de Silva, appeared to suggest noble ancestry—though many *conversos*, burying their identities, took surnames including places; a Portuguese village called Silva lies north of Oporto, just across the border from Galicia. Did Velázquez grow up with the impression that he was the scion of an ancient Portuguese house, although one whose family pedigree had dwindled in recent times? This conviction, this sense of aristocratic connections, making almost for an aura, went on surrounding him, buoying up his name well into the twentieth century. Palomino's assertions were followed by Carl Justi and many biographers, and amplified by the twentieth-century Spanish philosopher and historian José Ortega y Gasset, who felt "the principal motivating force in Velázquez's life was the desire to be a nobleman." Ortega wrote that Velázquez's family had believed it could trace its roots back to legendary times as far as Aeneas Silvia, "king of Alba Longa." Taking Velázquez at his own word, Ortega saw him as a man with noble qualities, "a genius in the matter of disdain." He came "of a noble family which had emigrated and become impoverished, and in which moreover the preoccupation with their lineage must have been obsessive. . . . In the initial and deepest layer of his soul, Velázquez found this commandment: 'You must be a nobleman.'" Just how this supposedly aloof aristocrat could become a working painter, who was paid for his skills, yet who later claimed that he didn't really practice a craft, would become a matter of dispute not long after he had put paint to canvas in *Las Meninas*. The facts of his ancestry continued to be swallowed in the fog of the artist's upwardly mobile aspirations and even now arouse scholarly argument.

I FOLLOW HERE not Palomino or Ortega but two living historians, the Spaniard Julian Gallego and Kevin Ingram, an American professor of Spanish history in Madrid, who have both delved deeply into Velázquez's actual origins. According to Ingram, in an article for the *Boletín del Prado* in 1999, the painter's family had its roots in trade. Velázquez's grandparents most likely came into Spain from Portugal in the last quarter of the sixteenth century. His paternal grandfather was probably one Diego Rodríguez, of Portuguese origin, who was a tailor in Seville in the last part of the 1590s. Velázquez's mother Jerónima Velázquez was the daughter of a hose and trouser maker, Juan Velázquez Moreno; he and his wife, Juana Mexia, both died of the bubonic plague that struck Seville in 1599, about the time of Velázquez's birth. Velázquez's father Juan Rodríguez de Silva seems to have been a notary who worked for a church tribunal that dealt with the provisions of wills. The garment-business connection is germane to our inquiries—and to attempts made to distort or camouflage Velázquez's true origins—because many of the immigrants to Spain from Portugal in the late sixteenth century were converted Jews fleeing a revitalized Inquisition there for a country where the prosecution of Judaizers (Gallego's term) was less rigorous. The Jews had been exiled by Ferdinand and Isabella in 1492, and at this point no one still professing to be Jewish was legally allowed to live in either Spain or Portugal. Ingram points out that "two of the most popular surnames adopted by Portuguese *conversos* were Silva and Rodríguez." In *Don Quixote* one of Cervantes's characters says apologetically, "I'm sorry but I'm a tailor," a remark that would lead his audience immediately to suspect him of being wholly or partly Jewish. Another historian, Luis Mendez Rodríguez, has demonstrated that many of Velázquez's Sevillian relatives or connections worked in trades or occupations common to *conversos*. The profession of notary was also often practiced by Jews and *conversos*. From this it is easy to declare, as Ingram does, that "Velázquez's Portuguese roots may have been Jewish ones."

Given the Spanish desire for "pure blood," even suspicions on this score would have been incendiary. Problems in regard to Jewish ancestry would have been especially awkward when it came to the painter's aspirations to knighthood, qualifications for which included clean blood, good blood. Pacheco had observed Velázquez's ambitions in this respect. Velázquez had mentioned to his father-in-law in 1632 the story of how the king of France had heard that the Mannerist history painter Giuseppe d'Arpino was unhappy at being in a low order of knights and gave him much pleasure by appointing him to an order of greater prestige. At Philip's court word had spread of Velázquez's hopes. As noted, a newsletter in Madrid reported in July 1636 that he "was aspiring to become one day Gentleman of the Bedchamber and be knighted, following the example of Titian." Velázquez's portrait of Innocent X, painted in August 1650, was possibly intended to facilitate his ascent to knighthood. The pope not only gave Velázquez a gold medal and chain but his support for his chivalric ambitions because of the artist's "extraordinary" skill. Toward the end of that year Cardinal Panciroli sent a letter to the papal nuncio in Madrid giving the Vatican's backing to the artist's application for entrance to one of the Spanish military orders. But these things could take time, particularly in Philip's court, where even favorites had vocal and envious enemies; it wasn't until 1658 that the process of promoting Velázquez got properly under way. During Holy Week of that year, Palomino tells us, the king offered Velázquez his choice of membership in any of the three military orders: Calatrava, Santiago, or Alcantara. Velázquez preferred Santiago, Saint James of Compostela, whose name featured in the battle cry of the Spanish army and was his own patron saint—Diego being a form of Jago, for which the English is James. The order had been founded in 1165. Its knights promised to assist the poor, defend those making pilgrimages, and oppose those trying to invade Spain.

Velázquez must have felt gratified. The portals of the aristocracy were finally opened for him. However, everything was not yet quite done and dusted. An inquiry had to be conducted into his lineage before an investiture was performed. Under the Hapsburgs, knighthoods for painters weren't unachievable but they also weren't common: Titian and Rubens were exceptions. Apart from the matter of proving the purity of one's blood and the nobility of one's ancestry, there was a further sticking point: the rather obvious fact that most painters weren't amateurs; they worked with their hands; they painted for a living, and this down-to-earth artisan- or tradesman-like behavior was inadmissable. How do you get around that?

Velázquez acted as smartly as he could. He wrote for the Council of Military Orders a genealogy of his family "in his own hand." He then steered the two examiners for the Order of Santiago who had been appointed by the council toward the place in Portugal where, he said, his paternal grandparents—Diego Rodríguez de Silva and María Rodríguez—had come from. That was in Porto, in the north of the country. He claimed his maternal grandparents were Juan Velázquez Diaz de Rojas and Catalina de Zayas, both natives of Seville. (In fact, his parents' marriage certificate gave his mother's mother's name quite clearly as Juana Mexia—*not* Catalina de Zayas, the daughter of Andrés de Buenrostro.) In early October 1658 the royal recorder (and old friend of Velázquez) Don Gaspar de Fuensalida put up three hundred silver ducats for the inquiry expenses. The examiners took over a month looking into the family's Portuguese roots. Seventy-five people were interviewed, though well north of Porto, in Galicia, with a number saying they knew nothing about Velázquez's paternal grandparents and a few remembering only a little. The investigators couldn't cross the border because Spain and Portugal were at war and only vague accounts of the Silvas were picked up. There was a good deal of hearsay evidence to the effect that the grandparents were of noble and Old Christian stock, with no impurities of blood, Jewish or Moorish; they hadn't worked with their hands or in any low occupation. (The New Christians were Jews who had converted to Christianity, either willingly or under duress, and had blood that was by no means pure, clear, or good. The *conversos* were also called *marraños*, which meant swine.) Moving on to Madrid, the examiners listened to the testimonies of another twenty or so witnesses, some of whom were painters. Now was the time for old friends to stand up and be counted. Francisco Zurbarán, also from Seville, said he had known Velázquez for forty years and believed the Velázquezes were people of high standing and the Silvas came from northwest Portugal. Alonso Cano, who had been an apprentice of Pacheco's alongside Velázquez, a court painter in Madrid from 1638 to 1644, and godfather to Velázquez's granddaughter Inés del Mazo, stoutly maintained that Velázquez's parents were nobles, of untainted blood, properly married, and so on. He also testified (black is white, white is black) that he had "never heard that Velázquez exercised the craft of painter, nor that he ever sold a picture; he only practised his art for his own pleasure and in order to obey the King, for whom he decorated the Palace, and at whose court he fulfilled many honourable duties." Jerónimo Muñoz, a knight of Santiago, claimed that Velázquez hadn't taken the examination to become a master painter; he evidently painted for a hobby. Brushed under the carpet, apparently, were his many payments for freelance work and fees received for paintings done for the king.

Next came Seville itself, the hometown. There some fifty witnesses declared that Velázquez's maternal and paternal grandparents were *hijosdealgo*—from the lower nobility—and of clean blood. Velázquez's noble rank could be validated by showing that he sprang from people who were exempt from the meat tax. This particularly regressive levy favored the high born and well connected, in other words nobles, clerics, officers of the Inquisition, and holders of university degrees, not ordinary folk. The family tree Velázquez had provided, giving his grandparents' names and showing his maternal great-grandfather as one Andrés de Buenrostro, was checked with the city council meat-tax registers and declared to support the painter's claim. The examiners then went on to look at the records of San Pedro church, where the future painter or royal decorator had been baptized as a baby, and they confirmed his legitimacy.

WITH WHAT COLLUSION we are forced to guess, but wool was being pulled over many eyes. Velázquez or his lobbyists were going in for identity fraud on a considerable scale, especially on the maternal side of his ancestry. His mother's father was, as noted, Juan Velázquez Moreno, the hose and trouser maker, not Juan Velázquez Diaz de Rojas, and his true maternal grandmother was Juana Mexia Aguilar, not Catalina de Zayas; the names of both Juan Velázquez Díaz de Rojas and Catalina de Zayas, both real people, now dead, had been plucked into use presumably because they met the meat-tax exemption rule or had names that suggested links with nobility. "Andrés de Buenrostro" was similarly sequestrated; he was not Velázquez's great-grandfather. Kevin Ingram, the scholar who has exposed this deception in detail in the *Bulletin* of the Prado, adds: "Velázquez has lied about the paternal side of his family, too. . . . His paternal grandfather was merely a Rodríguez"— and not a "de Silva" as Velázquez had claimed, borrowing that name from his paternal grandmother in hopes, it would seem, of impressing the investigators of his noble links, going back to a misty Alba Longa, the legendary mother city of Rome. Ingram writes that the investigators for the Council of Orders failed to check the records of the marriage of Velázquez's parents; this would have brought into the open too much of the truth. Velázquez had petitioned Philip IV to have the investigators do their research work in Madrid, not on the Spain/Portugal border. Ingram concludes, "The painter was lying through his teeth; so too were the two investigators and all those witnesses who had stated that he was an *hidalgo*. Velázquez was not from a noble background." He believes that before his father got into the protective atmosphere of a cathedral office handling wills and estates, much of

Velázquez's family was in the rag trade. One reason Velázquez's parents were less in view, once their oldest son was in Madrid, may have been to protect him from searching scrutiny about his ancestry.

THE COUNCIL OF Orders had had in the past to put up with a lot of heavy persuasion from both the crown and its ministers when candidates for chivalric distinction were being presented. A number of great families including those of Medina Sidonia and Olivares had Jewish connections that they kept quiet about. At the request of Olivares, Philip IV handed out many a title, making many a duke, count, and marquis. The Order of Santiago had swollen from 242 *caballeros* in 1557 to 957 in 1625, and the rate of increase continued to grow under the count-duke's regime. Bankers became counts. The legal and banking professions harbored a number of *conversos*, many of them at court. One such was Manuel Cortizos, an accountant in the royal tax office and a city magistrate, who was often seen among the courtiers at the Buen Retiro; he was one of Philip IV's chief creditors. (In the 1680s Don Ventura Dionis—whose uncle had been an elder of the synagogue in Amsterdam—acquired the title of marquis from the Spanish king for 50,000 écus; his father had allegedly paid more for the Order of Santiago.) Many *conversos* had been caught out by the council's regulations; many a bribe was paid to sweeten the procedure and ensure a happy outcome. But the Inquisition had hardened its stance toward *conversos* after 1640. In 1653 a number of Sevillians were condemned as Jews, many of them of Portuguese extraction. Did Velázquez recall hearing in the Pacheco circle of the poet Ibn Sahl, a converted Jew who died in Seville in 1251? He was said to have drowned himself in the Guadalquivir so that, in his own words, "the pearl might return to its native land." Many people who had been Jews or were descended from converted Jews in Spain had become humanists, poets, and scholars, like the sixteenth-century author of *La Celestina*, Fernando de Rojas, a lawyer who was also mayor of Talavera, or Luis de León, a monk and poet from Salamanca, who was locked up by the Inquisition for five years. In the seventeenth century, many Jewish converts of Portuguese origin fled from Spain to Amsterdam where they went back to practicing their old religion, leaving their children to run their Spanish businesses under whatever cover they could find. However, a public relations exercise took place on behalf of Velázquez; in 1659 a courtier named Lazaro Diaz del Valle published an essay on the noble art of painting that mentioned Velázquez as a prime example *del nobilissimo arte.*

The council received its investigators' report on the Velázquez case in late February of that same year and at the beginning of April delivered its verdict. Velázquez's "purity of blood," his *limpieza,* met the councillors' test—there was no evidence, they said, that his family had Jewish or Moorish connections. But the meat-tax exemptions were insufficient on that score; they didn't satisfy the council as to the blueness of Velázquez's blood. He had therefore failed to prove that his family had noble origins. Further strings would have to be pulled if he was to gain entry into the coveted Order of Santiago. Palomino some years later suggested that Velázquez was held back because of the jealousies rife at court. The artist himself was not an envious sort, Palomino claimed. Palomino recalled the occasion on which the king told Velázquez that there were people who said his skill was limited to an ability to paint heads, and Velázquez had replied, "Sire, they favour me greatly, for I don't know anyone who can paint a head."

The Council of Orders had evidently not received any kickbacks on this occasion. The king was told a papal dispensation would be needed. So the Vatican was approached, and the pope, now Alexander VII, issued the necessary approval on June 9, 1659. After that, when the Council of Orders was still unhappy about Velázquez's purported lineage, the king ordered the Marquis of Távara to convene a special meeting of the Council of Orders, despite it being a holiday. A further dispensation or stroke of the whitewash brush was called for. The ambassador in Rome, Luis de Guzmán, was told to apply to the pope for the necessary exemptions; these attempted to ensure total compliance by naming all four Velázquez grandparents as proved noble. And Philip—who by then seems to have had enough of this protracted finagling—told the Council of Orders that Velázquez had no impediments. The king declared, stoutly, "I am certain of his nobility." Velázquez was therefore at last, by royal command, an *hidalgo.* The council conferred on him the title of knighthood on November 27, 1659, and a day later Velázquez was installed in the Order of Santiago.

The ceremony took place in the convent of Corpus Christi in Madrid. It was Saint Prosper's Day, the saint after whom the newest young heir to the throne was named, and—everyone hoped—a day of good omen. Velázquez received the costume of the order from the Count de Niebla. As a result of the artist's long career in the service of the crown, he was exempted from various onerous regulations of the order that most knights had to fulfill, such as the payment of certain taxes, naval service in the royal galleys, and the performance of religious duties in the order's convents. A year or so later the red cross of the Order of Santiago was painted on the black court uniform that Velázquez wore in his picture of the royal family, *Las Meninas*. It was traditionally said that Philip IV added this cross on Velázquez's chest with his own hand. Whatever the truth of that, the *pintor del rey* had made his supreme transformation.

We can more easily go along with Ortega's statement in *The Revolt of the Masses* that nobility was not simply a matter of inheriting noble blood, but of having qualities that set the concerned person apart from "the anonymous mass" because of an evident excellence and display of effort. "The noble life stands opposed to the common or inert life," wrote Ortega. To the Spanish mind the highest ideals of the time were honor, faith, and heroic action. On a less lofty level, Cervantes speaks on the subject of chivalry. The curate in *Don Quixote* says to the landlord of an inn, "You may put up your books"—that is, romances about knight-errantry—"and believe them true if you please, and much good may they do you. But I wish you may never halt of the same foot as your guest Don Quixote."

"There's no fear of that," says the innkeeper, "for I never design to turn Knight-Errant, because I find the customs that supported that Noble Order are quite out-of-doors."

Don Quixote himself admits elsewhere that things aren't easy in the knight business, in which he has been arduously, indeed quixotically, pursuing archaic glories: "I do not know yet what success I may have in chivalry in these deprav'd times."

ONE FURTHER NOTE in the saga of Velázquez's knighthood, which he acquired by hook and by crook. Despite the disclaimers, he was obviously a professional painter who had made a living from a position (for which he was not always promptly or overtly paid) in the royal household—a position that had been achieved because he *was* a painter, the king's painter. But on his behalf, though it was not made much of as a qualification for the honor of knighthood, I believe one should remember his famous temperament. That is, his phlegm and prudence, which Philip remarked on from time to time, in his ineffective letters of recall from Italy and in an audience with Gaspar de Fuensalida that Palomino cites. Velázquez got ahead at court without being pushy. Similarly, his paintings made their effect without conspicuous striving. There was an element of coolness in them and of the disdain referred to earlier. The fact that Velázquez didn't go overboard or get improperly, plebeianly mixed up with his pictures was regarded as a high virtue by some and by others as a fault—those for instance who were unhappy at not getting more of an erotic frisson from the *Rokeby Venus*. The distance that Velázquez puts between himself and his subjects wasn't simply a matter of using long-handled brushes. In modern parlance, Velázquez was cool. As the modern American painter Fairfield Porter has nicely put it, "He leaves things alone." He always takes a step back from the canvas to glance again at the person or persons posing for him. His use of paint was equally unexplosive, registering on the low side of the artistic temperature scale. The late-nineteenth-century Scottish art writer R. A. M. Stevenson talks of Velázquez's "unaccountable taste for certain cold harmonies, of a restrained kind, turning upon black and gray." There is nothing hotheaded about Velázquez's art. He is "wary of engaging," writes Svetlana Alpers, stressing "the pacific character of Velázquez's art, its avoidance of confrontation." Roger Fry, early in the twentieth century, in an essay on the Seicento, compared Caravaggio and Velázquez: the former combining melodrama and photographic realism; the latter also transposing mythology into the surroundings of peasant life but—unlike Caravaggio—with "distinction, detachment and scrupulous reserve." All in all, I think we can grant Velázquez his nobility not on grounds of meat-tax exemptions or ancestry but simply because of the sort of painter he was, self-possessed, thoughtful, and (Spinola's abbreviated embrace in mind) supremely empathetic.

XV. The Isle of Pheasants. Biscay and Madrid. 1660

ALL THIS TIME THROUGHOUT PHILIP'S REIGN A WAR WAS GOING on somewhere in the Spanish empire. Velázquez would have been physically close to one of the areas of fighting in Fraga, on the border between Aragón and Catalonia, where the Reapers' War, an insurrection within the war with France, went on for more than a decade. Indirectly he was aware of the conflict in the Low Countries whenever he thought about Breda. As we've seen, the city had been back in Dutch hands since 1637, after another siege, this time of only four months, conducted by Prince Frederick Henry. At that time Philip's brother the cardinal-infante had ill-advisedly shifted the king of Spain's army away from fending off the Dutch in order to take on the French elsewhere, and the Stadholder had seized his chance to encircle Breda. Then in May 1643 the veteran but threadbare Spanish Army of Flanders was routed by Condé's men at the Battle of Rocroi. Spain's hopes of regaining its dominions in the northern provinces slipped away—forever, as the 1648 Treaty of Westphalia indicated. Thereafter the arts of peace were to the fore in the United Provinces as far as Spain was concerned, and this wasn't necessarily good for business. The Dutch army was halved in size by 1650. Fewer soldiers meant fewer customers in shops and taverns; the States' income from beer excises slumped. Johannes Vermeer's uncle, a Dutch military supplier, went bankrupt within two years of the 1648 peace as less food and forage were needed. But the

Spanish empire, that widespread multinational organization, was unable to take advantage of the cessation of pressure from the Dutch. Getting an army together to put down the rebellious Portuguese proved to be an impossible task; Portugal remained outside the Hapsburg fold from that time. And France, with whom a war had been going on since 1635, presented no chance for Spanish military glory.

During the years between 1650 and 1660 the monarchy's most celebrated staff artist was especially stretched by his royal household duties, as chamberlain, curator, and decorator-in-chief. Velázquez performed the minimal tasks as royal painter, making the portraits we've seen of Princess Margarita, her mother (the king's second wife) Mariana, Mariana's stepdaughter María Teresa, and the new heir Felipe Próspero. The French reduced their hostility enough to ask for copies of the portrait Velázquez had made of María Teresa, so that Louis XIV could get acquainted with her looks. Velázquez was kept busy in both the Alcázar and Escorial palaces—the latter in greater use than for some time. Philip IV's renewed interest in the fate of his soul, and therefore in the consolations of religion, seemed to generate a zeal for improvements at his grandfather's giant monastic palace. The Hapsburg crypt, the Pantheon, was there and Velázquez was put in charge of furnishing and redecorating its sacristy. He made over one room into a gallery of Italian masters, a gallery in which Titian starred. Other chambers were redone to his orders. At the Alcázar, the king continued to look in and chat about painters and attributions with his collection's chief curator, who was concerned to ensure that His Majesty was seen by the court in as grand a setting as could be contrived. When a delegation from the French court arrived to discuss the arrangements for the proposed wedding of María Teresa and Louis XIV, who was Philip's nephew, Velázquez organized their reception in the Alcázar's Hall of Mirrors. This contained works by Rubens, Tintoretto, and Veronese, and four of his own paintings, including the *Mercury and Argus*.

The marriage was to seal a peace treaty between Spain and France, between a declining power and a reinvigorated one, both Catholic. Splendid ceremony and ornate decoration might make it look like a more equal union. An armistice in the quarter-century-long war between the two countries had been signed in May 1659, and Spain did not come too badly out of the articles in the treaty, which became known as the Peace of the Pyrenees, concluded in June 1660. Parts of Catalonia and of Flanders were to be given up by Spain to France. The surrender of María Teresa to Louis presumably wasn't going to mean a conjunction of the two monarchies, since Spain had a Hapsburg heir to hand, at least for now, in the frail form of Felipe Próspero, not yet three. The two kings were to meet between the lines, as it were, on the Bidasoa River, which divided their countries. There in midstream lay the Isle of Pheasants, close to where the river flowed into the Bay of Biscay and near what is now the town of Hendaye, west of Saint Jean de Luz. Velázquez, being chamberlain, was dispatched in advance in early April 1660 to organize the nuptial event. He was assigned a personal litter for the journey, a privilege given to only three other courtiers. His ground crew included the Surveyor of the Royal Works, José de Villa real, the Queen's Chamberlain, José Nieto, and various artisans—one being a carpenter who was ordered to ensure that there were working locks on the doors of the houses where the Spanish royal party was going to stay. The party went by way of Alcalá, Guadalajara, and Burgos, a journey of some twenty stages in twenty-three days. There were thus at least twenty halts for which the chamberlain had to reserve lodgings for the advance team and the lengthy, slow-moving royal caravansary that followed. The king's household traveled in fourteen coaches each pulled by a half dozen mules. Clothes, jewels, and costly trappings filled several hundred trunks, and fortunately—how armed the convoy was we don't know—no bandits stepped forth to raid it. The price of everything to eat and drink rose en route; for locals it was as if a plague of locusts was devouring everything in the royal path as the king and company stopped by on their journey. The royal procession barely accomplished six miles a day and took six weeks to cover the two hundred and fifty miles from Madrid to Fuenterrabía, where Velázquez had arranged lodgings for the king in the castle.

The main venue for the wedding was to be on the Isle of Pheasants. A conference hall needed to be refurbished, a bridge constructed, and everything splendidly decorated for the celebration. Palomino tells us that Velázquez went to the island by barge in order to prepare for the

big day, June 7, on which the infanta was to be handed over to the Most
Christian King of France, Louis XIV. Among the principal guests was
one who could be seen as a previous example of Spain's reaching out to
France, Philip IV's sister Anna, mother of Louis XIV and mistress of
Cardinal Mazarin, who also attended. But an air of competition was
strong. No expense had been spared by the Spaniards, who tried to put on
as good a show as they could. Velázquez had brought tapestries to liven
up the walls. The French had also brought tapestries of the struggle
between Scipio and Hannibal, and these were displayed as if in a duel
with the Spanish tapestries, four scenes from the Apocalypse. The underlying message of these was presumably one advertising their monarch
Philip as a defender of the one true faith (even if he was effectively
handing over the overlordship of Europe to Louis). The partygoers from
both sides were sumptuously dressed but the French males won the
battle of fashion in their long periwigs, fancy lace, and red high heels.
Velázquez did his best among the Spaniards, so Palomino later reported.
He had been asked to look after Philip's gift to Louis, a diamond-
encrusted watch, and Velázquez added to what Palomino called "his
gentlemanly bearing and comportment, which were courtly . . . his
natural grace and composure," and a distinction in dress. He seems to
have liked dressing up. On festive occasions at the Alcázar palace he
was noted wearing around his neck an exquisite gold chain the Duke
of Modena had given him in 1638. Here at Fuenterrabía Velázquez's
costume was trimmed "with rich Milanese silver point lace, according
to the fashion of the time, which favoured the golilla. . . . On his cloak
he wore the red insignia of Santiago. At his side was a very fine rapier
with silver guard and cap, with exquisitely chased designs in relief,
made in Italy. Around his neck was a heavy gold chain with a pendant
badge adorned with many diamonds, on which were enameled the
insignia of Santiago, and the rest of his apparel was worthy of such a
precious decoration." A very perfect knight, in fact. Velázquez watched
the king, with tears in his eyes, surrendering María Teresa to his nephew.
As he did so, Philip told Louis he was handing him a piece of his own
heart. It would have made a picture to hang alongside the affecting
image of Justin and Spinola as the Dutch gave up Breda.

* * *

IT WAS ANOTHER twenty days for the return journey from Fuenterrabia via Guadarrama, Valladolid, and the Escorial to Madrid. This time Velázquez's assistant José de Villareal went ahead preparing lodgings for the royal party while Velázquez kept in close attendance on the king. However, the journeys and his work for the ceremonies evidently took it out of the painter. Gold chains and silverpoint lace didn't balance the human scales that were weighed down with overwork and exhausting travel. Despite his claim on getting back to the capital at daybreak on June 26, that he was in good shape, he seems to have been very run down. Nevertheless his family was overjoyed to see him; there had been a rumor at court of his death while away.

From what we know, Velázquez lived up to Palomino's description of him as being "very pithy in his remarks and repartee"; he left very little correspondence; a rare letter from Velázquez—one of only two extant pieces from him—was sent on July 3, to a painter he had called on in Valladolid. This informed Diego Valentín Díaz, an old friend of Pacheco's, that Velázquez had returned to Madrid, tired but in good health. (The other letter, to Camillo Massimi of March 28, 1654, concerned some bronze fire dogs he seems to have commissioned in Rome, that had apparently just arrived in Spain.) Velázquez told Valentín that he had found his family all well, "thank God." Queen Mariana, "looking very pretty," had gone to meet the king who had returned on the same day; the royal couple had gone on to mass at the church of Our Lady of Atocha. Velázquez then told Valentín about a bullfight he had been to in the Plaza Mayor a few days after getting back, a straightforward fight without horsemen that made him remember the bullfight they had seen in Valladolid. He asked about the health of Valentín and his wife, and inquired what he could do for them. He ended:

> *Nothing is going on here of interest to you, unless it is that I*
> *pray God to preserve you for many years, as is my desire.*
> > Yours honours
> > *Diego de Silva Velázquez*
> > *g.s.m.b.*
> > (That was the abbreviation for the Spanish
> > phrase, "who kisses your hand.")

Health seemed to be uppermost in his mind, perhaps because he had intimations that his own was not good. But we don't know if he knew how imminent the peril was. As one gets older, one gets used to the idea that life is speeding up, and one may not notice until the last seconds—if then—that no time is left. A little over a month after his return to court, on the last day of July 1660, Velázquez was struck down by sickness. It was the feast day of Saint Ignatius Loyola. Velázquez had been in attendance on the king all morning, and he made his excuses to withdraw. The artist had severe burning pains in his chest and stomach. He was examined by his family doctor, Vicencio Molas, and the king sent another two court physicians to take a look at him as well. Palomino tells us that they diagnosed the beginnings of "an acute syncopal tertian fever, a condition very dangerous on account of the great weakening of the vital functions." Things looked particularly bleak because Velázquez was suffering from a constant raging thirst. Tertian ague, from which the poet Andrew Marvell is also said to have died, was the name then given to an illness which was probably malaria, but Velázquez's problem, despite the diagnosis of the royal doctors, sounds more like typhus or even yellow fever. In any event, the physicians at Velázquez's bedside in the Casa del Tesoro were soon replaced by priests. The seriousness of his condition was made clear by their high status: The king sent the Archbishop of Tyre, Patriarch of the Indies, who subjected the artist, as he lay dying, to a long sermon "for his spiritual comfort." Velázquez took the opportunity to name his old friend the Keeper of Records, Gaspar de Fuensalida, as his executor.

Then he received the Last Rites. These would have been consoling for a just-conscious believer, which by rote from childhood he may well have been. But what if there were no afterlife? What if this was it, the only life, parts of it dreamlike, and one went hereafter into dreamless nothingness? Then one had to be able to say or at least think now, I have done what I could. I have made some paintings that I hope may last for as long as paint and canvas hold together. Meanwhile, bury me in my robes as a knight of Santiago.

One imagines that as the mists formed he saw some of those pictures again: a black girl leaning over a kitchen table; a Virgin on a cloud; Juana; the field outside of Breda; an Italian Venus; his studio with the infanta and her companions. On August 6, at two o'clock in the afternoon Velázquez breathed his last. It was the cold sleep of death. No more paint; no more *flema*. He was sixty-one, and—Palomino added—a "wonder of the world."

THE REST OF Palomino's report on Velázquez's death is formal but nonetheless moving. "They put on his body the humble underclothing of the dead and then dressed him as if he were alive, as was customary with knights of military orders with the capitular cloak, with the red insignia on the breast, and with hat, sword, boots, and spurs. He was placed that night on his own bed in a darkened room, large candelabra with tapers on either side and more lights on the altar, where there was a crucifix, and he remained there until the Saturday, when they moved the body to a coffin with gilt nails and corner plates, and with two keys, lined with plain black velvet, trimmed and garnished with gold *passementerie* and surmounted by a cross with the same garniture."

Palomino might have paused here, to catch his breath or relieve any choking sensation he felt, before he went on: "When night came, and with its darkness put everyone into mourning, they carried him to his last resting place in the parish church of San Juan Bautista (near the Alcázar), where he was received by His Majesty's Gentlemen of the Bedchamber. They carried him to the catafalque that had been made ready in the middle of the principal chapel and the body was placed there on top. On both sides there were twelve large silver candelabra with tapers, and a great number of flames. The whole of his burial service was carried out with great ceremony, with excellent music from the Royal Chapel, with the softness and measure, the number of instruments and voices that were customary at functions of such great solemnity." All this was apparently based on an account given to Palomino by Juan de Alfaro, the painter from Córdoba who had been one of Velázquez's assistants. Alfaro also took the chance to sketch in black chalk Velázquez on his deathbed. The coffin containing Velázquez's body was borne by the Gentlemen of the Bedchamber to the burial vault belonging to his friend the Keeper of Records, Gaspar de Fuensalida. It was the funeral of a courtier, the elaborate ceremony owed to a high court official and knight of a military order. Alfaro called it a solemn event and in an epitaph wrote of Velázquez as "so great a man" who was now lying "in the company of heroes."

It was a time of deaths; a severe illness was clearly going around. The Italian fresco painter Agostino Mitelli, who had been working at court, had died four days before. And Juana Pacheco, Velázquez's wife, died a week after her husband—whether from the same sickness as that of Mitelli and Velázquez or simply because the shock and loss was too much for her. Sad to relate, we have little knowledge about their marriage apart from the fact of their two daughters. Were they by and large happy? He had painted her as a sibyl but how much Juana foresaw of their lives together, who knows? One suspects that he—like most geniuses—was not the easiest of men to live with; many of the concerns and niggles of his courtier's job would have been passed on to her; and then, too, he was an artist, which meant he was in pursuit of perfection, a striving in which could lie the seeds of much domestic disgruntlement.

The king, under whom Spain was going so rapidly downhill, stuck with Velázquez beyond the end. One wonders if Philip realized that his greatest achievement as monarch was his employment of the painter who ensured the king's image for posterity. But in the weeks after Velázquez's death the tongues of ill-disposed and envious colleagues in the household went on wagging. Velázquez's accounts were said to be in disarray. It was claimed that he owed the royal household's department of works a thousand ducats, and this was going to have to be repaid. Alongside a memorandum telling the king of these problems, a distressed Philip IV scribbled *Quedo abatido.* "I am still overwhelmed." The Alcázar studio room in which Velázquez had painted *Las Meninas* was officially examined so that the crown could attach some of the painter's possessions to cover his liabilities. It appeared that he had put aside some of the cash meant for salaries, for staff such as cleaners and sweepers. But Velázquez's defenders soon stood up to be counted. Fuensalida was among those who spoke for Velázquez's probity. The king himself said he thought Velázquez was "most prudent." Although some of his property was seized postmortem to cover the alleged debts, and not returned for several years, and the auditors found that he had indeed held on to 3,200 ducats for staff payments, he had been owed 1,600 ducats when he died (some of it for obligations to him going back seventeen years), and his estate eventually had to repay the crown only half the amount he had kept. Indeed, when the accounts were finally settled, it was reckoned that the royal exchequer owed Velázquez far more for overdue bills than he owed it. But the times were generally straitened: When Philip IV died in 1665 the city of Seville was broke and unable to commemorate immediately his death with the proper ceremonies.

INVENTORIES ARE INVALUABLE; they are often made at moments of crisis, when people become insolvent, have to move, or die. Velázquez's executors included his son-in-law del Mazo, who inherited Velázquez's post as court painter, Gaspar de Fuensalida, and Francisco de Rojas, the replacement *aposentador*, and they did a thorough job of listing his possessions. Velázquez's painting rooms in the Cuarto del Principe in the Alcázar and his family apartment in the Casa del Tesoro made clear both his worldly success and the sudden onset of his mortal illness. His studio contained a lay figure, some building plans, a model of a church, some pieces of sculpture, several bronze measuring devices, and much painting material, such as frames and stretchers. The canvases would now remain unpainted, at least as far as Velázquez was concerned— forever bare. There were also some paintings belonging to the king, possibly left for repair, and these included a Titian, *Spain Coming to the Aid of Religion.* In the studio there were paintings belonging to Velázquez, among them three portraits by El Greco, who had been taken up briefly by Philip II but then, falling out of favor with the king, had chosen his own way and retired to Toledo, proud of his independence. (Philip II preferred the Netherlands' painter of infernal scenes, Hieronymus Bosch, whose works decorated the royal bedroom.) Velázquez's two jobs, as court official and painter, were demonstrated in his studio by his account books as superintendent of special works and as chamberlain; the books were taken away for examination. In his apartment in the Casa del Tesoro a trunk was found to contain clothes not yet unpacked from his journey to the Isle of Pheasants. The inventory listed a great deal of silver, tapestries, draperies, and carpets. There was also jewelry aplenty, including gold medals (two were those given him by Innocent

X, bearing the pope's profile), chains, broaches, two gold scallop shells, and a ring set with nine diamonds. There were ten mirrors, much costly furniture, and several intricately decorated watches and clocks, one of which may have been that shown in the portrait he had painted of Queen Mariana in 1652.

That he was a learned man, an intellectual for that time if not a savant, was shown in his library. One hundred and fifty-four books displayed wide interests in various disciplines. Palomino said that Velázquez sought "the Proportions of the human body in Albrecht Dürer, anatomy in Andreas Daniele Barbaro, geometry in Euclid, arithmetic in Moya, architecture in Vitruvius and Vignola, as well as in other authors from all of whom he skillfully selected with the diligence of a bee all that was most useful." Velázquez owned volumes on art and aesthetics by Vasari, Leonardo, and Gracián, and collections of poetry by Góngora and Quevedo, both poets whom he had painted. Although no mention was made of any modern fiction—no Cervantes or Lope de Vega—Petrarch and Ariosto were on his shelves, together of course with Ovid, in both Spanish and Italian. He also had a number of books dealing with perspective and optical theory.

VELÁZQUEZ LEFT ABOUT 125 paintings; there is scholarly dispute about the attribution to him of several and about the amount of work he put into paintings that seem to be largely studio productions by his assistants. There are no contracts between the artist and those who commissioned his pictures. The numbers of the oeuvre rose relatively high in the mid-nineteenth century, peaking at 274 with the estimate of Charles Curtis in 1883, dropping to 83 with that of Aureliano de Beruete in 1898, and rising again to 130 with Juan Antonio Gaya Nuno in 1953. López Rey and Stratton Pruitt (most recently) agree on "about 125." Signed paintings are rare. His earliest dated painting is the *Old Woman Cooking Eggs* of 1618, and in the following two years are the *Adoration of the Magi* dated 1619, and the *Sister Jerónima de la Fuente*, signed and dated in 1620. Once in a while he inscribed himself "Velázquez" and very occasionally "Diego Velázquez" or "Diego de Silva Velázquez"—as, for example, on the *Philip IV in Brown and Silver* and the *Innocent X*, where the signature is fitted onto a sheet of paper or letter he has painted as part of the picture. Velázquez as we've seen was not an artist who painted as if there were no tomorrow; nor was he what the French call a *flaneur*. He knew *mañana* eventually comes. His court duties kept him busy, collecting, hanging, redecorating, remodeling, and masterminding ceremonies such as the Isle of Pheasants wedding. He had to cope with his notorious *flema*. In any event the numbers of paintings completed per year started fairly high but tailed off rapidly as the years passed. There were few drawings and no prints to be found—no etchings or engravings. Compared to many European artists—your average Dutch artist, for instance, who needed to paint at least one and preferably two paintings a week to make a living—his output was puny. This was so, Beruete thought, "because Velázquez never had an independent life." From entering the court at the age of twenty-three, he was always more of a servant of the king than a painter; the exercise of his household duties hindered him in the exercise of his art; and in the last eight years of his life "the artist disappeared almost entirely in the official." He didn't seem to mind.

XVI. PENULTIMATA

THERE ARE MANY LOOSE ENDS IN VELÁZQUEZ'S STORY AND NOT all of them can be neatly knotted. For instance, what happened to Juan de Pareja, once his slave? Was he at his former master's funeral? He was clearly not sent off the way Rozinante was by Don Quixote, with a brisk clap on the posterior and the parting words, "He that has lost his freedom gives thee thine." After Pareja's emancipation in 1654, Velázquez's assistant went on assisting and after Velázquez's death he went on painting; we know of religious works by Pareja such as *The Calling of St. Matthew*, which is in the Prado, and *The Baptism of Christ*, but these didn't show much influence of Velázquez, despite the long years of their attachment. After the death of Velázquez, Pareja stayed on with the family of Juan Bautista del Mazo, who as we've seen took over his father-in-law's job as painter to the king. With the license allowed to writers of fiction Elizabeth Burton de Trevino in 1965 wrote an affecting young people's novel *I, Juan de Pareja*, which has Velázquez's wife, Juana, dying before her husband and Philip IV making Velázquez a knight of Santiago after the artist's death. This gave the king himself the chance with Pareja's help to paint a posthumous red cross on the breast of the painter who a few years earlier had been seen at work on the giant canvas in *Las Meninas*. The portrait Velázquez had painted of Juan de Pareja in Rome, with Pareja as his assistant, was sold out of the Earl of Radnor's collection in 1971 and bought by the Metropolitan

Museum in New York for a then record price of $5,544,000. Palomino, a later court painter, did his best to flesh out the Velázquez life in 1724 in the third volume of his *El Museo Pictorico y Escala Optica*, in which he listed all the offices and honors Velázquez had received. Palomino had to hand the manuscript in which Velázquez's assistant Juan de Alfaro (who was seventeen when Velázquez died) had jotted down notes about the master. As for del Mazo, he remarried after Francisca's death but went on painting in his late father-in-law's style; many pictures once attributed to Velázquez are now credited to del Mazo.

Velázquez's granddaughter Inés remarried in Madrid in 1661 and the names of four other of his and Juana Pacheco's grandchildren are recorded: Gaspar, Baltasar, Teresa, and Melchor. One further unresolved aspect of things is what happened to Velázquez's natural son Antonio. Not long after the painter's death his friend and executor Gaspar de Fuensalida declared that Velázquez had made not two but three journeys to Italy. Fuensalida ought to have known the facts of this if anyone did, though the trip has never been substantiated. It might have been something wished for by Velázquez—going to see his son and his son's mother again—rather than something he actually accomplished. He may well have wanted to drink in again Italian air, Italian painting. He may have wanted to be seduced again. Throughout his career in the years after Seville, Velázquez borrowed ideas and themes from Italian artists and in particular quoted Titian and Tintoretto. However, as Jonathan Brown has observed, his "response to Italian art is circumspect." Unlike Rubens and Poussin, who threw themselves wholeheartedly into Italian art, "Velázquez kept his distance."

FOR A CENTURY or so thereafter others kept their distance from him. They were helped to do so by the fact that Spain and its empire had lost its clout; Spain was isolated from the rest of Europe and considered as at best a romantic, backward land of guitars and gypsies. Voltaire lumped it with the wilder parts of Africa and didn't want to know it any better. Most Europeans regarded Spain as dark and half dead, buried in royal bureaucracy and stifled by a Church that had lacked the invigorating reforming impulse of Protestantism. The long shadow of the Inquisition continued to fall over the Catholic faith in the eyes of most foreigners and many Spaniards, who found the Church's practices hatefully oppressive. As for Velázquez, he, too, seemed to have gone into hiding. No prints of his works were published until Goya made an etching after *Las Meninas,* circa 1778. The fact that most of Velázquez's works had been created for the king and that few were in private collections meant that no visible market for his paintings existed. They were sequestered in royal palaces and rarely seen publicly, except by those who as visitors were given access to the Escorial. The fire in the Alcázar of 1734 that destroyed many of the rooms Velázquez had designed and arranged, and many of the treasures he had collected to put in them, caused the loss of a number of paintings. Among them were his *Expulsion of the Moriscos* and three of the four mythological pictures he had painted for the Salon de los Espejos. But he was never lost, in the way some master painters have been—one thinks once again of Vermeer, whose identity was hidden in a muddled pack of other Dutch masters, and required rediscovery and disentanglement in the nineteenth century. In the years after Velázquez's death several artists who came to Madrid paid homage to the painter originally from Seville. Luca Giordano, a Neapolitan invited to paint at the court for King Carlos II, as we've seen expressed his fervent admiration for *Las Meninas* as the theology of painting, and painted a *Homage to Velázquez* (London: National Gallery), which was not very Velázquez-like. Apart from del Mazo there were (as Brown has noted) no followers, no "school of Velázquez." However, there was certainly an increasing awareness of him. Palomino's book in 1724 brought Velázquez to the attention of many, not just in Spain; a shortened English translation came out in 1739. In this period a copy of the *Innocent X* was brought to London for the prime minister Sir Robert Walpole and was sent on to the family seat of Houghton Hall in Norfolk. The portrait of Juan de Pareja, which also reached Britain, was purchased in 1788 by the Earl of Radnor. As time passed, word of mouth generated more and more interest in Velázquez among the English nobility and grand tour upper classes— the Earl of Carlisle, for example, who bought a copy of Velázquez's *Juan de Pareja* and (thinking it was by Correggio) Velázquez's *Baltasar Carlos with a Dwarf,* which is now in Boston.

It was not all admiration. Anton Mengs, a neoclassical German artist and writer on art who became court painter to Charles III, wasn't totally enraptured by Velázquez when Mengs first came to Madrid in 1761, although he gave Velázquez's naturalism full marks, just as Pacheco had done early on. Mengs saw how Velázquez had moved on from the realism of *The Waterseller* to a more loosely painted style in *The Spinners*, where, he wrote, "it seemed the hand played no role in the execution." A pupil of Mengs, Francisco Bayeu, had taught and become the brother-in-law of Francisco Goya (1746–1828). In 1778, when he was thirty-two, Goya had been made a painter to the king and had the job of making engravings after works in the royal collections. He was impressed by Velázquez's painting, not least his use of blacks and grays and his ability to create likenesses with a small number of powerful brushstrokes. Goya went on to paint a royal group portrait, *Charles IV and His Family* (Prado, 1800–1801), in which the painter stands in a *Las Meninas*–like shadow at his easel to one side of the family members, who are crammed, spotlit, at what seems to be the front of a stage. Goya's son said later that his father above all studied and looked at nature, which he declared to be his mistress (as Constable also would), but "he looked with veneration at Velázquez and Rembrandt." However, unlike Velázquez, Goya moved in his paintings from light to dark; his last paintings were as morbidly black as can be. There was moreover little of the deferential courtier about Goya. He kept no distance from the subjects of his pictures. The *flema* wasn't one of his obvious characteristics.

The "prime version"—Xavier Bray's term—of the *Juan de Pareja* arrived in England in the last decades of the eighteenth century with the help of its then owner, Sir William Hamilton, the British envoy in Naples. In 1801 Sir William was short of cash and asked John Christie to auction it; the sale price was £42. Another version had been bought by the fourth Earl of Carlisle on one of his two Italian tours and it ended up in the great house of Castle Howard in Yorkshire until sold to pay for reroofing in 1972. By the late eighteenth century Velázquez's coolness was being warmed to by many British visitors. The connoiseur and collector William Beckford called *Joseph's Blood-stained Coat Brought to Jacob*, then in the Escorial, "the loftiest proof in existence of the extraordinary powers of Velázquez." The diarist Henry Swinburne said the *Olivares* on horseback was "the best portrait I ever beheld." He didn't know which to admire most, "the chiaroscuro, the life and spirit of the rider, or the natural position and fire of the horse." In the late 1770s the British Ambassador to Spain, Lord Grantham, and his brother Frederick paid a German painter Wenceslaus Pohl to make small copies of the Velázquezes in the Spanish royal collection. Grantham also bought five sets of the etchings after Velázquez that Goya made in 1778 and had them sent to London, one set being for Sir Joshua Reynolds, president of the newly founded Royal Academy. Sir Joshua was said to have copied only two portraits in his life, one being Velázquez's *Innocent X*. Reynolds declared, "What we are all attempting to do with great labour, Velázquez does all at once." (However, as Mengs had observed, spontaneity takes much practice.) Reynolds's pupil James Northcote looked at a Velázquez portrait and said that "it seemed done while the colours were yet wet; everything was touched in as it were, by a wish; there was such a power that it thrilled through your whole frame, and you felt as if you could take up the brush and do anything."

The disasters of war, documented by Goya, were terrible for Spain and Spanish paintings but not completely disastrous for the Velázquez works in the country. The Peninsula War, the Spanish War of Independence (1808–13), and French armies marauding through Spain forced openings in the somewhat sealed envelope of that nation and brought its art, including Velázquez, into a gunsmoke-clouded daylight. Although Spain had established restrictions on the export of paintings in 1779, the continuous conflict loosened its grip. Some Velázquez paintings were taken as trophies or changed hands either under duress or in trade. The French Marshal Soult was among the Napoleonic soldiers who early on gathered up Spanish art for France. The British landscape painter George Augustus Wallis spent five years in Madrid from 1808 to 1813, acting as agent for a Scots art dealer named William Buchanan and acquiring pictures—among them *The Toilet of Venus*. Bartholomew Frere, the Briton sent to represent his country to the Spanish government, then sheltering in Seville, purchased two Velázquezes while there, *Saint John the Evangelist* and *The Immaculate Conception*, and took them home. An army officer, Lieutenant-Colonel Henry Packe, acquired the rather drab and disunited *Kitchen Scene with Christ in the House of Martha and Mary* in Seville, where it had apparently graced the house of the Duke of Alcalá. *An Old Woman Cooking Eggs* seems to have come to England about the same time and was sold in London in May 1813. Goya like many Spaniards welcomed into his country Napoleon's brother Joseph Bonaparte, who had been made King of Naples in 1806 but was thought to be a relative liberal. Goya worked for Joseph but hated the French troops and abhorred the atrocities they committed.

Goya also painted the British army commander the Duke of Wellington, who fought Joseph's army at the Battle of Vitoria, in the Basque country, in 1813, and achieved a valuable victory. The value lay not only in Wellington's success in practically freeing Spain from French domination, but in the booty captured. At the end of the all-day battle, the French abandoned 143 cannons, great stores of ammunition, three thousand wagons and carriages, fine wines, battle standards, and many chests containing money and treasure—more than a million pounds in sterling and the Bourbon crown jewels. There were also hundreds of horses and mules, pet monkeys and parrots, and numerous women, some "fancy," some less so: it was *"un bordel ambulant,"* as one female who was there described it. But the real treasure from our point of view was found in one carriage. The king and his immediate entourage had fled. In the king's carriage were a large number of state papers, love letters to the king from his mistresses, and his silver chamber pot. (This last trophy, according to Wellington's biographer Christopher Hibbert, was, in 1997, still owned by the King's Royal Hussars, the regiment of the officer who captured Joseph's carriage, and was used in the regimental mess for champagne toasts on officers' guest nights.) Picking over these trophies slowed down the pursuit of the French by the Allied army of British, Spanish, and Portuguese. But fortunately recognized at once as priceless were many rolled-up canvases. Among them were a Correggio *Gethsemane* and five paintings by Velázquez, *The Waterseller, Two Young Men at Table, Portrait of a Man (José Nieto), Mars at Rest,* and an *Innocent X.* The duke gave these pictures his protection and ensured that crucial items of "Joseph's Baggage" got safely to London rather than Paris. (*Two Young Men at Table* and *The Waterseller* were both attributed to Caravaggio when first in London, Italian rather than

Spanish painters having more *réclame* at that point and Caravaggio in particular having a splashier reputation.) When he got back home in 1815, the Iron Duke generously offered to return the paintings to Ferdinand VII, who regained the Spanish throne. But though the offer of the *Mars* was accepted and the painting was sent back to the Alcázar, the duke was given the others as thanks for getting rid of the French. We find in the bottomless resources of Cervantes an account of the occasion in which the Knight of the Wood tells Don Quixote, after their combat, that the Don's spoils "must now attend the Triumphs of my Victory, which is the greater." And furthermore, said the Knight of the Wood, "the Reputation of the Victor rises in Proportion to that of the Vanquish'd; and all the latter's Laurels are transferr'd to me." Despite similarities in words, this isn't quite what Spinola said to Justin of Nassau at Breda.

Goya was a man for most seasons and went back to working for the Spanish court under the restored Ferdinand VII from 1814 to 1824. The new Prado Museum was opened by the king in 1819, with the public being let in finally to see the royal collections now housed there. The British artist Sir David Wilkie visited the Prado in 1827 and waxed enthusiastic about Velázquez as a new artistic power, a master whom "every true painter must in his heart admire" and one who clearly was a great influence on such British artists as Reynolds, Romney, Raeburn, Jackson, and Sir Thomas Lawrence. William Hazlitt, portrait painter and one of the most perceptive writers of the time, showed the impact of Velázquez in his striking 1804 portrait of the essayist Charles Lamb, dressed all in black save for an off-white golilla collar. Lamb's pale face in the painting had an underlying olive tone, which made him look more like a native of Seville than of London. Hazlitt it was who wrote: "One is never tired of painting, because you have to set down not what you know already, but what you have just discovered. In the former case, you translate feelings into words; in the latter, names into things. There is a continuous creation out of nothing going on. With every stroke of the brush, a new field of inquiry is laid open; new difficulties arise, and new triumphs are prepared over them. . . . The air-wave visions that hover on the edge of existence have a bodily presence given them on the canvas." *The air-wave visions!* How this makes one think of Velázquez's paintings—visions, in Northcote's words to Hazlitt, touched in by a wish.

Meanwhile *The Surrender of Breda* continued to hang in Madrid. It never went far. It had been listed among the pictures in the Retiro palace in 1702, valued at five hundred doubloons. By 1772 it was in "the new palace"—Justi's term, presumably the eighteenth-century Palacio Real that had replaced the Alcázar and stood on the west side of the city, its east front facing the Plaza de Oriente—but by then the painting seemed to have lost some of its original bearings. Antonio Ponz, a Spanish art historian and guidebook writer, thought in 1775–76 that the hero of the *Breda* was the Marquis of Pescara. Ponz's contemporary Anton Rafael Mengs, who knew little about the painting's subject other than that it represented the capitulation of a fortress after a siege, believed the successful general was the Marquis of Leganes, Spinola's son-in-law and a kinsman of Olivares. At this stage the taxable value of the painting had increased to 120,000 reals. A little later the British traveler Richard Ford, a Devonshire gentleman who toured Spain on horseback in the early 1830s and whose vigorous handbooks on relatively unknown Spain were much read in the mid-nineteenth century, said that *The Surrender of Breda* was perhaps Velázquez's finest picture: "Never were knights, soldiers or national character better painted, or the heavy Fleming, the intellectual Italian, and the proud Spaniard more nicely marked, even to their boots and breeches; the lances of the guard actually vibrate." Constable's friend and biographer the Anglo-American painter Charles Leslie wrote about the thrill of coming on Velázquez and delight in the *Breda* in his *Handbook for Young Painters* (1855). Although he hadn't seen the picture in the flesh, only in reproductions, Leslie thought it testified to Velázquez's great dramatic powers. Leslie was moved by the way in which Velázquez showed Spinola's reluctance to take the keys of Breda from Justin. Spinola, he wrote, would not allow his recent antagonist to kneel but rather, "laying his hand gently on his shoulder, he seems to say, 'fortune has favoured me, but our cases might have been reversed.' To paint such an act of generous courtesy was worthy of a contemporary of Cervantes." However, Leslie then felt the need to acknowledge the natural *hidalgo* in Velázquez. "It is not," Leslie writes, "in the choice of subject, but in the manner in which he has brought the scene before our eyes, that the genius and mind of Velázquez are shown. The cordial unaffected bearing of the conqueror could only have been represented by as thorough a gentleman as himself." And Leslie notes that Richard Ford—affected by the same chivalrous inclination—had observed that the gentleman painter "had introduced his own noble head into this picture, which is placed in the corner with a plumed hat."

A less sedate afterlife than the *Breda*'s has been that of the *Venus with a Mirror*. By 1800 the *Venus* had passed from the de Haro/Guzmáns to the collection of the dukes of Alba. It was believed to have been a fond possession of the Duchess of Alba, and possibly therefore to have influenced the painting by Goya, the duchess's lover, of his two *Maja*s, one naked and one clothed. William Buchanan's agent George Wallis got his hands on it in Madrid in 1808, and Buchanan brought it to England in 1813; it was sold the following year to John Morritt of Rokeby Hall in Yorkshire. Sir Thomas Lawrence, the celebrated portrait painter, had advised Morritt to buy it. Morritt was a classical scholar, a member of parliament, and a friend of the historical novelist Sir Walter Scott. After Velázquez's nude arrived at Rokeby Hall, Morritt wrote to Scott:

> I have been all morning pulling about my pictures and hanging them in new positions to make room for my fine picture of Venus's backside which I have at length exalted over my chimney-piece in the library. It is an admirable light for the painting and shows it to perfection, whilst raising the said backside to a considerable height, the ladies may avert their downcast eyes without difficulty and connoisseurs steal a glance without drawing the said posterior into the company.

Since 1906 Venus's backside has been on public view in London, yet has continued to make difficulty for some of its viewers, their responses tugged between love, lust, embarrassment, and even—for a few— disgust. Velázquez's *Venus* doesn't exactly titilate today's hardened audience, but many earlier male viewers thought she was sexually exciting—and women assumed that men got an illicit frisson from looking at "the said backside." The *Venus*'s very existence in seventeenth-century Spain, in what Kenneth Clark called "the prudish and corseted court of Philip IV," seemed to unleash, as in recoil, all sorts of fantasies. Although to Clark's mind "a dispassionate work," she nevertheless prompted passionate acts. The *Venus* was acquired from the Morritt family by the London dealers Agnews in 1905. There were patriotic concerns that the painting was on its way to the Kaiser Friedrich Museum in Berlin, to the Louvre in Paris, or to a robber baron collector in the United States, and thirty thousand people went to Agnews to see it. The asking price of £45,000 needed to buy it for the National Gallery had to be raised. But the National Art Collections Fund drummed up support. Henry James and Roger Fry were among the many who dug deep into their pockets, as did King Edward VII, no prude, whose at-the-time last minute anonymous donation saved the *Venus* for the British nation.

At the National Gallery in London in March 1914, a few months before the declaration of war with Germany, a woman named Mary Richardson, armed with a meat cleaver, attacked the painting, slashing the beautiful buttocks. Ms. Richardson was a suffragette, a drum major in the militant organization's fife-and-drum marching band. She was dedicated to the excellent cause of gaining the right to vote for women, but she acted, she said, because "she hated the way men gawped at the *Venus*." Possibly, as some have suggested, sexual frustration was involved; perhaps, too, there was an element of simple power hunger behind her action. "Slasher" Richardson became in 1934 the head of the women's section of the British Union of Fascists. Before then the painting had received the expert attentions of Helmut Ruhemann, German-born chief restorer of the National Gallery, and today it looks completely unscarred. It is however now protected by shatterproof glass, and the gallery guards keep a cautious eye on visitors who dawdle for a suspiciously long time in front of the picture.

AN ANGLO-SAXON ATTACHMENT to and even acquisitiveness for Velázquez was matched in the mid-nineteenth century by the French. Indeed, the French infiltrated and took over the British liking for the Spaniard's art in such a way that they came to seem to have been there first. In 1688 André Félibien, the French architect, antiquarian, friend of Poussin, and writer on painting, had called Velázquez an "unknown." The Louvre had originally hung Velázquez in galleries marked "Italian School" but a *Galerie Espagnole* was established in the Louvre in 1838 by King Louis-Philippe, with some four hundred Spanish paintings acquired by his agents, Baron Taylor and the artist Adrien Dauzats, many of the works being bought for little and smuggled into France. Interest in Spanish painting was thereafter stimulated among French writers—Thoré, Taine, Michel, Baudelaire, and Faure, among others. Thoré in 1857 called Velázquez one of the supreme artists of all time and Faure found in him "a brother to Beethoven." Théophile Gautier, also a critic, famously asked of *Las Meninas*, "Where is the painting?" Moreover, French artists, Degas and Courbet among them, found much to marvel at in Velázquez's work. The world seemed to have changed in a way that took account of his art's complexity. One can say that above all it was other artists who saw the many dimensioned depths of his artistry and responded: They saw that Velázquez was among the truly great. The wait for worldwide fame had gone on long enough.

Toward the end of the nineteenth century, three painters from three countries took an exceptional interest in Velázquez: Vincent van Gogh (1853–90); Edouard Manet (1832–83), who frequently turned to Velázquez for inspiration and often used Velázquez's subjects as his own; and James McNeill Whistler (1834–1903). Manet, writing to Henri Fantin-Latour, described Velázquez as "the painter of painters," and announced to Baudelaire, "At last I've really come to know Velázquez and I tell you he's the greatest artist there has ever been. . . . He's greater than his reputation and compensates all by himself for the fatigue and problems that are inevitable on a journey in Spain." Manet paid homage to Velázquez in a number of pictures including an oil showing Velázquez painting. The empress Eugenie, Napoleon III's wife, was a Spaniard—she had been the Countess de Teba—and Paris was then full of everything Spanish, singers, dancers, and musicians such as the renowned guitarist Huerta. Manet's *Le Guitarrero* won an award at the salon in 1861. He wanted his mirror painting, *The Bar at the Folies-Bergère*, to be hung one day between a Titian and Velázquez's *Spinners, The Fable of Arachne*. Bizet's opera *Carmen* opened in Paris in

1875, based on the 1845 novella by Prosper Merimée, and after a shaky
start proceeded to become one of the most popular operas of all time,
throwing a melodramatic light on Seville and Spain by way of the fatal
love of the beautiful cigarette factory worker Carmen with corporal
Don José. In Marcel Proust's *In Search of Lost Time*, not set to music as
yet, the Duc de Guermantes affects to be the owner of a painting that
might just be (he hopes) a Velázquez. He had bought it from his cousin
Gilbert. "It was sold to me as a Philippe de Champaigne," the duke
tells the narrator Marcel, "but I believe myself that it's by someone
even greater. . . . I believe it to be a Velázquez, and of the very best
period." The duke then requests Charles Swann, who is also on hand,
to come up with an attribution. Swann, lover of Vermeer above all
painters, lightly suggests the painting is a bad joke, and this provokes
an outburst of rage from the duke.

As for van Gogh, toward the tragic end of the Dutch painter's life,
Velázquez was often in his thoughts. In mid-August 1888 he wrote
from Arles to his brother Theo, thanking him for some canvas and
paints, and telling him, touchingly:

> This restaurant where I am is very queer; it is completely grey;
> the floor is of grey bitumen like a street pavement, grey paper
> on the walls, grey blinds always drawn, a big green curtain in
> front of the door which is always open, to stop the dust coming
> in. Just as it is it is a Velázquez grey—like in the *Spinning
> Women*—and the very narrow, very fierce ray of sunlight
> through a blind, like the one that crosses Velázquez's picture,
> even that is not wanting, Little tables, of course, with white
> cloths. And behind this room, in Velázquez grey you see the
> old kitchen, as clean as a Dutch kitchen, with floor of bright
> red bricks. . . . There are two women who wait, both in
> grey. . . . I don't know if I describe it clearly enough to you, but
> it's here, and it's pure Velázquez.

People who otherwise got along not at all with one another could
at least be found agreeing about Velázquez as a painter at the forefront
of Spanish art, or of art anywhere. John Ruskin, the voluminous

critic and social theorist, included Velázquez among the great artists who had a "self-commanding, magnificent animality"—though what Ruskin's experience was of animality, the Lord knows. Ruskin also said that "considered as pieces of art only, the works of Velázquez are the only consummate pieces in the world." However, James McNeill Whistler, whose famous libel action against Ruskin won him not the £1,000 damages he wanted but a mere farthing, fulminated against Ruskin and other art critics in December 1878 for "crass idiocy and impertinence." Whistler's ire had been detonated by a London *Times* art writer who had found Velázquez "slovenly in execution, poor in colour—being little but a combination of neutral greys and ugly in its forms!" Whistler's paintings paid a purer respect to Velázquez—the portraits, for example, of Thomas Carlyle, of Whistler's mother, of Miss Cicely Alexander, and of himself in the late picture called *Brown and Gold*, which showed the painter appearing as a tall dark form out of spectral mist. Whistler owned a number of prints of paintings by Velázquez. He also possessed one particular prize, an early photograph of a detail from *Las Meninas*. An 1857 visit to the spectacular Art Treasures exhibition in Manchester had an immense influence on Whistler; back in London he pored over photographs of Velázquez works that he kept in his studio.

Many artists have used Velázquez as a foil—among them American artists as different as John Singer Sargent and Mary Cassatt. Sargent went to Spain in 1880 and took on board the influence of Velázquez, particularly as it was visible in Courbet and Manet: Sargent's scandalously successful *Madame Gautreau* of 1884 is evidence of this. Mary Cassatt like Sargent studied in France and seems to have been bowled over by the way the French had taken up Spanish art. (As well as American painters, American collectors such as J. P. Morgan and Henry Clay Frick began to get possessive about Velázquez.) Wyndham Lewis, the modern British artist and writer, painted a *Surrender of Barcelona* (1936–37), which combined cubist/vorticist forms and mechanistic figures, men in seventeenth-century visored helmets and armor, and both foot and horse soldiers bearing upright pikes in a nod to *Breda*. (The fluid post-Baroque forms of the Barcelona architect Gaudí appear to be more related to El Greco than Velázquez.) As for Pablo Picasso, the twentieth-century arch conjurer, though born in Málaga he made his cubist mark as a Parisian, French, and European showman—at a time when an increasingly strident mass media promised celebrity—rather than as a specifically Spanish artist. His skills in mimicry were indeed spurred by *Las Meninas* into a characteristic bout of overproduction. The result was more than fifty "variations" after that picture, mostly much whiter and lighter than the original. (They took up a mere two months of Picasso's time in Cannes in the summer of 1957.) Picasso's more genuine genuflection to his Spanish predecessor was to be found in his *Woman Ironing*, painted in Paris in 1904, though the angular, emaciated blue-gray female figure in that picture is more of a Sarajevo or Belsen victim than a Seville kitchen girl and again, in style if not in subject, maybe more El Greco than Velázquez.

A less prolific and less journalistic modern involvement with Velázquez than Picasso's *Las Meninas* series was that of Francis Bacon, whose obsession focused rather on the portrait of *Innocent X*. When in Rome, Bacon refused to go see the version of the painting itself, which hangs at the Galleria Doria-Pamphilj, but he bought reproductions of it for use in making studies of it. His 1953 *Study* conveys some of the horror and violence the Anglo-Irish painter found in Velázquez's picture, with the papal throne turned into what looks like an electric chair, the canvas a grid charged with a lethal current, and the pope's mouth jolted open in a rictus of death. In a confessional conversation with the critic David Sylvester, Bacon unburdened himself of thoughts prompted by the *Innocent X*, "one of the greatest portraits that have ever been." Bacon said that he admired Velázquez's desire to walk along the edge of a precipice and his ability to keep "so near to what we call illustration and at the same time so deeply unlock the greatest and deepest things that man ever can feel." Much of this may be more Bacon than Velázquez. Bacon's pope lets out a scream that seems to have a sadomasochistic origin. Velázquez's pope appears more on the defensive; if he is ready to strike a blow, it is only because he thinks it the best way of protecting himself.

Picasso and Bacon both bring us to the subject of value, as judged— often weirdly—in monetary terms. The art market is a strange beast. A herd mentality often prevails. At the moment Picasso rides high, Bacon high, van Gogh very high, Jackson Pollock immensely high. At this

Francis Bacon, Study after Velázquez's Innocent X,
1953, Des Moines Art Center.

writing a Pollock painted in 1948 holds the present record sale price of
$140 million, obtained in 2006. Picasso appears frequently in the
highest-prices-at-auction lists because he was so prolific an artist and is
currently so fashionable. But a painter like Velázquez is nearly invisible
in such lists. Few Velázquezes are sold. The museums that own them
can't or have no need to sell them and the smart owners don't want to
part with them: They are too valuable to sell, too wonderful, they are
priceless. They aren't gambling chips or stock certificates. The under-
stated yet inestimable value of Velázquez is nicely suggested in J. I. M.
Stewart's delirious 1949 thriller *The Journeying Boy*, written under the
pseudonym Michael Innes, where the eminent and well-to-do nuclear
scientist father of the much-threatened-with-kidnap youth Humphrey
has two portraits by the master discreetly hanging—amid Spanish

furnishings suitable for a modern grandee—in the library of his London mansion. Of the most recent sales of Velázquez paintings, among the few known are the *Juan de Pareja* sold in 1970 for £2,310,000 ($5,544,000), and the *Santa Rufina*, a painting of the early 1630s described as "a work of particular intimacy and simplicity," showing the woman who was martyred and became with her sister Justa one of Seville's patron saints. The *Santa Rufina*—probably modeled by Juana Pacheco, Velázquez's wife—was not seen in public between the 1640s, when in the Madrid collection of Olivares's nephew Don Luis de Haro, and 1868, when it reappeared on the walls of the Earl of Dudley in England; it was sold in New York in 1999 for just over eight million dollars and in July 2007 went at Sotheby's in London to a Seville foundation for £8.4 million, over seventeen million dollars. This was not only a world auction record price for Velázquez but the highest price ever achieved for a Spanish Old Master painting.

There are elements of guesswork, not so say blarney, in these figures. Both Picasso and Bacon have a certain notoriety value. Both acquire matter for their pictures cannibalistically from the works of earlier artists—Velázquez included. The *Juan de Pareja*, were it possible to sell it, might fetch a hundred million dollars today. And I believe Bacon would have willingly acknowledged Velázquez's top position. Unlike some of the contemporary auction-list champions, Velázquez combined in one masterwork after another the ability to feel, the ability to think, and the ability to apply paint. This is not to say that one doesn't admire Bacon's attempt to reach the heart of the matter. He was trying to pin down what Velázquez—"an amazingly mysterious painter"—was getting at. Bacon went on to say, "I think that Velázquez believed he was recording the [Spanish] court at that time; but a really good artist today would be forced to make a game of the same situation; photography has altered completely this whole thing of figurative painting." Furthermore—Bacon said with feeling—a sense of despair was now part of the artistic process: "Man now realises that he is an accident, that he is a completely futile being, that he has to play out the game without a reason." The Carthaginian early Christian thinker Tertullian wrote: *I believe because it is absurd.* In Velázquez's time, Bacon continued, an artist like Velázquez was still "slightly conditioned by certain types of religious possibilities, which man now . . . has completely cancelled out for him." Just how much Velázquez was conditioned by religion, by whatever Jewish blood he retained, or by the surrounding "sea of faith" that buoyed up so many and caused storms that scattered others, we don't know. We do know of his phlegm and his detachment. We detect a man, who, despite being a civil servant, cocooned in his courtier's garb, went on asking piercing questions and creating in his art a radiance of duality and doubt. For Velázquez, the haze of mystery was almost a fourth dimension (the dimension of dreams), and it took the place of any simple answer.

XVII. *LAS LANZAS*. BREDA AND SEVILLE.

O N WAKING IT CAN TAKE AN EFFORT TO CLIMB OUT OF A dream into the light and air. Deprived of personal detail from letters and conversations, one plunders pictures, connections, correspondences. In Schiller's play *Don Carlos*, which provided the gist for Verdi's opera *Don Carlo*, the revolt of the Netherlands against Spain and in particular the personal rebellion of the pro-Flemish, radicalized infante against his father, a malevolent Philip II, and against an even more menacing Grand Inquisitor, lies at the heart of the action. The play and opera set the tone for the historian Motley's slightly later take on that period, where plucky little Holland defeated a puffed-up and perverted Spain. (Don Carlos is madly in love with the queen, the twenty-two-year-old Elizabeth of Valois, his former fiancée but now stepmother, married to his father Philip II.) In George Bernard Shaw's play *The Doctor's Dilemma*, the young artist Dubedat, dying of consumption, says "I'm perfectly happy. I'm not in pain. . . . I've . . . fought the good fight. And now it's all over, there is an indescribable peace. I believe in Michelangelo, Velázquez, and Rembrandt; in the might of design; in the mystery of colour; in the redemption of all things by Beauty everlasting, and the message of Art that has made these hands blessed." Dying five years before his king, the king's painter didn't have to witness the demise of his greatest patron, Philip IV, who lived until 1665, leaving in Carlos II an heir who made a particularly impotent monarch—well-matched to his increasingly impoverished country. Golden Ages don't go on forever; by definition they have a beginning and an end; the Dutch found this, too, though more genially. Velázquez was fortunate to squeeze his life into the last part of one of the greatest Golden Ages. He did better still by growing all the way from young prodigy to mature genius.

I WENT RECENTLY to Breda to get the lie of the land and examine the terrain out of which Velázquez without ever going there conjured his martial masterpiece. I traveled by overnight ferry across a calm North Sea and then by train through Rotterdam, over the great rivers, Waal and Maas, past Dordrecht, south into Brabant. Mist hung over the low meadows, the air was filled with moisture, the land was like a giant sponge. Even the early June sunshine was watery. My hotel was on the edge of town and the bus drivers were on strike, but the hotel (*Het Scheephuis*, the Ship House) kept a half dozen bicycles for its clients. I cycled daily to the Breda town archives to read about Ambrogio Spinola and the Spanish occupation. I walked through the Grote Markt, where Descartes had strolled in contemplation during the period after the turfship success, when the Dutch had controlled Breda. *The Surrender of Breda* still hangs resplendently in the Prado in Madrid, but I looked at the two huge replicas of the painting that are here, one in the Town Hall, the other in the Breda museum, where a curator pointed out to me one mistake Velázquez had made and that these copies had copied: He had painted the Dutch ensigns as horizontal tricolors of (from the top down) blue, red, and white when in fact the United Provinces *Prinsen* flag, which served from 1572 to the 1630s, had been—from the top—orange, white, and blue; several years after the siege it became red, white, and blue. I walked, too, around the outside of the castle walls, through the pretty Valkenberg Park, and along the calm canals. The *castell*, now the Dutch military academy, its Sandhurst or West Point, stands at one corner of what was the old walled town. One of the remaining canals enters the walls at what is still called the Spaniards' Gate; alongside the quayside just outside this a big coal-black iron barge was moored. The vessel had been converted into a floating café-restaurant named *Spinola*. No hard feelings! Other conflicts have intervened—and other surrenders. One recalls news photos of terms being signed in the railway carriage at Compiègne, and Field Marshal Montgomery accepting the German surrender in 1945. The bars and cafés of Breda were awash with orange banners, flags, and scarves in anticipation of the football World Cup matches.

I made a thorough reconnaissance by bike of the country around Breda and found no natural eminence high enough for the view Velázquez posits in his *Surrender*. But although the generous suburbs have spread out into the low hinterland where Spinola's men set up their siege positions, one can still find the separate villages that Chaplain Hugo recorded as strategic sites, places of skirmish, concentrated defense, or armed confrontation. From Teteringen toward Wisselaar and Terheijden a narrow road runs across the old polders along the Zwarte Dijk, the Black Dike, that is visible in Velázquez's picture as a dark line above a flooded area of the countryside. I made a farther excursion one morning with a Dutch friend, Lies Vonkeman, a psychologist from IJist in Friesland, out past the spot near the Hertogenbosch gate in the walls where Justin is said to have handed over the keys of the town. We cycled northward to Teteringen and then, after asking directions at a village store, pedaled on past the church and several street junctions at the central square, and then westward across the Vucht Polder, which had been flooded during the siege. Part of a recently marked-out route called the *Spinolaweg* begins as a paved road and continues over the Black Dike as a dirt-and-gravel lane, with earthen verges and muddy ditches on each side. We were passed by one vehicle, a pickup truck, and one other couple on bikes came toward us. Otherwise Lies and I had the country to ourselves. An open expanse of flat farmland on the former polder stretched to woods on the right, and a tidy outskirts-of-Breda housing development filled the horizon on the left. The sky had a sprinkling of white clouds but—as is usually the case in the Netherlands— seemed immensely high. Our lane, still the Spinola Way, made a sharp bend northward toward the woods and past a farm called the Hartel. Here we found the river Mark, now canalized, a broad waterway with not a single vessel in sight upon it. And here, in a small empty parking area near a highway called the Nieuw Bredasebaan, we dismounted, locked up the bikes, and walked eastward on a gravel path into the woods. Here Spinola's name was also remembered in the remains of a small fort or *schans*, where his engineers had built a redoubt to but-tress the double line of ramparts and entrenchments encircling Breda. This circuit of the inner *contravallie* and outer *circumvallie* was gener-ally made with the siege lines at a distance one from the other but was here built with the lines close together, because of the natural obstacles available and useful features of the terrain. The gap between the *vallies* varied from a stone's throw, as here, to as much as a kilome-ter near Terheijden in the north and Gineken in the south. The double circuit was to keep the Dutch garrison of Breda penned in and repel any Dutch relieving force planning to attack the Spanish besieging army from without.

The *schans* was now overgrown, the grass on its twenty-feet-high banks a foot or so tall except where it had been flattened by walkers, though we were alone here today. The trees were mostly ash and alder, not large but dense enough to obscure any view. A light breeze ruffled the leaves. In the center of the roughly square grassed area of the *schans*, about half a football pitch in size, a red tubular metal pole was impaled in the earth—meant to suggest a lance, we gathered, and to indicate that this site was on the Spinola Way; the pole's color, bloodred, helped give the impression that it was an offensive weapon rather than just an old piece of scaffolding. Outside the green ramparts lay a moat of dark water beyond which the supposedly firm ground looked wet. The moat had apparently been dug in already boggy soil by Frederick Henry's troops a decade after the Spanish siege.

Lies and I sat on the highest part of the bank for a snack of *Fries suikerbrod* and apples she had brought. We kept our eyes open for the wildlife that presumably was not much different from that almost four centuries before: frogs, hedgehogs, crows, blackbirds, sparrows. The place was immensely peaceful. No distant traffic sounds intruded. As on other battlegrounds I've been to, at what the French call Azincourt in the Normandy countryside and in the fields along the river Boyne in Ireland, this site gave little help in prompting images of violent action. Passages of fighting then were of course intermittent. For the partici-pants, wars were as now spent most of the time waiting for something to happen and then, suddenly, there one was, in the swirl of lethal thrust and parry, amid moments of panic and horror, cowardice and blind bravery. Father Herman Hugo's record of the siege of Breda gave few figures for military fatalities or casualities. In the *schans*, here and elsewhere around the siege lines, the small units guarding the operation posted sentries who were meant to raise the alarm when needed and call the men nearby to hold the ground against the Orange attackers until a reserve force from the Army of Flanders could come to help.

The ten-month siege was for the most part a conflict of excavation and construction. Spades were the essential if unremarked Spanish weapon. Spades were at hand for peat digging; they could deliver knockout blows and, sharpened, served to disfigure and dismember. The siege works were formed primarily of the four-mile circuit of ditches, trenches, earth-and-turf ramparts strengthened here and there with oak palisading, and redoubts like this *schans*. In appropriate spots both sides fought water wars. The Dutch dammed watercourses and tried to inundate Spinola's army. The Spanish replied with engineering works that they hoped would drown or at any rate impede the Dutch. There were frequent skirmishes and sallies, with attempts being made to break through the lines by patrols or by groups escaping from the city. It was a war of constriction and attrition, and there were—from what the records tell—few out-and-out battles. Father Hugo details one exception, numbering the casualties suffered in one more than usually bloody incident when English troops serving Prince Frederick Henry attacked a *schans* at Terheijden garrisoned by Italians of the king of Spain's army, and according to Hugo, Spinola's spokesman in this, "a great slaughter" ensued: Nearly two hundred of the prince's men were killed by the defenders of the *schans* with the loss of a dozen or so of their own. (About five hundred United Provinces' horses were also captured.)

In Breda today the "surprise" of the turfship is still commemorated every year, but the anniversary of the success of Spinola's army is unremarked by festivities. However, the Spanish siege of Breda has featured in several works of fiction: in Calderón's play of that name not long after the surrender and more recently in an adventure novel, *The Sun over Breda,* by the Spanish writer Arturo Pérez-Reverte—one of a series of swashbuckling tales about a squad of seventeenth-century Spanish diehards and their taciturn leader, Captain Alatriste. Much of the detail

in Pérez-Reverte's book rings true, and there are some nice touches—
for example, the presence, toward the end back in Madrid, of Alatriste's
young servant Íñigo who is asked to advise an artist named Diego
Velázquez as he paints *The Surrender of Breda*. But much of the action
of the book seems offstage or indirect in presentation, with a consequent etiolation of character. Captain Alatriste comes across—despite
his macho mustache and a reputation for robust swordplay—as a thinly
portrayed fellow, morose and speechless. Here at Breda, where our
author puts Alatriste in the thick of it, one suspects the actuality of the
ten-month siege was a good deal less violent and more tedious, though
possibly just as deadly. According to Father Hugo, five thousand inhabitants of Breda, about a third of the town's population, died during the
siege, mostly it would seem from sickness and malnutrition. The war
cry that arose from Spanish ranks as the *tercios* went into battle with
arquebus, lance, sword, and spade was *"Santiago cierra España!"* ("Saint
James! And close ranks, Spain!"). Yet the occasions for yelling it would
have been infrequent, compared with the hours spent digging or sitting in lice- and rat-ridden shelters waiting for the skimpy rations to
arrive at waterlogged redoubts. This was the cockpit of Europe, where
enraged captive birds peck and claw at each other. Flanders Fields—
even then closer to a wet hell than heaven. Sancho Panza exclaimed
from the dry heart of Spain, "If any more Devils or Horns come hither,
they shall as soon find me in Flanders as here!" A century and a bit
later Uncle Toby recalled in *Tristram Shandy*, of one of Marlborough's
wars, "Our army swore lustily in Flanders." The Dutch and Spanish
artillery salvoes at Breda were only a tiny taste of what was to come in
1914–18, but were effective for all that in maiming and killing. Even so,
the mud was a more tiresome foe than pike-tip or musket-shot; trench
foot and death by pneumonia brought on by damp clothing and wet
blankets were common, albeit unrecorded by Chaplain Hugo.

There were deaths, too, from friendly fire and military punishment.
Breda natives caught attempting to smuggle out messages or smuggle
in tobacco and provisions were executed, often by being hanged from a
gibbet and then shot for target practice. This was done within view of
the town walls, to discourage others. Callot drew a graphic scene of such
an event in his map of the siege, with a mounted officer shown super-

vising the fatal occasion. It was diffficult to identify spies accurately at
that time because no one wore recognized uniforms. Soldiers distinguished their loyalties by scarves and sashes, the Dutch with blue and
orange, the Army of Flanders with red, or by standards—the Spanish
favoring the red Saint Andrew's cross of Burgundy or the "ragged cross"
flag showing two red-colored bumpy wooden clubs on a white background. Spinola, however, used his discretion in decreeing penalties.
Some hungry escapees from Breda were simply shepherded back to the
town walls to be let back in; that way the garrison inside still had the
increasingly difficult job of feeding them. Three young Frenchmen tried
to get away from the town and were carried back to a gate in the captain-
general's own coach. Spinola, riding hither and yon, monitored the sentries and lookouts and ensured reinforcements were stationed at points
where enemy assaults might occur. He had a charmed life, he and his
horse being nearly hit on several occasions by Dutch cannon fire.

Apart from the birds and frogs, all was fairly quiet at what is now
called *Spinola-schans* on the day we stopped there. The sylvan morning
allowed for peaceful meditation but interfered with any imaginative
connection with 1625. No ghostly, furious calls of *"Santiago!"* or *"España!"*
could be heard. I had a few grateful thoughts about European union
and the inevitable bureaucracy that has at any rate suppressed national
war-lust for the last sixty-five years. Lies and I gave the symbolic
lance—planted like a javelin in the earth—a parting look and walked
back around the top of the rampart and then along the uneven trail to
the parking place where our bikes awaited. Here, across the Mark
River, Spinola's men had built a pontoon bridge to enable supplies to
reach the siege ring. We cycled back into Breda and lunched at a
bedecked café where the orange flags and pennons proclaimed support
for the Dutch football team. The Spanish victory in the final left the
Netherlanders naturally disappointed, but it was one they put up with;
they found it preferable to a German victory. After three hundred and
eighty some years, old enmities undergo metamorphoses. Serious griev-
ances are replaced by irony and humor. In the Breda Museum the next
afternoon I spotted inside a glass exhibit case a large rusty key, a hand-
span long, which looked as if it had fitted an old mortice lock from an
immense door or gate. Alongside it lay a piece of paper on which was

inscribed a handwritten poem by the Breda artist who had made the key: Pieter Laurens Mol, born in 1946.

> *Dear Diego Velázquez*
> *Let's make it up*
> *No more fuss.*
> *At last I found the bloody key*
> *Of my bloody home town.*
> *Pedro de Barca*

Below this Mol had drawn an array of lances.

DURING THE YEARS of the "protectorate" in which Cromwell ruled England, the Stuart pretender and future English king Charles II lived in Breda, not far from his sister Mary, who had married the second Prince William of Orange. When the Cromwellian regime faltered, Charles delivered in 1660 his Declaration of Breda, laying down the conditions on which he would accept the restored crown of England. In the First World War Holland managed to stay neutral, unlike Belgium, but during the Second World War German armies occupied all of the Low Countries, north and south, including Breda, on their way into France.

The German occupation—and the collaboration of occupied people with the enemy—were cleverly foreseen in Jacques Feyder's very stylized film of 1935, *La Kermesse héroique* or *Carnival in Flanders*, starring Jean Murat and Louis Jouvet and set in the former Spanish Netherlands. The year is 1616, and the male residents of the Flemish town of Boom panic at the prospect of the Army of Flanders moving in on them. The female residents demonstrate greater ambivalence about the threat. Much fun is made of the craven cowardice of Boom's burgomaster and councillors. Much sport is also made of the cupidity of the town's merchants who regard the pike-carrying foreign soldiery as good for trade. One burger takes comfort in the notion that a captured town gets a year's exemption from taxes. Signs go up: "Welcome to our visitors." The womenfolk of Boom reckon that, given the supine behavior of their husbands, the Spaniards offer the chance of amorous entertainment. The keys of the town are eagerly handed over with the unspoken suggestion that a key can unlock more than a city gate. The welcome ceremonies become a feast, with oysters, wine, and love-play. One good wife of Boom says longingly, "The Spaniards are supposed to rape and pillage. And I've waited all day." Another declares, "These Spanish have been maligned—this is just a dream." Life is a wonderful dream, and rape, it turns out, is unnecessary in Boom. At the time the film was regarded by some Belgians and French as unpatriotic, promoting appeasement, and slanderous toward the Flemings. A few years later the Wehrmacht panzer divisions gave them more serious worries.

In Lope de Vega's play of 1606, *Don Juan de Austria en Flandes*, a Netherlander orders his daughter to be branded and sold as a slave because she has taken up with a Spanish soldier, but on the ground the collaboration went both ways—or even three ways: There was reluctance, under duress, or even actively helping out. Many Spaniards developed an affection for the Low Countries that outweighed their love of their homeland. Some officers of the Army of Flanders learned French and adopted Flemish customs and titles. Not a few Netherlanders learned Spanish. A small number of Spanish words came into common use in the southern provinces. The Dutch begin to celebrate Christmas on December 5, the feast of Saint Nicklas, when the good saint turns up to bring small presents to good children, accompanied by his young black sidekick, Zwarte Piet, a Morisco, before heading south to Spain. According to the historian Geoffrey Parker, speakers of Dutch and Flemish particularly adopted Spanish swearwords; terms that were much in use had to do with sex, violence, and deceit. Marriages often occurred across the divide. Less permanent relationships took a notorious toll: *el mal galico*, venereal disease, the French pox, consumed many, while others were brought low by *el mal de corazón*, a heart illness that was possibly a war-induced stress disorder or a fatal homesickness, like the *nostalgie* identified by British army surgeons as the reason many of their soldiers fighting the American rebels in the Revolutionary War pined away and died. The men of the Army of Flanders were generally much farther from home than their United Provinces opponents, and desertions from their ranks were more frequent, especially when they hadn't received their pay for six months or more. But the distances to Lombardy or La Mancha made it a long hike back.

* * *

HEADING SOUTH TO Seville, I paused in Madrid. The Prado, originally a natural sciences museum first opened up to the Hapsburg art
collections in 1819, had gained a new wing at the rear stretching
toward the Retiro park and the few remaining buildings of the Retiro
palace. This wing housed an exhibition devoted to Velázquez's "Fables,"
thirty some paintings from various points of his career that had to do
with mythology, classical legends, and religious subjects. *The Rokeby
Venus*, here called *The Venus with a Mirror*, had been shipped from
London for the occasion. I spent longer with the less familiar to me
Mercury and Argus and *The Fable of Arachne* before climbing into the
older parts of the Prado where *Las Meninas* and *The Surrender of Breda*
were to be found. On the way I noted in several paintings by Brueghel
premonitions of Velázquez: how the bare trees in the superb *Hunters in
the Snow* stand up like the pikes in *Las Lanzas*; and how Spanish pikes
were also to be seen, menacingly, in Brueghel's *Massacre of the Inno-
cents*. Moreover, one observed in the same painter's *Corn Harvest* that
the ground fell away from a foreground elevation to a distant plain, in
very much the same way as the terrain depicted in Velázquez's *Breda*.

In front of that painting I found myself losing certain peripheral
areas of vision and planes of consciousness. Some of the surroundings
became less perceptible; one's focus narrowed and sharpened; the *Breda*
was all that mattered. Footfalls, other viewers, people nearby who might
or might not impede one's view and concentration, all faded, and I was
left insulated in a private gallery almost my own. One can look at some
pictures many times and on each occasion notice different things. On
this occasion I was aware that from the viewer's standpoint, the foreground of the painting presented some crucial backs—the back of the
Dutch soldier, for example, wearing a light brown coat and carrying a
short pike with a orange pennon attached, while to that soldier's right,
beyond the genuflecting figure of Justin and the welcoming presence of
Spinola, the viewer comes up against the gleaming chestnut brown rear-
end of the massive warhorse from which the Spanish captain-general
has dismounted. These backs cause us to focus more intently on the
faces shown. Justin's bearded profile looks scarcely that of a veteran of
sixty-six but doesn't catch the light in the way that Spinola's even more

elegantly bearded countenance does. Seeing the commanders again reminded me that here, at the heart of what was a public picture, Velázquez had put a private moment—one which made the original point that Justin's and Spinola's roles were reversible. The Spanish army's senior officers formed up behind their general earned their rights of recognition and can be identified. As noted, they include Prince Wolfgang von Neuburg; Don Gonzalo de Córdoba; Count Salazar; Count Henry van den Bergh; and two Saxon princes. Carl Justi tells us that "the old man on the left" of the Spanish party "with both hands on a stick" is probably Albert Arenbergh, Baron of Balancon, commander of the Flemish cavalry. In armor, next to Arenbergh, might be Wolfgang von Neuburg. And behind him is possibly Don Carlos Coloma, "head of the infantry, who had risen from the ranks." We have appreciated the painting's epic force but this documentary quality gives it another dimension: as with the *Iliad*, in which the leading warriors have names.

Between the fawn-coated Dutch soldier and the huge horse a sort of porthole is created under Spinola's right arm, an aperture partly occluded by the black iron key which Justin proffers. Through this window we have one of Velázquez's split-screen images. A transient view is given of the surrendering Dutch garrison marching past. And over Spinola's dramatically outstretched arm, in the larger gap between the standing Dutch soldiers and the commanders of the Army of Flanders in their attendant phalanx behind their general's horse, in a space further delimited by the fence of Spanish lances on the right and smoke drifting skyward behind the shorter Dutch pikes and battle-axes on the left, we see out across the flooded Vucht polder to a high horizon and a sky with a few breaks in the clouds.

The foreground figures stand in pools of shadow. At least three of the score of more or less recognizable men meet one's eye. The young Dutchman wearing a black hat, arquebus over his shoulder, seems curious to know what the viewer—or the artist who is sizing him up—intends. The bare-headed and bearded Spanish senior officer standing behind Spinola, a sash over his right shoulder, gives us a detached, thoughtful gaze; he obviously has a lot to think about. And on the far right, framed by the head and flank of the general's horse and by a large checkered blue-and-white flag drooping toward him is a man, glimpsed at the last, who without much to go on we take for a civilian, wearing pale garments, head topped by a pale hat. He appears to be without weapons, a participant perhaps only in being brought on as a privileged spectator of the occasion. But he is someone seen before. The broad *W*-shaped mustache, the hint of beard on the chin, the mass of curly hair, and the complicit gaze of a man regarding himself in a mirror before putting brush to canvas—he is to be found in several self-portraits and working before the easel in *Las Meninas*. He is interested in what we think although he looks a trifle unsure of what we will make of him. Here he is staring into the eye of history, which he has aimed to focus on himself. Will the message he is now half-sending actually carry to us? How in the end will this pan out?

IN SEVILLE I went searching for traces of Velázquez. As a person, he remains private, scarcely documented where his feelings and behavior are concerned. We are stuck with the one special fact that at any rate he was a painter—which is why we are interested in him—and there are his paintings to ponder and marvel at. Is it wrong, as some critics say it is, to take the works of an artist as autobiographical documents? Don't they shed light on the artist who painted them? Now and then, as if just waking from a tantalizingly almost tangible dream, I've had the feeling that he was about to be revealed; a fully formed individual was on the point of announcing himself; he was going to let us know which was the real man, the title-seeking courtier or the painter whose works indicated such acute recognition of shammery. But then the mists thickened again around the nearly visible figure. Was he, like Don Quixote, in the thrall of an enchanter?

Seville helped. His hometown is *south*, inland south. Indeed, lacking the moderating influence of the Mediterranean or the Atlantic, it seems farther south than Málaga or Cádiz, despite its well-embanked river, the Guadalquivir, curving gently through it with a way to go still before reaching the sea. This is a place that for five months of a year is blindingly bright. It is a city where you step out of doors and immediately seek shadow—which side of the street is it going to be preferable to walk on? It is a city where one feels the proximity less of Europe than of Africa, and one remembers the Moors. Much of its low-scale jumbled townscape suggests Paris before Baron Haussmann. The narrow, twisting streets form mazes; you don't always come out where you expect to, and then you may have to look for the position of the dazzling sun to work out which way you are heading. The Moors were here from the early eighth century. Seville was recaptured by the army of King Ferdinand III of Castile in 1248 and the seven-hundred-year-long Reconquest of Spain was accomplished in 1492, the year Granada fell to the forces of Ferdinand and Isabella, "the Catholic monarchs," and the year the navigator they were sponsoring on an optimistic westward voyage to the Orient found not what he was looking for but the West Indies. Certainly it was, for Spanish purposes, a New World. Cristo foro Colombo was, one recalls, like Ambrogio Spinola, one of the Spanish empire's useful Genoese.

I began my Velázquez reconnaisance in the Alameda de Hércules, a long, empty avenue surfaced with sand-colored clay hoggin. A pair of columns rise at one end of the Alameda; on them used to stand statues of Hercules and Julius Caesar, the Greek god who was the mythical founder of Seville and the Roman general; now next to the columns is a modern statue of Manolo Caracol, a noted flamenco singer. Overlooking this spot Velázquez had had—courtesy of Juana Pacheco's dowry—a couple of houses which he rented out before he headed for Madrid. It seemed in the sharp sunlight a surreal, de Chirico sort of space. From here I walked south into the labyrinth of the Santa Cruz district, once heavily Jewish, and got my bearings now and then in the twisting alleyways from the tower of the Giralda seen over the rooftops. I paused in the Plaza San Francisco outside the sixteenth-century Town Hall. Nearby were the law courts, the site of public executions, and of the prison in which Cervantes to his grief was locked up on two or three occasions (in 1592, 1597, and possibly 1602). Then I made my way to the Giralda, the magnetic pole of these parts.

Giralda means weather vane. A bronze figure of Faith turns in the light breeze at the summit of the tower, the former minaret, three hundred and twenty feet high, that is planted next to the remains of the old mosque and its courtyard full of orange trees. The adjacent fifteenth-century cathedral bulks large, overshadowing the Muslim relics; only

Saint Peter's in Rome and the later Saint Paul's in London are larger European religious edifices. Within, immense columns rise to support great arches which spread the load of the vaulting, two hundred feet above the transept. In the south transept is Columbus's tomb, an ornate nineteenth-century affair showing the coffin of the explorer being carried by four bronze pallbearers, the kings of León, Castile, Navarre, and Aragón. There isn't much here to remind us of Velázquez's father's occupation, working on testamentary business for the cathedral chapter. One can stretch out a long hand to the past more readily in the gardens of the nearby Alcázar. Reached through a man-sized keyhole gateway, these have a sense of structured beauty laid down in the late twelfth century by Yacoub Al Mansur, the sultan who commissioned the Giralda. In the gardens, fountains plashed into stone basins. Orange blossom gave a sweet scent to the warm air. Not much is left of the Moorish Almohad Alcázar, but enough survives to give one an idea of how the following Christian monarchs were influenced by the palace's carved stone, gilded iron, and intricate cedarwood decorations; these carried the fluid rhythms of Muslim artifice into the Iberian kingdoms of Charles V and Philip II—whose Sevillian *palacio real* the Alcázar became. Visiting this royal part of the city on childhood errands for his father, Velázquez may have been impressed by the calm shade and the birdsong. He may have realized early on that a working connection with a palace had advantages.

My return walk took me around the high walls of the bullring in the Plaza de Toros, close to the left bank of the Guadalquivir. Not far away in a restored friary, founded after the Reconquest, is the Seville Fine Arts Museum, with an airy cloister at its heart. There were no Velázquezes but among other things two Zurbarán Crucifixions, a splendid Ribera painting of Saint James the Apostle—*Santiago!*—with full beard and red cloak, and several Pacheco portraits that allowed one to see again that Velázquez's parents had acted smartly when they moved young Diego away from Herrera's mastership in 1611. Pacheco's own work can seem wooden and programmatically pious, but the double portrait here of an elderly couple, himself and his wife, their heads touching the top of the canvas, was simply done and moving. From the museum it was eastward up the Calle Alfonso XII, a main shopping street that becomes the Calle Larana and then the Imagen before narrowing and taking a dogleg at a church that blocks its way. This was San Pedro. Dark inside, with the smell of incense lingering. A priest entered a confessional and awaited talkative sinners. This church is where Diego Velázquez de Silva was baptized on June 6, 1599, by the San Pedro curate Gregorio de Salazar, the infant's godfather being Pablo de Ojeda. I went back into the daylight and crossed a rectangular square, the Plaza Cristo de Burgos, with a children's playground in the middle but otherwise given over to parked cars.

Here I needed assistance. No one I'd yet asked in Seville could give me precise directions for finding Velázquez's birthplace. I'd inquired in my hotel, not far from here, and the reply hadn't been reassuring. "We used to have someone here who knew where it was. . . ." The city information office I'd visited had been of little use. "It's somewhere around San Pedro, I think. . . ." One problem was that the street where his parents had lived in 1599 had changed its name; it was no longer Calle Gorgoja, a name no one now recognized, but Calle Padre Luis María Llop, a name that also aroused no sudden smiles of recognition. In the early seventeenth century the square, the Plaza Cristo de Burgos, had been the Plaza Buen Suceso. Velázquez's 1906 biographer, Aureliano de Beruete, had found at the time no trace of the painter's family's house. I walked around the neighborhood, getting blank looks and shrugs in bars and shops in return for my question about the whereabouts of Velázquez's birthplace; it might have helped if my enunciation had been more Spanish, with the "V" of Velázquez sounding correctly like a blurred mixture of "V" and "B." But eventually my luck turned: in the Cristo de Burgos someone thought the Calle Padre Luis María Llop (also a Spang-lish mouthful) was "back that way"—pointing into the far right-hand corner of the plaza. In that direction I found a parked mover's van. Several workmen were unloading wheeled trolleys and rolls of padded matting. I approached a man who was wearing a suit and carrying a clipboard, and asked my question. "Follow us," he said. Their van was apparently too large to get any farther into the warren of small streets. We left the square and hastened down a street called Morería, whose name suggested that people of Moorish or Morisco origin had lived there. We turned off into what felt like a brief cul-de-sac, though it had no end in immediate sight. This was the Calle Padre Luis María Llop! Around a bend to the left we stopped outside number 4. Before it a member of the moving team was sitting on a trolley. A small plaque was to be seen in a recess of the wall below an upstairs window: "VELÁZQUEZ CASA NATAL."

The front door was open. It wasn't the perfect moment for an uninvited call but a woman at a desk inside seemed to think that with the movers arriving, things couldn't get any worse. "Look around," she said phlegmatically in Spanish. Today was the day her company, a firm of fashion designers, was moving out to new premises. Her phone rang and I made a quick tour of the ground floor, where the movers had begun to put stuff in plywood crates and cardboard boxes. The ceilings of the downstairs rooms had exposed beams, through which one could see the undersides of the floorboards of the rooms above; the beams rested on intricately carved wooden columns. The windows at the front were low and small, iron-barred outside. The sound of splashing water came from an open trough in an interior courtyard—a good place for filling water jugs. The house extended to the rear in a series of rooms that seemed like former open patios, now roofed over—rooms which at the back had a dark, cavelike feeling, with small doorways that made me think of the serving hatches in Velázquez's early split-screen pictures. If this arrangement had an effect on the future artist, it must have been in an almost *in utero* or *ex utero* fashion, just before or soon after birth, because his parents moved away from the Calle Gorgoja soon afterward, possibly because Velázquez's maternal grandparents Juan Velázquez Moreno and Juana Mexia had died of plague in this house that year. A change of scene on health grounds was advisable. The family moved from the San Pedro to the San Vicente district, north of the Merced friary which is now the Fine Arts Museum, between the river and the Alameda de Hércules.

Next day I took a look at the Velázquez *casa natal* again. The front door was locked, the shutters shut. It felt as if Velázquez had gone away—to San Vicente; to Madrid and the court; to fame and glory; or simply returned to one's dreams—and I would have to take any remaining questions to a higher plane, back to his paintings.

A Note on Money

(SEE ALCALA-ZAMORRA, *LA VIDA COTIDIANA*,
IN BIBLIOGRAPHY, BOOKS, BELOW)

A *maravedi* minted of copper was the smallest coin, the equivalent roughly of the British farthing, or less than what would be a U.S. cent.

One *real* (mixed silver and copper) was worth approximately 34 *maravedis*.

One *ducat* or *ducado* was the equivalent of 11 silver *reales*.

One gold *escudo* was worth 440 *maravedis*. *Escudos* meant "coats of arms" and they came in denominations of eight (hence "pieces of eight," particularly in pirate lore), four, two, and one.

A *doblones* or *doubloon* was two *escudos*.

According to Kevin Ingram, "an average monthly rent for a property in Seville at the end of the sixteenth century was 20 *reales*." (*Boletín del Museo del Prado*, XVII, 35, 1999, p. 84, n. 31.)

BIBLIOGRAPHY

BOOKS

Alcala-Zamorra, J. N., ed. *La Vida Cotidiana en la España de Velázquez* (Daily Life in the Spain of Velázquez) (Madrid, 1994).

———. *Philip IV—the Man & the Kingdom* (Madrid, 2005).

Aleman, Mateo. *Guzmán de Alfarache* (1599), tr. Edward Lowdell (London, 1883).

Alpers, Svetlana. *The Vexations of Art* (New Haven and London, 2005).

Bailey, Anthony. *A Concise History of the Low Countries* (New York, 1972).

———. *Vermeer: A View of Delft* (New York and London, 2001).

Ballemans, Koen. *Historische Canon van Breda* (Breda, 2007).

Beaujean, Dieter. *Diego Velázquez* (Cologne, 2000).

Beruete, Aureliano de. *Velázquez* (Madrid, 1906).

Borton de Trevino, Elizabeth. *I, Juan de Pareja* (New York, 1965; Harmondsworth, 1968).

Braudel, Ferdinand. *The Mediterranean and the Mediterranean World in the Age of Philip II* (1949), two volumes, English translation (London, 1973).

Brenan, Gerald. *The Literature of the Spanish People*, 2nd ed. (Cambridge, 1953).

Brown, Dale, and the editors of Time-Life Books. *The World of Velázquez* (Amsterdam and New York, 1969).

Brown, Jonathan. *Velázquez, Painter and Courtier* (New Haven and London, 1986).

Brown, Jonathan, and J. H. Elliott. *A Palace for a King*, new ed. (New Haven and London, 2003).

Calderón de la Barca, Pedro. *Three Plays Including Life's a Dream,* adapted by Adrian Mitchell and John Barton (London, 1998).

Cervantes, Miguel de. *Don Quixote* (part 1, 1605 and part 2, 1615), tr. P. A. Motteux (London, 1700–1703; new ed., New York and London, 1991).

Clark, G. N. *The Seventeenth Century* (Oxford, 1929).

Clark, Kenneth. *The Nude* (New York, 1959).

Corrigan, Gordon. *Mud, Blood and Poppycock* (London, 2003).

Dickens, A. G., ed. *The Courts of Europe* (includes J. H. Elliott, "Philip IV of Spain, Prisoner of Ceremony") (London, 1977).

Dominguez Ortiz, Antonio, and Bernand Vincent. *Historia de los moriscos* (1978) (Madrid, 1984).

Elliott, J. H. *The Count-Duke of Olivares* (New Haven and London, 1986).

Evelyn, John. *The Diary of John Evelyn*, ed. E. S. de Beer (Oxford, 1959).

Ford, Richard. *A Handbook for Travellers in Spain* (London, 1845).

———. *Gatherings from Spain*, new ed. (London, 2000).

Gallego, Julian. *Velázquez en Sevilla*, 3rd ed. (Seville, 1999).

Gracian, Baltasar. *The Hero* (1630), tr. (London, 1726).

Grosvel, J. *Het Turfschip van Breda* (Breda, 1990).

Harris, Enriqueta. *Velázquez* (Oxford, 1982).

Hazlitt, William. *Conversations of James Northcote* (London, 1949).

———. *Selected Writings*, ed. Ronald Blythe (Harmondsworth, 1970).

Helfferich, Tryntje. *The Thirty Years War* (Indianapolis, 2009).

Hibbert, Christopher. *Wellington* (London, 1997).

Hugo, Herman, S.J. *Obsidio Bredana* (Antwerp, 1626); *The Siege of Breda*, tr. by "CHG" (Antwerp, 1627).

Huizinga, Johan. *The Waning of the Middle Ages* (1924) (Harmondsworth, 1972).

Israel, Jonathan. *The Dutch Republic, 1477–1806* (Oxford, 1982).

Jones, David. *The Dying Gaul and Other Writings* (London and Boston, 1978).

Justi, Carl. *Diego Velázquez and His Times*, tr. A. H. Keane (London, 1889).

Kamen, Henry. *A Concise History of Spain* (London, 1973).

Lea, Henry Charles. *The Moriscos of Spain* (London, 1901).

Lenihan, Padraig. *Confederate Catholics at War 1641–49* (Cork, 2001).

Leslie, Charles. *A Handbook for Young Painters* (London, 1855).

Lopez-Rey, José. *Velázquez: Complete Works* (Cologne and Paris, 1996).

McKim-Smith, Gridley, and others. *Examining Velázquez* (New Haven and London, 1988).

Mendez Rodríguez, Luis. *Velázquez y la cultura sevillana* (Seville, 2005).

Muller, Joseph-Emile. *Velázquez*, tr. Jane Brenton (London, 1976).

Ortega y Gasset, José. *The Revolt of the Masses* (London, 1932).

———. *Velázquez* (Madrid, 1954).

———. *Velázquez, Goya, and the Dehumanization of Art*, tr. Alexis Brown (New York, 1972).

Ovid (Publius Ovidius Naso). *Metamorphoses*, tr. David Raeburn (London, 2004).

Pacheco, Francisco. *Arte de la Pintura* (Seville, 1649), tr. E. Harris, in *Velázquez* (Oxford, 1982).

Palomino, Antonio. *El Museo Pictorico y Escala Optica* (Madrid 1715–24), tr. E. Harris, in *Velázquez* (Oxford, 1982).

Parker, Geoffrey. *Spain and the Netherlands* (Short Hills, N.J., 1979).

———. *The Army of Flanders and the Spanish Road*, 2nd ed. (Cambridge, 2004).

Pater, Walter. *The Renaissance* (London, 1877).

Pérez-Reverte, Arturo. *The Sun over Breda* (New York and London, 2007).

Pike, Ruth. *Aristocrats and Traders: Sevillian Society in the Sixteenth Century* (Cornell, 1972).

Rodriguez Villa, Antonio. *Ambrogio Spinola* (Madrid, 1904).

Scott Shawe, Wilfred H. *Sea of Seas* (Princeton and London, 1961).

Stevenson, R. A. M. *Velázquez* (London, 1910).

Stratton-Pruitt, Suzanne, ed. *The Cambridge Companion to Velázquez* (Cambridge, 2002).

———. *Velázquez's Las Meninas* (Cambridge, 2003).

Thomas, Hugh. *Madrid* (London, 1988).

Tietze-Conrat, E. *Dwarfs and Jesters in Art* (London, 1957).

Trevor-Roper, H. R. *Princes and Artists* (London, 1976).

White, Jon Manchip. *Velázquez* (London, 1969).

EXHIBITION CATALOGUES

Manet/Velázquez: The French Taste for Spanish Painting, ed. Gary Tinterow (New Haven and London, 2003).

Velázquez in Seville (includes Peter Cherry, "Artistic Training and the Painters' Guild") National Gallery of Scotland, Edinburgh, 1996.

Velázquez, ed. Dawson W. Carr, with others (includes Javier Portus, "Nudes & Knights") National Gallery, London, 2006.

Velázquez y Sevilla. Seville, 1999.

PERIODICALS

Anales de Historia del Arte 2008. 18, pp. 111–39, José Manuel Cruz Valdovinos, "Oficios y mercedes que recibio Velázquez de Felipe IV."

The Art Bulletin, December 1988. Simone Zurawski, "New Sources for Jacques Callot's Map of the Siege of Breda."

Boletín del Museo del Prado, tomo XVII, número 35, 1999. Kevin Ingram, "Diego Velázquez's Secret History."

Burlington Magazine, CXXV, 1983. Jennifer Montagu, "Velázquez Marginalia."

Burlington Magazine, CXXXXIII, 1991. Peter Cherry, "New Documents for Velázquez in the 1620s."

The Independent, July 10, 2010. Felipe Fernández-Armesto, "Two Nations, One World Cup Final, and 440 Years of Hurt."

Nineteenth Century Art Worldwide, 3, 1, Spring 2004, Alisa Luxenberg review of exhibition, "Manet/Velázquez," Paris, 2002–2003 and New York, 2003.

INDEX

Page numbers in *italics* refer to illustrations.

ABOUT THE AUTHOR

ANTHONY BAILEY, a writer for *The New Yorker* for thirty-five years, has been called "one of the best descriptive writers of his generation" (John Russell, the *New York Times*). Among his many books are two on Rembrandt, one recently on Vermeer, and most recently a biography, *John Constable: A Kingdom of His Own.*